The Marriage of
Heaven and Earth

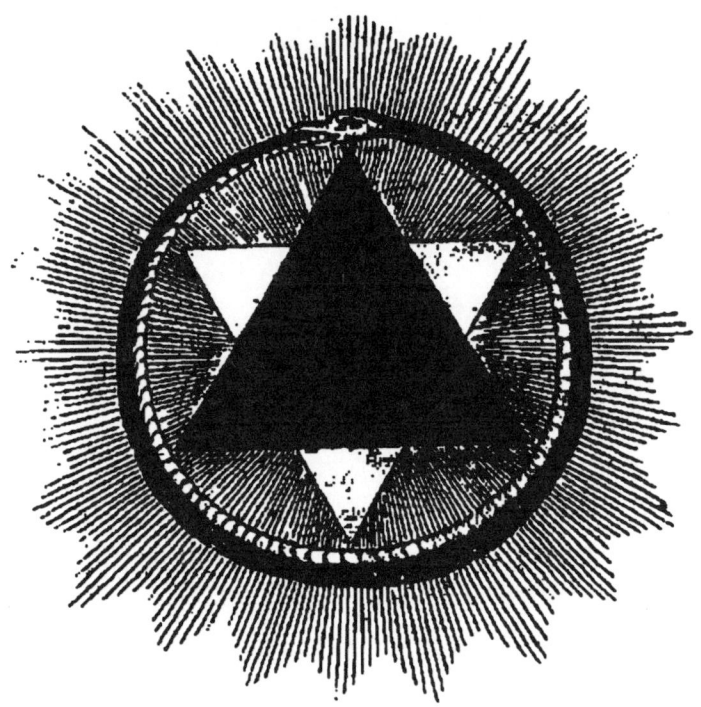

Frontispiece from Margaret Fuller's *Woman in the Nineteenth Century* (1846).

The Marriage of Heaven and Earth

Alchemical Regeneration in the Works of Taylor, Poe, Hawthorne, and Fuller

RANDALL A. CLACK

Contributions to the Study of American Literature, Number 6

Greenwood Press
Westport, Connecticut • London

Library of Congress Cataloging-in-Publication Data

Clack, Randall A., 1958–
 The marriage of heaven and earth : alchemical regeneration in the works of Taylor, Poe, Hawthorne, and Fuller / Randall A. Clack.
  p. cm.—(Contributions to the study of American literature, ISSN 1092–6356 ; no. 6)
 Includes bibliographical references and index.
 ISBN 0–313–31269–9 (alk. paper)
 1. American literature—19th century—History and criticism. 2. Alchemy in literature. 3. Taylor, Edward, 1642–1729—Criticism and interpretation. 4. Poe, Edgar Allan, 1809–1849—Criticism and interpretation. 5. Hawthorne, Nathaniel, 1804–1864—Criticism and interpretation. 6. Fuller, Margaret, 1810–1850—Criticism and interpretation. 7. Regeneration in literature. I. Title. II. Series.
 PS217.A43 C57 2000
 810.9'37—dc21   99–058878

British Library Cataloguing in Publication Data is available.

Copyright © 2000 by Randall A. Clack

All rights reserved. No portion of this book may be reproduced, by any process or technique, without the express written consent of the publisher.

Library of Congress Catalog Card Number: 99–058878
ISBN: 0–313–31269–9
ISSN: 1092–6356

First published in 2000

Greenwood Press, 88 Post Road West, Westport, CT 06881
An imprint of Greenwood Publishing Group, Inc.
www.greenwood.com

Printed in the United States of America

The paper used in this book complies with the Permanent Paper Standard issued by the National Information Standards Organization (Z39.48–1984).

10 9 8 7 6 5 4 3 2 1

Copyright Acknowledgments

The author and publisher gratefully acknowledge permission for use of the following material:

Randall A. Clack. " 'Strange Alchemy of Brain': Poe and Alchemy." In *A Companion to Poe Studies*, ed. Eric W. Carlson, 367–87. Westport, Conn.: Greenwood Press (an imprint of Greenwood Publishing Group, Inc., Westport, CT), 1996.

Randall A. Clack. "The Alchemy of Love: Hawthorne's Hermetic Allegory of the Heart." *ESQ: A Journal of the American Renaissance* 41 (1995): 307–38.

Randall A. Clack. "The Transmutation of Soul: The *Opus Alchymicum Celestial* and Edward Taylor's 'Meditation 1.8.' " *Seventeenth-Century News* 50 (Spring/Summer 1992): 6–10.

Jeffrey Steele. "Freeing the 'Prisoned Queen': The Development of Margaret Fuller's Poetry." In *Studies in the American Renaissance*, ed. Joel Myerson, 137–75. Charlottesville: University Press of Virginia, 1992.

Michael Maier. *Atalanta Fugiens: An Edition of the Emblems, Fugues and Epigrams*. Trans and Ed. Joscelyn Godwin. Grand Rapids, Mich.: Phanes, 1989.

To the memory of my father, Ralph A. Clack,
William T. Booth, and Reginald H. Ward

Contents

	Acknowledgments	xi
	Abbreviations	xiii
1.	Alchemy in Early America	1
2.	Edward Taylor and the Transmutation of Soul	13
3.	Alchemical Spirits in Eighteenth-Century America	41
4.	Poe's Alchemy and the Regeneration of Imagination	49
5.	Hawthorne's Alchemy of Love	83
6.	Fuller and the Golden Seed	113
	Epilogue	133
	Works Cited	137
	Index	149

Acknowledgments

Parts of chapters 2, 3, and 5 first appeared in *Seventeenth-Century News* and *ESQ: A Journal of the American Renaissance*. I would like to thank the present editors of these journals for permission to reprint these articles in revised form. Parts of chapter 4 appeared in *A Companion to Poe Studies*.

During the course of writing this book, I had the pleasure of working in many fine libraries. I would like to thank the staffs of The American Antiquarian Society, Worcester; The Beinecke and The Cushing/ Whitney Medical Libraries, Yale; The John Hay Library, Brown; The Homer Babbidge Library (especially the talented staff at Inter-Library Loan), University of Connecticut; The New York Public Library; The Woodruff Library, Emory; and The Pullen Library, Georgia State.

I would also like to thank Louis Bastien, Jr., Eric W. Carlson, John Gatta, Jr., J. D. O'Hara, and Barton Levi St. Armand for their suggestions and encouragement. Finally, I would like to thank Jamie and Max for more reasons than I could ever list here.

Abbreviations

CE	*The Centenary Edition of the Works of Nathaniel Hawthorne*, ed. William Charvat et al., 23 vols.
CW	*Collected Works of Edgar Allan Poe*, ed. Thomas Ollive Mabbott, 3 vols.
EF	*The Essential Margaret Fuller*, ed. Jeffrey Steele
ER	*Edgar Allan Poe: Essays and Reviews*, ed. G. R. Thompson
HM	*The Hermetic Museum, Restored and Enlarged*, ed. Arthur Edward Waite, 2 vols.
Letters	*The Letters of Edgar Allan Poe*, ed. John Ward Ostrom, 2 vols.
Poems	*The Poems*, Edward Taylor, ed. Donald Stanford

Chapter 1

Alchemy in Early America

Alchemy: the very word conjures up the image of a bearded old magician laboring over smoking glass beakers and vials in a dark castle dungeon, a wizard attempting to turn lead into gold by mixing putrid substances in his alembics (the alchemical vessels used in the distillation process) while heating them over sweltering fires. What does alchemy have to do with early American literature? To note in passing that Edward Taylor ridiculed the figure of the alchemist in *Meditation* 1.9; that Edgar Allan Poe used the alchemist as the focal point for his hoax "Von Kempelen and His Experiment" (1849); or that Nathaniel Hawthorne included the figure of the alchemist in two of his most memorable stories, "The Birth-mark" (1843) and *The Scarlet Letter* (1850), almost trivializes the influence that alchemical transformation had on their creative imaginations. These three writers, along with Margaret Fuller, drew upon the tropes and metaphors of alchemical philosophy to illustrate their visions of regeneration. Although the concept of regeneration is intrinsic to early America and its literature,[1] in the following chapters we will examine how Taylor, Poe, Hawthorne, and Fuller distilled the essence of alchemical philosophy into a figurative *elixir vitae* emphasizing the theme of regeneration that underscores their work.

What is alchemy? Stated simply, alchemy is the process of transforming a substance of little or no worth into a substance of great value, yet behind this definition is both a scientific and a mystic tradition, the roots of which reach back to ancient Mesopotamia.[2] According to hermetic legend, Hermes Trismegistus, the father of alchemy and author of the sacred alchemical text *Tabula Smaragdina* (Emerald Tablet), was said to have imparted the secret of transmutation to the Egyptians

2500 years before Christ.[3] In fact, ancient Egypt's wealth was once thought to have come from alchemical knowledge. This myth, popularized through the ages, was accepted as fact by the Roman emperor Diocletian, who, after conquering Egypt in A.D. 290, decreed that all books in Egypt that dealt with metals or the making of gold were to be destroyed to prevent the Egyptians from rebuilding their empire.

From Egypt the "royal art" was disseminated throughout Greece and the Middle East, and Near Eastern culture contributed elements of Gnosticism to the art of alchemy. Although the early Christian Church attempted to suppress both alchemy and Gnosticism, hermetic science was preserved by the Arabs, who absorbed the system from the Greeks. With the advent of the Crusades of the Middle Ages, Europeans were introduced to alchemical lore, and many a would-be adept soon began chemical experimentation with the hope of transmuting lead into gold.[4]

While there were many noteworthy alchemists to emerge during the Middle Ages—Thomas Norton, Basilus Valentinus, Raymond Lull, and Nicholas Flamel, to name a few—there were just as many charlatans all too willing to take advantage of the popular belief in the transmutation of metals, as Geoffrey Chaucer intimates in "The Canon's Yeoman's Tale." There were, however, two interesting developments in alchemy during the Middle Ages. First, many alchemists adopted the literary convention of allegory to encode their chemical operations and hide what they believed to be the secrets of transmutation from the profane (Poe and Hawthorne used this technique to veil their own concepts of transformation). Second, those alchemists connected with the Church, such as Lull, Petrus Bonus, Thomas Aquinas, and George Ripley, often noted the connection between the regenerative properties of the philosophers' stone and Jesus Christ (the idea at the heart of Taylor's divine alchemy).[5]

By the 1600s, the popular conception of alchemy focused upon the transmutation of lead into gold through the agency of the philosophers' stone. Although the exact composition of the magical stone was shrouded in secrecy by adepts, its attributes included the purification of matter (transmuting lead into gold) and curative and regenerative powers through the *elixir vitae*—a theme that Hawthorne exploits in "Dr. Heidegger's Experiment," "The Birth-mark," "Etherege," the "Septimius" stories, and "The Dolliver Romance." As the alchemist Arnold of Villanova notes, "The Philosopher's Stone cures all maladies. In one day it cures a malady which would last a month, in twelve days a sickness which would last a year, and a longer one in a month. It restores youth to the old."[6]

During the alchemical process the *prima materia* (prime matter) was said to be subjected to extreme heat and treated with chemical compounds (often involving mercury and sulfur) until it crumbled into a black powder. Further chemical operations, often involving the addition of mysterious chemical elements such as antimony, were then performed on the substance, changing its color from black (*nigredo*) to white (*albedo*) and finally to red-gold (*rubedo*), announcing the creation of the philosophers' stone.[7]

While the transmutation of lead into gold was a complex and intriguing idea, in reality it was a chemical fantasy. But even in the face of hundreds (if not thousands) of failed attempts at transmutation, the hermetic science of alchemy could boast such royal patrons (and practitioners) as Emperor Rudolph II (1577–1612) and Charles II of England (1660–1684).

Yet if alchemical transmutation was a fantasy, why then did alchemy remain popular? First and foremost, we should not underestimate the place of greed in human nature: many patrons of alchemy expected to be repaid tenfold for their support, and many a professed alchemist was merely a con man hiding under the guise of mystical scientist. Second, many of those who claimed to possess the secret of transmutation could boast not only a noteworthy reputation but also influence over their royal patrons. Hence, many alchemists wielded a Faustian power in European courts during the Renaissance. A more noble explanation for the interest in alchemy, however, lay in the academic (scientific) interest in unlocking the secrets of nature, and the chemical experimentation of the alchemists paved the way for great scientific advances in both chemistry and medicine during the Middle Ages and the Renaissance. By the mid-sixteenth century, the alchemist Paracelsus (Theophrastus Bombastus von Hohenheim, 1493–1534) and his followers had revolutionized the field of medicine by pioneering the practice of iatrochemistry (chemical medicine).[8]

In addition, scientific figures of the British Renaissance, such as Elias Ashmole, Robert Boyle, John Dee (and his son Arthur), Kenelm Digby, Robert Fludd, Samuel Hartlib, and Isaac Newton, were greatly influenced by alchemical philosophy.[9] While alchemical experimentation underscored many of the scientific endeavors during the British Renaissance, writers such as John Donne, Ben Jonson, Andrew Marvell, and William Shakespeare adapted alchemical thought to literary convention.[10]

In addition to the scientific discoveries achieved under the aegis of alchemy, hermetic science also offered a metaphor for the perfection of the human race, an idea that recalls the influence of ancient Gnosticism. The philosophy of the Gnostics posits that the soul has lost touch with the divine spirit (Sophia) of the universe (with which it was once closely linked) and has become imprisoned in matter (flesh); the soul, however, longs for reunion with the divine spirit, and through gnosis (knowledge) the soul achieves a reunion with the divine. In sum, Gnosticism represents the liberation of the soul through knowledge, or what alchemists like Martin Ruland referred to as "the separation of the impure from the purer substance";[11] the separation of the pure seed (gold) from imperfect matter. According to the American alchemist Eirenaeus Philalethes, "The main ground for the possibility of transmutation, is the possibility of reduction of all Metals and such Minerals as are of metallick principles, into their first Mercurial matter."[12] Ronald Gray illuminates this idea as follows:

> The whole chemical process rested on the assumption that all metals were endowed by Nature with a common quality. By virtue of this quality each bore within itself a tendency to develop into the highest form of all metals, gold. This tendency, sometimes called the "seed of gold," was, however, obstructed by natural imperfections, with the result that a variety of metals, conventionally recognized as seven in number, had come into existence. These were arranged, according to degree of perfection, in the order lead, tin, iron, copper, quicksilver, silver and gold. . . . It was the task of the alchemist to assist the more imperfect metals to attain their highest possible form by removing as far as possible the obstructions in their path.[13]

Thomas Norton illustrates this idea in "The Ordinall of Alchimy": "*Mettals* of Kind grow lowe under ground, / Soe above the erth appeareth corruption, / Of mettals, and in long tyme destruction, / Whereof noe Cause is found in this Case, / But that above Erth thei be not in their place."[14] Edward Taylor also alludes to this process in "The Description of the Great Bones Dug Up at Claverack":

> Herein doth lie the Path of Natures race
> She runneth ore from goal to goale apace . . .
> Her darksom root bears melancholy Rocks,
> Breeds Stones, Lead, Churlish iron in their plots.
> Her brighter Spirits with good warmth refinde
> Through her rich Calender breed richer kinde
> And so hath Silver bright and Gold more fine
> And sparkling Gems that mock the Sun and 'ts Shine.[15]

By the time of the Renaissance, the philosophy behind the alchemical process was being interpreted by alchemists with a religious bent (as well as by certain religious personages) in Christian allegorical terms. Even Martin Luther (1483–1546) saw the allegorical uses of alchemy in connection with Christianity:

The science of alchymy I like very well, and indeed, 'tis the philosophy of the ancients. I like it not only for the profits it brings in melting metals, in decocting, preparing, extracting, and distilling herbs, root; I like it also for the sake of the allegory and secret signification, which is exceedingly fine, touching the resurrection of the dead at the last day. For, as in a furnace the fire extracts and separates from a substance the other portions, and carries upward the spirit, the life, the sap, the strength, while the unclean matter, the dregs, remain at the bottom, like a dead and worthless carcass; even so God, at the day of judgement, will separate all things through fire, the righteous from the ungodly. The Christians and righteous shall ascend upwards into heaven, and there live everlastingly, but the wicked and the ungodly, as the dross and filth, shall remain in hell, and there be damned.[16]

The idea that I wish to emphasize here, however, involves the comparison of base metal (such as lead) with the state of the human race after its fall from grace and its expulsion from Eden. Mystical (or spiritual) alchemy, in addition to exploiting the core idea of metallic transmutation, emphasized a millennial outlook. In other words, those alchemists who recognized the spiritual implications of alchemy viewed the hermetic science as a means to speed up time, to facilitate the perfection of the soul, and to move toward (forward into) a new, golden age. For these alchemists gold was indeed a symbol of spiritual perfection and immortality.[17] As the medieval alchemist Gerhard Dorn aptly put it: "Transmute yourselves from dead stones into living philosophical stones."[18]

Just when the spiritual/mystical side of alchemy came into existence is a matter of conjecture, yet by the publication of *The Chemical Wedding of Christian Rosencreutz* (1616), the spiritual allegory of perfecting human nature suggested by the alchemical opus began to have wide-ranging implications (both spiritual and political), especially in light of the mystical order of the Rosicrucians.[19] Some alchemists with a mystical inclination even suggested that the earth could be restored to its original edenic splendor, an idea that recalls the Puritan typology of America as the New Jerusalem, exemplified in John Winthrop's "Model of Christian Charity."

Even for its earliest explorers America offered the promise of wealth and regeneration; Hernando Cortez's City of Gold (Eldorado), Ponce de Leon's Fountain of Youth, Francisco Coronado's Seven Cities of Gold, and Peter Martyr's Golden Tree of Hispañola all evoke the possibility of a transformation (material and physical regeneration) to be found in the New World. For example, Martyr writes the following:

> They [the explorers of Hispañola] have found by experience that the Vein of gold is a living Tree, and that the same by all ways spreadeth and springeth from the root, by the soft pores and passages of the Earth, putteth forth branches, even to the uppermost part of the Earth; and ceaseth not until it discover it self unto the open air: at which time it sheweth forth certain beautiful colours in the stead of flowers, round stones of golden Earth in the stead of fruits, and thin plates in stead of leaves. These are they which are dispersed throughout the whole Island [Hispañola] . . . by the course of the Rivers, eruptions of the Springs out of the Mountains, and violent falls of the flouds. For they think such grains are not engendered where they are gathered, especially on the dry land, but otherwise in the Rivers. They say that the root of the golden Tree extendeth to the center of the Earth, and there taketh nourishment of increase: for the deeper that they dig, they find the trunks thereof to be so much the greater, as far as they may follow it, for abundance of water springing in the Mountains. Of the branches of this Tree, they find some as small as a thred, and others as big as a mans finger, according to the largeness or streightness of the rifts and clefts. They have sometimes chanced upon whole Caves, sustained and born up as it were with golden pillars, and this in the ways by which the branches ascend: the which being filled with the substance of the trunk creeping from beneath the branch, maketh it self way by which it may pass out.[20]

In a sense, these early explorers of America carried with them the zeitgeist of alchemy, and though their descriptions of the New World carry subtexts designed to justify colonization and exploitation of the Western Hemisphere, their stories of vast riches and the water of youth intimate a belief in the twofold quest of the alchemist (gold and the elixir of life) that still flourished among peasants and nobles alike in the Old World. Christopher Marlowe even alludes to the alchemical promise of the New World when Faustus refers to America as the land of the golden fleece, a popular alchemical image referring to the philosophers' stone.[21]

This persistent engagement with imagination relates to cultural myths of America as a New World, a golden land where baser elements of human nature might indeed be transformed. A little more than two centuries after the first Spanish explorers arrived in America, Hector De Crèvecoeur would use the alchemical/metallurgical image of the melting pot to suggest that America was a land of transformation.[22] Preceding De Crèvecoeur's arrival in America, however, there were alchemists—sons of the fire—in New England. Hermetic and alchemical lore arrived in America with the first settlers from England and continental Europe, who also brought with them a belief in astrology and witchcraft.

In seventeenth-century America, experimental alchemy was confined (for the most part) to the areas of Massachusetts, Connecticut, and Rhode Island, and connected with many of the Puritan alchemists was Connecticut Governor John Winthrop, Jr. (1606–1676). Around Winthrop grew a circle of correspondents that included Rhode Islander Christian Lodowick (ca. 1640); Jonathan Brewster of Manheken (Norwich), Connecticut (ca. 1656); and Boston residents Robert Child (1613–1654); George Starkey (1628–1665); and William Avery (ca. 1684).[23] In addition to Winthrop's circle of illuminati, colonial America could also lay claim to Eirenaeus Philalethes, a mysterious figure whose alchemical works, *Secrets Reveal'd* (London, 1669) and *Ripley Reviv'd* (London, 1678), were brought to the attention of Hartlib, Newton, and other prominent European scientists with alchemical interests by Starkey upon his arrival in England from America.[24]

Winthrop, a chemical physician in the Paracelsian tradition and a member of Hartlib's scientific circle, amassed an alchemical library of well over 250 volumes, many obtained from contacts in Europe. A brief survey of the authors represented in Winthrop's library reads like a "Who's Who" of Medieval and Renaissance alchemy. Some of the more prominent authors include Elias Ashmole, Gerhard Dorn, Nicholas Flamel, Robert Fludd, Raymond Lull, Michael Maier, Paracelsus, George Ripley, Martin Ruland, George Starkey, and Basilius Valentinus.[25]

So great was Winthrop's reputation as an alchemical scientist that Cotton Mather, writing after Winthrop's death, called him the "Hermes Christianus" of America yet noted that Winthrop "was not more an *Adeptist* in those Noble and Secret *Medicines*, which would reach the *Roots* of the Distempers that annoy Humane Bodies, and procure an *Universal Rest* unto the *Archæus* on all Occasions of Disturbance, than he was in those *Christian Qualities*, which appear upon the Cure of the Distempers in the Minds of Men, by the Effectual *Grace* of our Lord Jesus Christ."[26] Benjamin Tompson, a New England schoolmaster and physician, also wrote of Winthrop's alchemical knowledge in his "Funeral Tribute" (1676) to the Connecticut governor:

> [Alchemical] Projections [experiments] various by fire he made
> Where Nature had her common Treasure laid [the seed of gold].
> Some thought the tincture *Philosophick* [elixir of life] lay
> Hatched by the Mineral Sun in *WINTHROPS* way;
> And clear it shines to me he had a [philosophers'] Stone
> Grav'd with his Name which he could read alone . . .
> His fruit of Toyl Hermetically done
> Stream to the pure as light doth from the Sun.[27]

Tompson included a second elegy for Winthrop in *New-Englands Tears for her Present Miseries* (1676), and he again underscored Winthrop's hermetic ability:

> *Monarch* of Natures Secrets, who did hold,
> Its grand Elixir named the *Star* of *GOLD*. . . .
> He had been round the Philosophick sea,
> And knew the Tincture if any there be:
> But all his Art must lie, there's no Disease
> Predominant, where he doth take his Ease:
> Outliving *Theophrast* [Paracelsus], he shew'd thereby
> Himself Hermetick, more surpassing high
> *TRISMEGESTOS* I'll tile him; first in Grace,
> Thrice great in *ART*, the next deserving place.[28]

Bad poetry to be sure, yet in both of these elegies Tompson demonstrates his own familiarity with both alchemy and Winthrop's reputation as an alchemist and stresses that the governor's hermetic ability was second only to his Christian qualities.

Indeed, more than a century after Winthrop's death, his reputation as an alchemist was remembered in New England folklore and recounted by Ezra Stiles:

> Govr Trumbull has often told me that this [the mountain known as *Governors Ring*] was the Place to which Gov. Winthrop of N. Lond. used to resort with his Servant; and after spend^g three Weeks in the Woods of this Mountain in roast^g Ores & assaying Metals & casting gold Rings, he used to return home to N. Lond. with plenty of Gold. Hence this is called the Gov. Winthrop's Ring to this day. Gov. Winthrop was an Adept, in intimate Correspond. with Sir Knelm Digby and first chemical & philosophical Characters of the last Century.[29]

Such was the occult reputation of the man who would remain governor of Connecticut for five years after Taylor arrived at Westfield, Massachusetts. During this period, Taylor, preacher and physician of Westfield, was writing his *Preparatory Meditations*. While Taylor rejected the claims of alchemical transmutation (perhaps in response to the reputations of those Puritan practitioners of alchemy, including Winthrop),[30] throughout his *Meditations* Taylor (almost paradoxically) adapted the tropes and metaphors of alchemy to illustrate the redeeming grace of God upon the fallen soul.

As a final note to the history of alchemy in early colonial America, Hermeticism and alchemy were not isolated with Winthrop and his

New England circle. In 1694, the German emigrant Johannes Kelpius established a mystical Rosicrucian settlement, "Woman of the Wilderness," outside Philadelphia on the banks of the Wissahickon River. Practicing an amalgam of Hermeticism, Gnosticism, and Christianity, Kelpius and his followers sought to distill the *elixir vitae* in order to "remove all seeds of disease from the human body, thereby renewing youth and lessening the infirmities of age, if not repelling death."[31] This colony of adepts survived until Kelpius' death in 1708, when its remaining members joined the colony at Euphrates, Pennsylvania.

Although I am not suggesting that alchemy was openly practiced by the Puritan settlers of New England, there was an undercurrent of both fascination and belief in the hermetic science of alchemy in early America, as there was in Europe during this time. Winthrop and his circle of illuminati practiced it, and that hoary old Puritan divine, Cotton Mather, if his short biography of Winthrop is any indication, seems to have tolerated its practice (at least in the context of physick).

In the following chapters we will examine how Taylor, Poe, Hawthorne, and Fuller incorporated the tropes and metaphors of alchemical philosophy into their own works. Our survey of alchemical imagination in the works of these writers will evoke as well a wide range of possible alchemical sources. It is useful to remember, however, that although it is possible to illuminate a particular author's work with evidence from alchemical texts that he or she may have encountered, we should keep in mind that each author was adapting alchemical philosophy to artistic expression.

The tropes and metaphors of alchemy provided Taylor, Poe, Hawthorne, and Fuller with not only a variation of the transformation theme but also a temporal link in their metaphors with the unknown, the end result of which promised knowledge, freedom, and regeneration. Our authors returned to the idea of transformation throughout their work, and it was the philosophy of the alchemists that gave them a unique way of imagining the transformation/regeneration process.

NOTES

1. For a detailed analysis of the regeneration theme in early American literature, see Richard Slotkin, *Regeneration Through Violence*.

2. Mircea Eliade, *The Forge and the Crucible* (19–26), traces the origin of alchemy to the myths surrounding the metalworkers of Mesopotamia ca. 1200 B.C.

3. For background on the history and legend of Hermes Trismegistus and the Emerald Tablet, see Lyndy Abraham, *A Dictionary of Alchemical Imagery* (100–1); Johannes Fabricius, *Alchemy* (214, 225); Charles Nicholl, *The Chemical Theatre* (49); and C.J.S. Thompson, *The Lure and Romance of Alchemy* (31).

4. For a good general discussion of early alchemy, see Henry Carrington Bolton, "The Literature of Alchemy"; John Read, *Prelude to Chemistry*; H.M.E. De Jong, *Michael Maier's* Atalanta Fugiens (21–39); and Stanton J. Linden, *Darke Hierogliphicks* (6–36).

5. For a historical survey of "The Lapis-Christ Parallel," see C. G. Jung, *Psychology and Alchemy* (345–431).

6. Quoted in Eliade (167). According to Petrus Bonus, in *The New Pearl of Great Price*, "Our Medicine [*elixir vitae*] has also power to heal all infirmity and diseases, both of inflammation and debility; it turns an old man into a youth" (348).

7. See Mark Haeffner, "Colours" (88–90) and "Stages" (235–38, esp. 236), in *The Dictionary of Alchemy*; and Abraham, "*Albedo*" (4–5), "Black" (26–27), "Colours" (44), "*Nigredo*" (135–36), and "*Rubedo*" (174–75), in *Dictionary*.

8. For further information concerning iatrochemistry, see Allen G. Debus, *The Chemical Philosophy*; and Abraham, *Dictionary* (104–5).

9. See Betty Jo Teeter Dobbs, *Alchemical Death and Resurrection*; *The Foundations of Newton's Alchemy*; "Studies in the Natural Philosophy of Sir Kenelm Digby," Parts 1–3; William Newman, "Newton's *Clavis* as Starkey's *Key*"; Richard S. Westfall, "Alchemy in Newton's Library"; Ronald Sterne Wilkinson, "The Hartlib Papers and Seventeeth-Century Chemistry"; and Lyndy Abraham, *Marvell and Alchemy* (1–29).

10. See Eugene R. Cunnar, "Donne's 'Valediction: Forbidding Mourning' and the Golden Compasses of Alchemical Creation"; Abraham, *Marvell*; Linden, for Jonson (118–53) and Donne (154–89); and Nicholl, for Jonson and Donne (107–35) and Shakespeare (136–239).

11. Martin Ruland, *A Lexicon of Alchemy* (20).

12. Eirenaeus Philalethes, *Ripley Reviv'd* (3). He also writes, "As then it is with those who are Redeemed, their Old man is crucified, [and] after that the New man is restored . . . even so it is after a sort in our Operations, for first of all our old Body dyeth . . . which is as it were the Purgatory of this old Body. . . . And when it once is purged, and made clean and pure, then are the Elements joyned . . . so that from henceforth there is nothing but concord and amity to be found in all our habitations" (354–55).

13. Ronald D. Gray, *Goethe the Alchemist* (15–16). For further information on the generation of metals, see Abraham, *Dictionary* (84–85).

14. Elias Ashmole, *Theatrum Chemicum Britannicum* (18).

15. Quoted in Donald Stanford, "The Giant Bones of Claverack" (56–57).

16. Martin Luther, *The Table Talk of Martin Luther* (326).

17. Eliade (78). Also see Abraham, "Gold and Silver" (86–88), in *Dictionary*.

18. Quoted in Jung, *Psychology and Alchemy* (148).

19. For further information on esoteric (spiritual) alchemy, see H. J. Sheppard, "Gnosticism and Alchemy"; and Daniel Merkur, "The Study of Spiritual Alchemy." For further background on the Rosicrucian Order, see Christopher McIntosh, *The Rosicrucians*; Arthur Edward Waite, *The Real History of the Rosicrucians*; Frances A. Yates, *The Rosicrucian Enlightenment*; De Jong (39–48); and Haeffner, "Rosicrucians" (222–23).

20. Quoted in John Webster, *Metallographia* (48–49).

21. Christopher Marlowe, *The Tragical History of Doctor Faustus* (act 1, scene 1, line 132).

22. See Abraham, "Crucible" (50), in *Dictionary*.

23. For further information on New England alchemists, see Harold Jantz, "America's First Cosmopolitan"; George Lyman Kittredge, "Dr. Robert Child the Remonstrant"; Herbert Leventhal, *In the Shadow of the Enlightenment* (126–36); William Newman, "Prophecy and Alchemy" and *Gehennical Fire* (14–53); G. H. Turnbull, "George Stirk, Philosopher by Fire (1628?–1665)"; and the following articles by Ronald Sterne Wilkinson: "The Alchemical Library of John Winthrop, Jr. (1606–1676) and His Descendants in Colonial America," Parts 1 and 2; "The Problem of Identity of Eirenaeus Philalethes"; "George Starkey, Physician and Alchemist"; "Hermes Christianus: John Winthrop, Jr. and Chemical Medicine in Seventeenth Century New England"; and "New England's Last Alchemists."

24. For further information on Philalethes, see Newman, *Gehennical Fire* (14–53); Newman argues that Philalethes was the pseudonym for George Starkey.

25. See Wilkinson, "Alchemical Library," Parts 1 and 2.

26. Cotton Mather, *Magnalia Christi Americana*, Vol. 1 (262).

27. Benjamin Tompson, *Benjamin Tompson 1642–1714*, (100).

28. Ibid. (85). For further information on the tincture/elixir, see Haeffner, "Elixir" (116–18); and Abraham, "Medicine" (123), "Red Elixir" (169), and "Ticture" (200), in *Dictionary*.

29. Ezra Stiles, *Literary Diary*, Vol. 3 (266).

30. There are, however, no records of correspondence between Taylor and Winthrop.

31. Quoted in Julius F. Sachse, *The German Pietists of Provencial Pennsylvania, 1694–1708* (111). Kelpius and his followers practiced a form of spiritual alchemy influenced by Rosicrucian philosophy. Their work also suggests a type of hermetic millennialism.

Chapter 2

Edward Taylor and the Transmutation of Soul

Very little is known of Edward Taylor's life before he arrived in America.[1] Born into a family of dissenters from Leicestershire, England in 1642, Taylor left England on April 26, 1668; seventy days later, he arrived in Boston. For the next three and a half years Taylor studied at Harvard College.

On May 5, 1671, Taylor and four fellow members of his Harvard senior class met to present their final declamations. Among the 212 lines of heroic couplets that Taylor wrote for this occasion appears the first reference to alchemy written by the Puritan poet: "no such spirits flow / From mine alembick, neither have I skill / To rain such honey falls out of my still."[2] Taylor offers the preceding as an apology and evokes the image of the alchemical vessel, the alembic and its medicinal spirits, with which he contrasts the product(s) of his own unrefined poetic imagination.

Although it may seem strange to some scholars that the poetry of a Puritan preacher finds its way into a study of alchemical imagination and early American literature, the work of Joan Del Fattore and Cheryl Oreovicz has laid a foundation by which scholars may note the alchemical references and tropes in Taylor's *Meditations*.[3] A closer examination of Taylor's *Meditations*, however, illuminates how his Puritan mind encountered and incorporated the tropes and philosophy of alchemy into his poetic work to illustrate his vision of regeneration.

Upon first encountering Taylor's *Meditations*, it is apparent that the poet held the figure of the earthly alchemist in utter contempt. In *Meditation* 1.9 Taylor describes the alchemist:

> The Boasting Spagyirst (Insipid Phlegm,
>   Whose Words out strut the Sky) vaunts he hath rife
> The Water, Tincture, Lozenge, Gold, and Gem,
>   Of Life itselfe. But here's the Bread of Life.
>   I'le lay my Life, his Aurum Vitae Red
>   Is to my Bread of Life, worse than DEAD HEAD. (*Poems* 19–20)

In the first few lines of this passage Taylor chides the alchemist ("Boasting Spagyirst") for his attempts to create the stone of transmutation ("Lozenge, Gold and Gem") and the *elixir vitae* ("Water, Tincture . . . Of Life"). Taylor's reference to "Aurum Vitae Red" is also interesting, for it refers to the liquid that the alchemists called the "Gold of Life"—the tincture of the philosophers' stone (i.e., the alchemical elixir of life) that was reported to prolong life and in rare cases to restore the dead.[4] While this stanza in the midst of a *meditation* on the Living Bread of the communion at first seems out of place, Taylor intimates that the aims of the alchemist—the creation of the philosophers' stone and the elixir of life—are worthless ("DEAD HEAD," or chemical dregs) compared with the regenerative power of God's "Bread of Life."[5]

Although he was familiar with the philosophy behind the transmutation of metals, gleaned from his study of John Webster's *Metallographia*,[6] Taylor used the spiritual metaphors of alchemy to illustrate what he saw as the regenerating powers of God's grace through the theanthropy of Christ. The Puritan poet fashioned a paradigm that drew heavily from Christian alchemists and that part of their worldview concerned with the transformation and regeneration of the soul. Stanton Linden cogently summarizes the connection of Christ and the philosophers' stone perceived by Christian alchemists of the seventeenth century:

> Along with other concerns, alchemical authors of this period were especially interested in setting forth the sacred implications of the art by devising or reaffirming intricate systems of correspondence that existed (or were thought to exist) between chemical processes and interactions occurring within their alembics and spiritual transformations taking place within their own hearts and souls. In each case the desired end was purification and perfection: the attainment of the philosopher's stone or the moral and spiritual regeneration of a believer whose soul, through God's grace, has been fitted for salvation. Central to this analogical system is the ancient idea of Christ as the philosopher's stone: the agent of healing, deliverer from sin and baseness, rewarder of merit, author of grace and salvation, and creator of new heavens and a new earth. . . . In its most extreme form, this analogical mode of thought leads to a direct identification of Christ, or his attributes, or God,

with the master alchemist who creates, directs, and will someday end the world and the course of human history.[7]

Although Taylor fell heir to this alchemical tradition, he rejected the claims of the mundane alchemist. For Taylor, God alone possessed the power of transmutation, the power to regenerate the fallen soul into a redeemed member of the elect.

Taylor encapsulates this idea in *Meditation* 1.7. Perhaps the one meditation to which scholars frequently turn for an example of Taylor's use of alchemical tropes, this short meditation is rich in alchemical imagery and begins with the poet's vision of Christ as an alchemical still:

> Thy Humane Frame, my Glorious Lord, I spy,
>   A Golden Still with Heavenly Choice drugs filld;
> Thy Holy Love, the Glowing heate whereby,
>   The Spirit of Grace is graciously distilld.
>   Thy Mouth the Neck through which these spirits still.
>   My Soul thy Violl make, and therewith fill. (*Poems* 17)

The golden color of the still suggests the value of its contents, "Heavenly Choice drugs" that have been distilled by God's "Holy Love, the Glowing heate." From this still flows the "Spirit of Grace"—the regenerative "Tincture" (or *elixir vitae*) of stanza two—that Taylor needs distilled into his alembic soul.

In the second stanza, Taylor specifically refers to God's Grace in five of the six lines as a "tincture" distilled:[8]

> Thy Speech the Liquour in thy Vessell stands,
>   Well ting'd with Grace a blessed Tincture, Loe,
> Thy Words distilld, Grace in thy Lips pourd, and,
>   Give Graces Tinctur in them where they go.
>   Thy words in graces tincture stilld, Lord, may
>   The Tincture of thy Grace in me Convay. (*Poems* 17)

Although Taylor has chosen Psalms 45:2, "Grace in thy lips is poured out," as the text for this meditation, the reference to both the alchemical distillation process and the tincture is of particular interest. According to Paracelsus, the tincture had the power to transform base metal (or base material) into gold.[9] In Webster's *Metallographia* (a work that Taylor transcribed in condensed form and bound by hand), the poet found such passages as the following:

> Gold in essence is threefold, 1. *Cœleste & est solutium*, celestial and loosed. 2. *Elementare*, and that is fluid. 3. *Metallicum*, and

that is corporeal. Further, it is to be known that the first *ens*, that is to say, the first composition of Gold, which as yet remains a liquor not coagulated, doth renew and restore whatsoever it takes; not only men, but also all Beasts, Fruits, Herbs, and Trees.

We may now consider whether this *primum ens auri* may be had in an hard and coagulated form or not. And it appeareth plainly that it may; for the Philosophers that sought after that great secret of Nature and Art, the Physical Tincture, or Grand Elixir, do certainly affirm it.

The Philosophers often make mention of another sort of *aurum potabile*, or the tincture of Gold, which is not drawn forth of common Gold, but forth of another subject; and this we touched where we spake of Astralish [Celestial] Gold.[10]

I have cited these passages from Webster to indicate how Taylor transformed the "Grand Elixir" (the *elixir vitae*) of the alchemists into a metaphor for the tincture of God's grace. In the final stanza of *Meditation* 1.7, Taylor moves from Christ's words as tincture to Christ's words as gold:

> That Golden Mint of Words, thy Mouth Divine,
>   Doth tip these Words, which by my Fall were spoiled;
> And Dub with Gold dug out of Graces mine
>   That they thine Image might have in them foild.
>   Grace in thy Lips pourd out's as Liquid Gold.
>   Thy Bottle make my Soule, Lord, it to hold. (*Poems* 17)

Here the association of grace with gold ("Golden Mint of Words" and "Gold dug out of Graces mine") culminates in the image of "Grace" as "Liquid Gold"—the *primum ens* of gold created in the alchemical opus—with Taylor's soul figured as an alchemical vessel, or alembic, to hold the precious substance.[11] Implicit in this passage is the idea that God's "Grace" is tantamount to His joy and love given form in Christ. For Taylor this "Grace" becomes a most transmutative substance having the ability to redeem the poet's soul.

First and foremost for Taylor, Christ is the agent of transmutation through which the soul moves to a state of grace. Throughout the *Meditations* Taylor emphasizes this point: Christ is comparable with the philosophers' stone, created by God-the-alchemist to regenerate the fallen soul. Additionally, Christ, in his role as philosophers' stone, possesses the power to move Taylor's imagination from a state of despair that begins many of his meditations to a state of grace that seems to end these poems. As Taylor states in *Meditation* 2.153:

> With Christs rich praises whose lips do distill
> Upon his Spouse such ravishing dews to gust
> With Silver Metaphors and Tropes bedight.
> How fair, how pleasant art, Love, for delight? (*Poems* 359)

In the context of Taylor's *Meditations*, Christ also transmutes or regenerates the poet's imagination.

Returning to *Meditation* 1.7 and Taylor's image of the "Golden Still with Heavenly Choice drugs filld," we may glean a clue as to the extent of Taylor's alchemical knowledge, for this line suggests the poet's familiarity with Paracelsian (alchemical) medicine. Indeed, as town physician of Westfield, Taylor was exposed to alchemical theories of medicine through his studies of physick.[12]

Of the many alchemists whose work influenced the artistic imagination of Taylor, by far the most influential was Theophrastus Bombastus von Hohenheim, or Paracelsus. Insulted by his detractors for having no respect for the traditional Galenic school of medicine and accused of habitual drunkeness, this self-proclaimed medical reformer (along with his followers) reenvisioned the medical profession during the European Renaissance and laid the foundation for the study and practice of iatrochemistry, the use of chemical compounds to treat illnesses. Opposed to the Galenic school of medicine, which treated illnesses on the assumption that one or more of the humors was out of balance in the patient's body, Paracelsus and his followers relied heavily on the chemical procedures and discoveries developed by the alchemists during their experiments. As Paracelsus proclaimed in the subtitle to The *"Labyrinthus Medicorum"*: "Concerning The Book of Alchemy, Without Which No One Can Become a Physician."[13]

While Taylor did not possess any specific writings of Paracelsus, the Westfield physican-preacher's personal library contained three major sources of Paracelsian medical thought: John Woodall's *The Surgion's Mate, or a treastise discovering faithfully the due contents of the surgions chest* (London, 1617); Simeon Partlitz's *A New Method of Physick* (translated by Nicolas Culpeper, London, 1654); and the *Pharmacopoeia Londinensis* (translated by Nicholas Culpeper, London, 1649, 1650).[14] Woodall, heavily influenced by Paracelsean hermetic medicine, included in *The Surgion's Mate* an eighty-six page section on alchemy as well as some verses that illustrated what he saw as the relationship of the Trinity with the Paracelsian *tria prima* (the sulfur-salt-mercury theory of alchemy).[15] While the Puritan preacher would have rejected Woodall's notion of the Trinity, Taylor appears to have been influenced by the Paracelsean doctrine of the *tria prima*, for it correlates with that part of Taylor's own system of correspondence that emphasized God-the-alchemist and the fire of love (sulfur), Christ as mercurial solvent, and the soul as object of transmutation.

A second text that holds importance with regard to Taylor's knowledge of alchemical medicine is Culpeper's translation of Partlitz's *A New Method of Physick*. Here Taylor discovered such statements as the following:

> Medicine cannot want Alchymie, the one is so helpful, to another as man & wife, and therefore they ought not to be separated.

> Look upon one of *Galens* Apothecaries Shops . . . so many simples are in one Composition, that they hinder one anothers operation, and therfore how can they ease the sick without calling the help of an Alchymist to resolve, separate, and exhale what is obnoxious, thereby producing the hidden Natures of things for use . . . Also the Alchymist searcheth after the strength and Temperature of things, the Causes and Originall of their actions and by Mediation of a certain pure body sets the very species and forms of things before your eyes . . .

> The Art of an Alchymist is to separate this which nature hath mixed: As the Maseraick veynes separate from the pure Chyle from the impure dung in the body of man; So Alychmie separates from the spirits the medicine, and rejects the impure dross.[16]

Partlitz's *Physick* was clearly proposing a conjunction of alchemy and medicine—the iatrochemical thought introduced by Paracelsus.

The third source of alchemical medicine found in Taylor's library was the *Pharmacopoeia Londinensis*, translated by Culpeper. The *Pharmacopoeia*'s chapter on "Chemical Oyls and other Oyls or Herbs and Flowers" offers this suggestion: "Your best way to learn to still Chymical Oyls, is to learn of an Alchymist: for I rest confident the greatest part of the [London] College [of Physicians] had no more skil in Chemistry, than I have in building houses; but having found out certain Models in old rusty Authors, tell people SO they must be done."[17] This brief excursion into Taylor's medical library is intended to emphasize the alchemical foundation behind Taylor's own medical knowledge.[18] We might indeed say that Taylor was a physician of the body as God was physician of the soul.

In addition to Taylor's background in physick, the Puritan preacher also had an interest in metallurgy, a fact that is evidenced by his personal copy of Webster's *Metallographia*. In this treatise, an alchemical history of metals, Webster draws heavily on the writings of Paracelsus for the bulk of his study. As Allen G. Debus notes, "Webster sought to make available in translation the views of the major authors who had written of this subject [alchemy]. . . . Webster singled out Paracelsus for special praise, because he had described chemical processes in plain words, thus making alchemy available to a new audience."[19] Webster presents his thesis in the first chapter: "The most noble of all Arts, the Transmutation of Metals [alchemy], and the curing of all diseases by an universal Medicine . . . is no where to be had but forth of the Mineral Kingdom."[20] Taylor transformed Webster's thesis to emphasize God's ability to transmute the soul from its base life of sin (spiritual sickness) to a state of salvation, or regeneration.

Webster, however, was not concerned with salvation, and his main theme in *Metallographia* focuses on the transmutation of metals as it relates to alchemy and the alkahest (the Paracelsian universal solvent), as the following chapter titles attest:

Chap. 8. *Of the several sorts of Gold according to the mystical Authors; also of the Primum Ens of Gold, and of some other things of the like nature.*

Chap. 12. *What may be thought of common Gold, whether it be an ingredient into the Philosophers Tincture or not? What may be said of* Aurum Potabile, *or the Tincture of Gold? And what of the white Body when the Tincture is taken from it? and something of the Alkahest.*

Chap. 24. *Of the several sorts of Mercuries, according to the mystical Philosophers or Adeptists.*

Chap. 26. *Of several sorts of Medicaments prepared forth of common Mercury, both by the way of vulgar Chymistry, as also by the mystical way; and of the* Pæcipiolum *of Paracelsus and Helmont.*

Chap. 29. *Of the Transmutation of Metals.*[21]

Of special interest to our study of Taylor is Webster's account of the *Aurum Potabile* and the alkahest and their connection to Taylor's use of *aqua vitae*. *Aurum Potabile* was a term used by Paracelsians to denote potable gold used in medicines; the alkahest was purported to be a universal solvent capable of dissolving even the hardest of metals.[22]

A fine example of Taylor's use of the alkahest is located in *Meditation* 1.10 (the biblical text is John 6:55: "My blood is drink indeed"). While the image of Christ's blood (and the sacrament) is primary for the poet here, Taylor's subtle use of chemical images and apparatus in the midst of this meditation (stanzas two through five) signals the secondary alchemical metaphor of the distillation process at work.

After Taylor's praise of God's "Stupendious Love!" (*Poems* 20) in the first stanza of *Meditation* 1.10, the second stanza demonstrates how the poet's thirst for this love is quenched by God's "Aqua-Vitae":

My Soule had Caught an Ague, and like Hell
    Her thirst did burn: she to each spring did fly,

> But this bright blazing Love did spring a Well
> Of Aqua-Vitae in the Deity,
> Which on the top of Heav'ns high Hill out burst
> And down came running thence t'allay my thirst. (*Poems* 21)

Although Taylor associates *aqua vitae* with Christ's blood (the wine of the sacrament), Ruland, in his *Lexicon of Alchemy*, notes that "AQUA VITAE is Mercury," a solvent often used in the alchemical process to dissolve impurities (dross) from metallic substances.[23] *Aqua vitae* also connotes the alchemical *elixir vitae*, the water of life, and when consumed was reported to have restorative powers. In the context of *Meditation* 1.10, the spiritual *aqua vitae* has the power to dissolve the sin that surrounds the soul and restore its spiritual state. Thus, at the end of this stanza, Taylor's use of *aqua vitae* evokes both the alkahest and the *elixir vitae*.

In the third stanza Taylor clearly identifies the *aqua vitae* with Christ's blood, yet the "golden" adjectives the poet uses conflate the concept of heavenly perfection with the golden product of the alchemical opus:

> But how it came, amazeth all Communion.
> God's onely Son doth hug Humanity,
> Into his very person. By which Union
> His Humane Veans its golden gutters ly.
> And rather than my Soule should dy by thirst,
> These Golden Pipes, to give me drink, did burst. (*Poems* 21)

At the beginning of this stanza Taylor presents the image of Christ as alchemical mediator—wedding God with Taylor (heaven with earth)—through whose "Union" with humanity Taylor receives *aqua vitae* through "golden gutters" and "Golden Pipes." Taylor's golden images reflect the subtle alchemical nuances that the poet is already working into *Meditation* 1.10, for as we have observed, Taylor's image of "Golden Pipes" suggests the contents of the still at the end the opus (*Medication* 1.7). Furthermore, Taylor's use of Christ as mediator between heaven and earth evokes the description of the philosophers' stone found in Eirenaeus Philalethes' "The Fount of Chemical Truth" (1678): "Join heaven to earth in the fire of love, and you will see in the middle of the firmament the bird of Hermes [the philosophers' stone]" (*HM* 2: 263).[24] Indeed, Taylor's vision of the Christ-figure reconciles heaven and earth (God and Taylor) and prepares the way for the soul's regeneration.

In stanza four, Taylor shifts from the image of *aqua vitae* flowing from Christ's "Golden Pipes" to a more literal image of wine:

> This Liquour brew'd, thy sparkling Art Divine
> Lord, in thy Chrystall Vessells did up tun,
> (Thine Ordinances,) which all Earth o're shine
> Set in thy rich Wine Cellars out to run.
> Lord, make thy Butlar draw, and fill with speed
> My Beaker full: for this is drink indeed. (*Poems* 21)

While the "Liquour brew'd, thy sparkling Art Divine" refers to Christ's blood (as *aqua vitae*), Taylor's use of "Chrystall Vessells" to store the heavenly wine recalls the alembics used to catch and hold the distillates of the alchemical process created by the "Art Divine," God's heavenly alchemy.[25]

Thus far we have noted the alchemical subtext of *Meditation* 1.10 in Taylor's use of *aqua vitae*, Christ's union with man, and the distillation of wine, but there is also an important connection between the philosophers' stone (the tincture) and the blood of Christ that further helps to illuminate this poem. According to H.M.E. De Jong, "In the Middle Ages, when the passion, dying and resurrection of Christ was made analogous to the transmutation process, from which the Philosophers' Stone would arise, the red colour of Christ's blood, by which the world was redeemed, counted for that reason also as the colour required for the Philosophers' Stone."[26] The equation of Christ's blood with the philosophers' stone allows us to observe how Taylor conflates his theme of communion (wine) with the divine alchemy of God's grace. The wine of which Taylor writes holds the power of transmutation for those who consume it. In essence, the communion wine is a spiritual physick, what Taylor refers to elsewhere as a "Heavenly Alkahest" (2.68[B] *Poems* 207), which regenerates the soul.[27]

TAYLOR'S ALCHEMICAL PARADIGM

To this point we have observed how Taylor reenvisioned specific tropes from alchemy and hermetic physick and incorporated them into his *Preparatory Meditations*. Taylor also fashioned an interesting paradigm reminiscent of the system of correspondences used by Christian alchemists. Taylor's hermetic paradigm contains four major points: (1) the poet and his soul as both an "alembick" and an object of transmutation; (2) God as alchemist; (3) Christ as the philosophers' stone; and (4) grace as philosophical gold and healing tincture. Taylor used this system of correspondence throughout his *Meditations* to underscore his vision of regeneration.

In his study of Taylor, John Gatta notes that the *Preparatory Meditations* exhibit "two broad categories of metaphor—one signifying containment, the other transmutation."[28] Both metaphors serve as important illustrations of Taylor's adaptation of alchemical thought in his poetry. Although Taylor uses many different images to symbolize his soul, those images that appear as alchemical vessels, such as alembics and vials, help to illuminate Taylor's vision of the alchemical opus as a primary metaphor for the transforming and transmuting power of God's grace. For example, in *Meditation* 1.28 Taylor appeals to God:

> Let thy Choice Caske, shed, Lord, into my Cue
>   A Drop of Juyce presst from thy Noble Vine.
> My Bowl is but an Acorn Cup, I sue
>   But for a Drop: this will not empty thine.
>   Although I'me in an Earthen Vessells place,
>   My Vessell make a Vessell, Lord, of Grace.
> My Earthen Vessell make thy Font also:
>   And let thy Sea my Spring of Grace in't raise.
> Spring up oh Well. My cup with Grace make flow.
>   Thy Drops will on my Vessell ting thy Praise.
>   I'l sing this Song, when I these Drops Embrace.
>   My Vessell now's a Vessell of thy Grace. (*Poems* 46)

Here Taylor first presents his body as a "Vessell" (for his soul), yet this image quickly transforms to a vessel that catches and holds the distillate of God's redeeming grace.

The metaphor of the soul as vessel also finds expression in *Meditation* 1.48, where Taylor notes, "My Soule seems an Alembick doth possess / Love stilld into rich Spirits by thy Art" (*Poems* 78). This passage offers a superlative example of Taylor's use of alchemical tropes, and a close look at the meditation will further illustrate this point. In its first stanza, Taylor appears struck by what he sees as the unequal exchange of his love in return for God's "Joy":

> When I, Lord, eye thy Joy, and my Love, small,
>   My heart give in: what now? Strange! Sure I love thee!
> And finding brambles 'bout my heart to crawl
>   My heart misgives mee. Prize I ought above thee?
>   Such great Love hugging them, such small Love, thee!
>   Whether thou hast my Love, I scarce can see. (*Poems* 77)

Here, God's "Joy," or grace, is bestowed freely upon Taylor, yet the poet bemoans the small amount of love that he returns to God. Taylor's recognition of this unequal exchange leads the poet to banish his love of earthly things in the second stanza: "Avant adultrous Love. From me depart" (*Poems* 77).

In the third stanza Taylor moves to his alchemical motif, which begins as if by free association. During stanzas one and two, Taylor refers to his heart's love of earthly things as "brambles 'bout my heart to crawl" and "a thorn bush" (*Poems* 77). In the third stanza, "Puddle Water boyld by Sunn beams till / Its Spiritless, and dead" (*Poems* 77–78) feeds the brambles of his heart. The water, "spiritless and dead," recalls the alchemical *nigredo*—the alchemical stage of blackness, despair, and death at the beginning of the opus. Although water boiled by the sun's beams is the best that the earth can offer (i.e., nature's alchemy), Taylor realizes that God's water of life far surpasses what the earth might offer:

> nothing more thin
> Tasts wealthier than those thou dost distill.
> This seems to numb my heart to think that I
> Should null all good to optimate a toy. (*Poems* 78)

In the fourth stanza, the "beamings . . . of thy [God's] rich Joys [Grace]" guild Taylor's soul, and the poet states:

> meethinks I'm sure I Love thee.
> They Calcine all these brambley trumperys
> And now I'm sure that I prize naught above thee.
> Thy beams making a bonefire of my Stack
> Of Faggots, bring my Love to thee in'ts pack. (*Poems* 78)

Here God's joy burns through the dross (the corruption of Taylor's earthly love) surrounding the poet's heart. Finally, in the fifth stanza Taylor's heart is transformed from a brambled nest to an alembic for God's love:

> For when the Objects of thy Joy impress
> Their shining influences on my heart
> My Soule seems an Alembick doth possess
> Love stilld into rich Spirits by thy Art.
> And all my pipes, were they ten thousand would
> Drop Spirits of Love on thee, more rich than gold. (*Poems* 78)

Through what can best be described as God's divine alchemy ("Art"), Taylor's soul is transformed into an alchemical vessel that catches the distilled spirit of God's grace, a love "more rich than gold."

There remains, however, one more observation to be made concerning Taylor's use of the image of alchemical vessel in *Meditation* 1.48: Taylor's poem functions as a figurative alembic into which the poet places the *prima materia* of his imagination. In a creative sense, Taylor becomes the poet-alchemist, shaping and transmuting his own imagination into a work of art. Although Taylor often bemoans his own (vain) labors as a poet, he locates a mercurial-like catalyst (inspiration) in the figure of Christ (and the experience of grace) to complete his work, as in *Meditation* 2.153: "Christs rich praises whose lips do distill / Upon his Spouse such ravishing dews to gust / With Silver Metaphors and Tropes bedight."[29] Thus, each meditation may be viewed as a poetic vessel into which the poet places his despair, only to have it transmuted by his experience of God's grace into joy and love for God.

Further understanding of how Taylor develops the metaphors of transmutation in the *Meditations* may be derived from his handling of images to describe his own soul:

> a Dish of Dumps: yea ponderous dross,
>   Black blood all clotted, burdening my heart,
> That Anger's anvill, and my bark bears moss. (2.25 *Poems* 127)

> I'm Common matter: Lord thine Altar make mee.
>   Then sanctify thine Altar with thy blood:
> I'l offer on't my heart to thee. (Oh! take mee)
>   And let thy fire Calcine mine Altars Wood,
>   Then let thy Spirits breath, as Bellows, blow
>   That this new kindled Life may flame and glow. (2.82 *Poems* 233)

> My Lumpish Soule, enfir'd with such bright flame
>   And Quick'ning influences of this Sight
> Darting themselves throughout my drossy frame
>   Would jump for joy, and sing with greate delight. (2.93 *Poems* 249)

All three of these passages illustrate Taylor's recognition of his soul as unrefined *prima materia* ("ponderous dross," "Common matter," "Lumpish Soule," and "drossy frame").[30] Only God can redeem this base matter of the poet's soul. As Taylor states in *Meditation* 1.24: "My minde is Leaden in thy Golden Shine. / Though all o're Spirit, when this dirty Dross / Doth touch it with its smutting leaden lines" (*Poems* 40). The above lines offer a fine example of Taylor bemoaning the fact that both his soul and imagination are corrupt, unrefined, and unworthy of praising God. Although Taylor's despair finds alchemical correspondence in the idea of the *nigredo* and the cleansing of the *prima materia*,[31] the transformation of the imagery here is fascinating: from earthy lead (Taylor's imagination) to heavenly gold, from the "dross" of Taylor's imagination to heavenly spirit.[32] Taylor's imagery suggests a transformation from a state of sin (dross or base metal) to regeneration (gold or perfection) with recourse to language of a decidedly alchemical nature. As Webster notes: "Transmutation is when a thing loseth its form, and is so altered, that it is altogether unlike its former substance and form, but assumeth another form, another essence, another colour, another virtue, another nature or propriety."[33]

We find Taylor again adapting Webster's concept of alchemical transmutation within the context of the soul's regeneration in *Meditation* 2.12. Once again, Taylor begins in a state of despair, "I finde my Spirits Spiritless, and flat" (*Poems* 101), but at the end Taylor entreats God to transmute the poet's soul:

> Spare me, my Lord, spare me, I greatly pray,
>   Let me thy Gold pass through thy Fire untill
> Thy Fire refine, and take my filth away.
>   That I may shine like Gold, and have my fill
>   Of Love for thee. (*Poems* 102)

Although Taylor's primary trope in this passage is drawn from the refining process of gold, it is worthwhile to note that Webster acknowledged alchemy's historical relationship with metallurgy. In *Meditation* 2.12, Taylor emphasizes the refining fire of God that purges the dross surrounding Taylor's soul so that the true spiritual gold of the soul (the alchemical seed of gold) is revealed. As Taylor remarks in *Meditation* 2.5, "Lord with thine Altars Fire, mine Inward man / Refine from dross" (*Poems* 89). Thus, in the holy, purifying fire, Taylor's Christian metal is proven.[34] Indeed, throughout the *Meditations* we may observe frequent references to the poet's soul as dross or base metal, but through Taylor's experience of grace (in its many forms) his soul is transmuted into "Heavens gold" (1.30, *Poems* 49).[35]

In the preceding examples from the *Meditations* we have observed how Taylor used the tropes of esoteric alchemy to embody his vision of the soul's regeneration. While Taylor rejected claims that the human alchemist could create the stone of transmutation, Taylor often referred to God as an alchemist-physician whose work of spiritual regeneration evoked images of the earthly alchemist.

In *Meditation* 1.4, for example, Taylor envisions God as an "[al]Chymist" who creates a regenerating elixir from the Rose of Sharon:

> God Chymist is, doth Sharons Rose distill.
>   Oh! Choice Rose Water! Swim my Soul herein.
> Let Conscience bibble in it with her Bill.

> Its Cordiall, ease doth Heart burns Causd by Sin.
> Oyle, Syrup, Sugar, and Rose Water such.
> Lord, give, give, give; I cannot have too much.
>
> But, oh! alas! that such should be my need
>   That this Brave Flower must Pluckt, stampt, squeezed bee,
> And boyld up in its Blood, its Spirits sheed,
>   To make a Physick sweet, sure, safe for mee.
>   But yet this mangled Rose rose up again
>   And in its pristine glory, doth remain. (*Poems* 13)[36]

Here God's chemical distillation of the elixir (of life) from "Sharons Rose" (Christ) leads to the only cure that Taylor recognizes for his weary soul. As Taylor intimates, the risen Christ embodies the healing elixir that will purge the spiritual sickness from the poet's soul and facilitate his union with the Lord:

> My Dear-Sweet Lord, shall I thy Glory meet
>   Lodg'd in a Rose, that out a sweet Breath breaths.
> What is my way to Glory made thus sweet,
>   Strewd all along with Sharons Rosy Leaves.
>   I'le walk this Rosy Path: World fawn, or frown
>   And Sharons Rose shall be my Rose, and Crown. (*Poems* 13)

While the rose garden of the philosophers is one of alchemy's best-known emblems, the rose was often used by the alchemists as a symbol of the *rubedo*, the red-gold stage of the opus that proceeds the creation of the philosophers' stone.[37] In *Meditation* 1.4 the Christ-Rose with its alchemical resonances yields the alchemical tincture, the "oyle" of salvation. "Sharons Rose," in fact, becomes analogous with the philosophers' stone, formed by the alchemical conjunction of the "Pure White, and Red" (*Poems* 13)—the conjunction of the *albedo* and the *rubedo* of the opus—that is distilled by the celestial alchemist in stanzas seven through nine. Furthermore, "Sharons Rose" displays the "Beauties of all Flowers" (*Poems* 12)—the rainbow colors of the *cauda pavonis*, the alchemical stage that announces the philosophers' stone.[38]

A further treatment of the Rose of Sharon theme is located in *Meditation* 2.60:

> I am thy Vally where thy lilly grows
>   Thou my White and Red blesst lilly fresh;
> Thy Active and thy Passive 'bedience do
>   Hold out Active and Passive Right'ousness.

Pure White and Red making a lovely grace,
Present thee to our Love to hug and 'brace. (*Poems* 373)

The white phase of the opus, the *albedo*, was often symbolized by the whiteness of the moon, the lily and silver, whereas the red phase, or *rubedo*, was symbolized by the sun, the rose, and gold.[39] To illustrate the alchemical conjunction of white and red, William Bloomfield writes, "Joyne thow in one Body with a perfect unity / First the red Man, and the white Woman";[40] and according to Thomas Norton, "Then is the faire White Woman / Married to the Ruddy Man."[41] Against this backdrop of alchemical symbolism Taylor's image of "Pure White and Red" evokes the conjunction of the alchemical *albedo* (white) with the *rubedo* (red). The product of this conjunction is the spiritual gold that Taylor calls "a lovely grace"—the redeeming grace of Christ that has the power to transmute Taylor's soul from a state of sin into a state of grace.

Taylor again alludes to this alchemical conjunction of white and red in *Meditation* 2.21:

Make mee thy Lunar Body to be filld
   In full Conjunction, with thy Shining Selfe
The Sun of Righteousness: whose beams let guild
   My Face turnd up to heaven, on which high Shelfe
I shall thy Glorys in my face that shine,
Set in Reflected Rayes. Hence thou hast thine. (*Poems* 117)

This passage recalls the alchemical conjunction of Sol (the sun, gold, and Christ) and Luna (the moon, silver, the poet's soul) that leads to the final step in the alchemical opus: the bursting of the alchemical vessel and the returning of the soul to God.[42] Taylor's imagery here has for its source the following passage from Webster's *Metallographia* (which is quoted from Paracelsus):

First we are to know that every Metal, as long as yet it lies hid in its first being, or *ens*, hath its peculiar stars. So Gold hath the star of the Sun, Silver hath the star of the Moon, &c. But so soon as they are come unto their perfection, and are coagulated into a fixt metallick body, their stars do recede from every one of them, and leaves its body dead. From whence it follows, that all their bodies are from thenceforth dead, and inefficacious; and the invincible star of the Metals doth overcome them all, and convert them into its nature, and make them all so to be Astral.[43]

For Taylor this final step was reflected in the fallen soul's redemption (purification) through God's love (imaged alternatively as sun, son, and furnace or refining fire). When we apply Webster's observation to Taylor's *Meditation* 2.21, we find that the conjunction of Christ (sun) with the poet (moon) yields both the "death" of Taylor's earthly body and the ascension of Taylor's regenerated spirit to heaven.

In *Meditation* 1.34, Taylor again refers to God's divine plan for man's redemption (through physical death) in alchemical-medicinal terms:

> And still thou by thy gracious Chymistry
>   Dost of his [Christ's] Carkass Cordialls make rich, High,
> To free from Death makst Death a remedy:
>   A Curb to Sin, a Spur to Piety.
>   Heavens brightsom Light shines out in Death's Dark Cave.
>   The Golden Dore of Glory is the Grave. (*Poems* 55)

In this passage, heaven's "gracious Chymistry" transforms Christ, reducing the body to a "Carkass" from which medicinal cordials are made to facilitate the soul's regeneration. In fact, this short passage in the midst of *Meditation* 1.34 suggests a concentrated allusion to the divine alchemical opus. Christ's death evokes the alchemical *nigredo*, and from his "Carkass" God transforms death into an elixir of life. Even Taylor's use of the grave recalls the symbolism of the alchemical grave (or alembic) illustrated in many alchemical texts.[44] "Heavens brightsom Light" heralds the yellowing of the *citrinitas*, and the "Golden Dore of Glory," the entrance to the spiritual kingdom of God, recalls the golden color at the end of the opus.[45] Thus, through death's doorway the poet's soul returns to God-the-creator, "Say I am thine, My Lord" (*Poems* 55).

In *Meditations* 2.4 and 2.32, we may also observe the poet's further reference to God as "[al]Chymist."[46] In the former Taylor entreats God to

> Distill thy Spirit through thy royall Pipe
>   Into my Soule, and so my Spirits feed,
>   Then them, and me still into praises right
>   Into thy Cup where I to swim delight. (*Poems* 88)

Here Taylor puns on "Spirit" to suggest both God's spirit and alchemical essences that flow from the "Pipes" of heaven's still to Taylor's soul (as receptacle or alembic). Taylor's final image of the soul swimming in a cup of spirits evokes the alchemical *ablutio*, or cleansing, and suggests that through the distilled spirit(s) of grace the poet's soul is purified. We might suspect that Taylor had a baptismal image in mind here, but the image of the poet swimming in God's "Cup" also recalls the alchemical illustrations of base material purified during the alchemical process.[47]

The final three stanzas of *Meditation* 2.32 (an unfinished meditation) also recall the image of God as alchemist (although there does not appear to be any connection here with the fragmented theme presented in the first eight stanzas of this poem). In these last passages Taylor first implores the divine alchemist:

> O let thy lovely streams of Love distill
>   Upon myselfe and spoute their spirits pure
> Into my Viall, and my Vessell fill
>   With liveliness, from dulness me secure.
> And I will answer all this Love of thine
> When with it thou hast made me all Divine. . . .
>
> If thou my dross dost but refine from mee.
>
> Lord! Make my Leaden Whistle metall good. (*Poems* 142)

In these first lines Taylor refers to God's grace ("Love") as an alchemical distillate; Taylor puns on "spirits" and "Viall" while referring to himself as a "Vessell" into which God's grace will be siphoned. In the last two stanzas Taylor further emphasizes his alchemical theme as he alludes to God's ability to refine (transmute) the dross of Taylor's soul. In language that recalls the words of Partlitz, "So Alychmie separates the spirits from the medicine and rejects the impure dross," the poet anticipates a time when God's tincture of love will transmute Taylor's dross (his "Leaden Whistle" or earthly voice) into what we may surmise to be a golden voice of praise, "metall good." Taylor's use of "Leaden" especially evokes the metal lead, a favorite object of alchemical transmutation.

Just as Taylor often portrays God as the heavenly alchemist, the poet also draws parallels between Christ and philosophers' stone. Referred to as the carbuncle, elixir, lapis, pearl, phoenix, and quintessence, the philosophers' stone was also envisioned as a mediator between heaven and earth. One of the oldest Christ-lapis references is found in Petrus Bonus' *The New Pearl of Great Price*:

> The hidden Stone may be called the gift of God. . . .
>   It is God alone that perfects our Stone . . .
>   Though heathens [pre-Christian philosophers], they knew that there would come for this world a day of judgment and consummation; and of the resurrection of the dead, when every soul shall be reunited to its body, not to be severed from it thenceforward for ever. Then they said that every glorified body would be incorruptible, and perfectly penetrated in all its parts by the spirit, because the nature of the body would then resemble that of the

spirit.... Our substance conceives by itself, and is impregnated by itself, and brings forth itself—and this, the conception of a virgin, is possible only by Divine grace. Moreover, the birth leaves our substance still a virgin, which, again, is a miraculous event. ... Alphidius tells us that [of] our Stone ... its mother is a virgin, its father knows no woman. These ancient Sages also knew that God must become man, because on the last day of our Magistery that which generates, and that which is generated, become absolutely one; then the old man and the child, and the father and the son, are indistinguishably united. Hence they concluded that the Creator must also become one with the creature; moreover, they knew that man was, alone of all created beings, made in the image of God.[48]

In this passage Bonus intimates that the philosophers' stone comes from God alone and that Christ is the embodiment of the stone's redemptive and regenerative powers.[49] Taylor draws upon this tradition, and in many of his meditations he incorporates metaphors and images of the philosophers' stone to illustrate the redemptive (and transformative) power of Christ. Indeed, the metaphor of the heavenly alchemist (God) and his creation, the philosophers' stone (Christ)—also known as the philosophers' son[50]—is one of the most powerful examples of Taylor's adaptation of esoteric alchemy, and an examination of particular meditations reveals Taylor's innovative use of this alchemical tradition.

One of the most interesting (and traditional) images of the philosophers' stone that Taylor employs is that of the pearl. According to Paracelsus, "The matter of the Tincture [elixir of life], then, is a very great pearl and a most precious treasure, and the noblest thing next to the manifestation of the Most High and the consideration of men which can exist upon earth. This is the Lili of Alchemy and of Medicine, which the philosopher's have so diligently sought after."[51] The alchemical equation of Christ with the pearl or philosophers' stone is further strengthened by John Pordage's description of the stone:

Now is the stone shaped, the elixir of life prepared, the love-child or the child of love born, the new birth completed, and the work made whole and perfect: O wonder of wonders! You have the tincturing tincture, the pearl of the virgin.... This is the Son of the Virgin, this is her first-born, this is the noble hero, the trampler of the serpent, and he who casts the dragon [of death] under his feet and tramples upon him.[52]

Here Pordage clearly equates the stone ("tincturing tincture, the pearl of the virgin") with Jesus Christ. While the biblical reference to the pearl as Christ is paramount for Taylor, the related metaphor of the Christ-pearl as philosophers' stone functions on a secondary level in many of Taylor's meditations and enhances the poet's vision of Christ's power of regeneration.

The first instance of Taylor's use of the Christ-pearl metaphor occurs in *Meditation* 1.2. In the first two stanzas Taylor notes:

> My Dear, Deare, Lord I do thee Saviour Call:
>   Thou in my very Soul art, as I Deem,
> Soe High, not High enough, Soe Great; too small:
>   Soe Deare, not Dear enough in my esteem.
>   Soe Noble, yet So Base: too Low; too Tall:
>   Thou Full, and Empty art: Nothing, yet ALL.
>
> A Precious Pearle, above all price dost 'bide.
>   Rubies no Rubies are at all to thee.
> Blushes of burnisht Glory Sparkling Slide
>   From every Square in various Colour'd glee
>   Nay Life itself in Sparkling Spangles Choice.
>   A Precious Pearle thou art above all price. (*Poems* 5–6)

Although Taylor's first task in the opening of *Meditation* 1.2 is to emphasize Christ's theanthropy—the heavenly royalty of Christ's spirit and his base, human frame—Taylor's description of Christ in the first stanza also recalls the paradoxical descriptions of the philosophers' stone from the *Rosinus ad Sarratatam Episcopum* (one of the oldest Arabian alchemical texts): "This stone is below thee . . . above thee . . . about thee."[53] As Taylor notes, Christ is "Nobel . . . Base . . . Low . . . Tall . . . Nothing, yet All," and in the second stanza the Christ-stone becomes "A Precious Pearle . . . above all price." The descriptions of both Taylor's Christ-pearl and the philosophers' stone in the above passages suggest a reconciliation of opposites, or what the alchemists referred to as the marriage of heaven and earth. And indeed, for Taylor, Christ possesses the power to reconcile the fallen soul with God.

In the first stanza of "The Return," Taylor also uses the image of the "Pearl of Price" to symbolize Christ:

> Inamoring Rayes, thy Sparkles, Pearle of Price
>   Impearld with Choisest Gems, their beams Display
> Impoysoning Sin, Guilding my Soule with Choice
>   Rich Grace, thy Image bright, making me pray,

> Oh! that thou Wast on Earth below with mee
> Or that I was in Heaven above with thee. (*Poems* 9)

In this passage, the Christ-pearl has the power to guild the poet's soul with the heavenly grace that Taylor often associates with gold. The last two lines of this stanza, "that thou Wast on Earth below with me / Or that I was in Heaven above with thee," become a refrain to which Taylor returns at the end of each of the nine stanzas. Apart from the poet's wish to be with Christ, these lines recall the words of Philalethes, "Join heaven to earth in the fire of love," and intimate that Christ is a spiritual bridge from heaven to earth wedding the two realms, as Taylor notes in stanza five:

> Heavens Golden Spout thou art where Grace most Choice
>   Comes Spouting down from God to man of Clay.
> A Golden Stepping Stone to Paradise
>   A Golden Ladder into Heaven! I'l pray
> Oh! that thou wast on Earth below with mee
> Or that I was in Heaven above with thee. (*Poems* 10)

For the poet, Christ, the "Golden . . . Stone to Paradise," becomes the mediator between God and man, heaven and earth.

Taylor again draws on images of the mediating Christ and the wedding of heaven and earth in *Meditations* 1.23 and 2.33:

> I know not how to speak't, it is so good:
>   Shall Mortall, and Immortall marry? nay,
> Man marry God? God be a Match for Mud?
>   The King of Glory Wed a Worm? mere Clay?
>   This is the Case. The Wonder too in Bliss.
>   Thy Maker is thy Husband. Hearst thou this? (1.23 *Poems* 39)

> Who is the Object of this Love? and in
>   Whose mouth doth fall the Apple of this tree?
> Is't Man? A Sinner? Such a Wormhol'de thing?
>   Oh! matchless Love, Laid out on such as Hee!
>   Should Gold Wed Dung, Should Stars Wooe Lobster Claws,
>   It would no wonder, like this Wonder, cause. (2.33 *Poems* 143)

In these passages Taylor evokes the alchemical marriage of heaven and earth through images of the poet's spiritual marriage with God—"Man marry God? God be a Match for Mud" and "Should Gold [the divine] Wed Dung [man], Should Stars [heaven] Wooe [marry] Lobster Claws [earth]." While Taylor's image-pairs of God and mortal, God and mud, gold and dung, and stars and claws may at first seem unusual, they recall the words of Philalethes, who claimed that the philosophers' stone initiated a "reconciliation of Contraries, a making friendship between Enemies."[54] This marriage of heaven and earth evokes the Christ-lapis parallel and serves as a touchstone for Taylor in "The Return" and in *Meditations* 1.23 and 2.33.

Taylor's association of Christ with the philosophers' stone is further strengthened by an examination of the fifth stanza of *Meditation* 2.45. Here Taylor compares Christ to

> a Sparkling Carbuncle up Caskt
>   Within a Globe of Chrystall glass most cleare
> Fills't all with Shine which through its sides are flasht
>   And makes all glorious Shine: so much more here
>   These treasures of thy Wisdom shine out bright
>   In thee. My Candle with thy Flame, Lord, Light. (*Poems* 163–64)

Although the impetus for this is Colossians 2:3, "In who are hid all the treasures of wisdom," this passage reveals a literal comparison of Christ with the philosophers' stone ("a Sparkling Carbuncle") in an alchemical vessel ("a Globe of Chrystall glass").[55]

Given Taylor's previous association of Christ with the stone, we may better appreciate how Taylor's use of the word "Lump" in *Meditations* 1.14 and 2.2 serves as further reference to the philosophers' stone. In the former Taylor refers to Christ as

> A Lump of Glory flaming in her bright
>   Devouring Flames, to be my Sacrifice
> Untill her Fire goes out well Satisfide:
> And then he rose in Glory to abide. (*Poems* 27)

Here Christ is pictured as "A Lump of Glory" prepared in alchemical fashion, in "Devouring Flames," that ascends (here Taylor puns on rose) at the end of the opus, "in Glory to abide." In the latter Taylor presents a similar image of Christ:

> Oh! that my Soul was all enamored
>   With this First Born enough: a Lump of Love
> Son of Eternall Father, Chambered
>   Once in a Virgins Womb, dropt from above.
>   All Humane royalty hereby Divin'de. (*Poems* 85)

Although Taylor's primary image here is of the Christ-fetus ("Lump of Love") in the "Virgins Womb," this passage recalls Pordage's alchemical metaphor of the philosophers' stone-son in the alchemical womb (still) uniting heaven and earth in the supreme alchemical conjunction.

Thus far we have observed Taylor's poetic vision of his soul as alchemical vessel and *prima materia*, of God as alchemist, and of Christ as philosophers' stone (or philosophers' son). The final aspect of Taylor's alchemical paradigm is his equation of God's grace with alchemical or philosophical gold. This idea correlates with Christ as philosophers' stone, for it is through God's golden grace that divine love and regeneration manifest through Christ.

While we previously noted Taylor's reference to golden grace as *elixir vitae* and liquid gold in *Meditation* 1.7, in 2.126 the poet again employs the golden trope to impart the value of God's redeeming grace. In stanzas three through five, Taylor presents four distinct images of golden grace:

> The golden Current of Sweet Grace sprung in
>   Thy Heart, Dear Lord comes Wafting on thy Tast
> Sweetning thy Palate passing by its ring,
>   And rowling in our borders thus begrac'te.
>   Come tast and see How sweet this Current is.
>   Oh! sweet breath passage. Sweetend sweet as bliss.
>
> The golden mine of Sanctifying Grace
>   That in thy heart is glorious indeed
> In Golden Streames come flowering out apace
>   Through thy rich golden pipe, and so in Speed,
>   As golden liquour, running thence all ore
>   Into thy Spouse's heart from Graces Store.
>
> The golden Crucible of Grace all sweet,
>   Is thy sweet Heart, The golden pipe of Fame
> Is thy sweet Windpipe, where thy Spirits reech
>   Comes breizing sweet perfumes out from the Same.
>   This is the golden gutter of thy Lungs
>   And through thy mouth, by th'Palate sweetly runs. (*Poems* 311–12)

Through what might best be described as the poet's free-association of gold, Taylor shifts from the image of "The golden Current of Sweet Grace" to "The golden mine of Sanctifying Grace" from which a "golden liquour" (of grace) flows in "Golden Streames." In stanza five the poet transforms his image of grace into that of a "golden Crucible of Grace all sweet, / Is thy [Christ's] sweet Heart." In the final four stanzas Taylor returns to his biblical source, "His Mouth is most sweet" (Canticles 5:16), but even so, Taylor associates Christ (and by implication, God's grace) with gold. Thus, Taylor again evokes the image of God as heavenly alchemist preparing the regeneration of man through the golden stone of grace.

Taylor's association of grace with gold is also apparent *Meditation* 1.35. Here Taylor's imagery recalls the alchemical theme of transmutation of soul from base, common matter (sin) to spiritual enlightenment. In using "enlightenment" here I am referring to a feeling, a mood, a state of mind. This is a key point with regard to Taylor's *Meditations*, for as we have already observed, Taylor begins many of his *Preparatory Meditations* in a seeming state of despair. However, through the course of each of these works, Taylor's mood seems to "lighten up," or change color. His imagination, his outlook, his way of seeing and perceiving, as well as his spiritual condition, is transmuted. As Taylor states in *Meditation* 1.35: "That Grace might in get and get out my dross! / My Soule up lockt then in this Clod of Dust / Would lock up in't all Heavenly Joyes most just" (*Poems* 57). Here Taylor intimates that God's grace possesses the transmutative power to remove the "dross" of the soul—the corrupt matter or sin that surrounds the soul—and move the soul to experience the feeling of "Heavenly Joyes most just,"or regeneration.

As we have noted, throughout the *Meditations* Taylor incorporates the tropes of alchemy to enhance his vision of regeneration. It is fascinating to observe how the poet transmuted alchemical imagery into a paradigm for salvation. Unlike Governor Winthrop, Taylor was not an alchemist; he came by his knowledge of alchemy through his study of medicine and metallurgy. It was from this background that Taylor reenvisioned the key ideas of alchemy and worked out his own system of correspondence between alchemical tropes and his own religious sentiments.

During Taylor's tenure as physician and minister of Westfield, he witnessed the breakdown of the New Jerusalem of the New World. The return to the primitivistic, biblical state of New Jerusalem had failed, and the only sense of return left for Taylor and his congregation was the return to God through regeneration. This return to God brings us to the spiritual and alchemical image of the marriage of heaven and earth, for out of the rubble that was to have been the "City upon a hill," the individual (as Taylor perceived the situation) could rise through Christ's redemptive powers (and God's grace) to a new life in a spiritual paradise.

The Puritan dream of a spiritual New World was already beginning to shatter into economic reality during Taylor's years at Westfield, so it was to his own soul and the souls of his congregation that Taylor focused his attention. It was God's "Alchemy of Grace," as Oreovicz aptly calls it, that gave Taylor the hope and the promise for a better life, not in the New World, but in the Next World. Indeed, Taylor's knowledge of esoteric alchemy and hermetic physick provided him with the metaphors and tropes to express his vision of God's love and redeeming grace: regeneration.

NOTES

1. Taylor may have attended Cambridge before he arrived in America. See Willie T. Weathers, "Edward Taylor and the Cambridge Platonists."

2. Quoted in Norman S. Grabo, *Edward Taylor's Christographia* (96).

3. See Joan Del Fattore, "John Webster's *Metallographia*"; Cheryl Z. Oreovicz, "Edward Taylor and the Alchemy of Grace" and "Investigating 'The America of Nature'" (108–9); Randall A. Clack, "The Transmutation of Soul"; and Leventhal (128–29).

4. For more on the *Aurum Vitae* ("Gold of Life"), see Abraham, "Red Elixir" (165–66), in *Dictionary*; and Ruland (65). Taylor's source for this image appears to be John Webster's *Metallographia*: "As *Johannes Rhumelius* (whom I have quoted before, though not to this very purpose) doth confess in these words: That his *tincture Solis* was made forth of a Rubie-coloured, red, thorough-shining, or transparent, bright golden Ore, & c. And his *Aurum vitae* was prepared forth of a certain, pure, or shining Mineral; which in its first coagulation, was found of a red colour" (222).

5. See Oreovicz, "Edward Taylor" (33); and Abraham, "*Caput Mortuum*" (31), in *Dictionary*.

6. Taylor's Library Catalogue Number 52 (*Metallographia*) in Edward Taylor, *The Poetical Works of Edward Taylor* (208).

7. Linden (201).

8. It is probably no coincidence that Taylor refers five times to the tincture, for the number 5 represents the alchemical quintessence, the philosophers' stone. For more on the quintessence, see Abraham, "Fifth Element" (75–76), in *Dictionary*; and Haeffner, "Quintessence" (215–16).

9. Paracelsus, "The Hermetic and Alchemical Writings, Vol. 1 (28–29). Also see Abraham, "Tincture" (200), in *Dictionary*; and Haeffner, "Tincture" (246–48).

10. J. Webster (118, 122, 127, 191). For more on "Aurum Potabile," see Abraham, *Dictionary* (14); and Haeffner (58).

11. Del Fattore locates Paracelsus' concept of *primum ens* as a direct influence on Taylor's *Meditation* 2.47 (234–35).

12. For further discussion on Taylor-as-physician, see Catherine Rainwater, "'This Brazen Serpent Is a Doctors Shop.'"

13. Paracelsus, Vol. 2 (165). Although Paracelsian chemical medicine was supported by Puritans during Oliver Cromwell's tenure, physicians during the reign of Elizabeth I were also influenced by the theories of Paracelsus. For further discussion on this subject, see Allen G. Debus, "The Paracelsian Compromise in Elizabethan England"; P. M. Rattansi, "Paracelsus and the Puritan Revolution"; and C. Webster, "English Medical Reformers of the Puritan Revolution."

14. Taylor's Library Catalogue Numbers 10 (*Surgion's Mate*), 58 (*Pharmacopoeia*), and 147 (*New Method of Physick*). See Taylor, *Poetical Works* (205, 209, 216).

15. See John Woodall, *The Surgions Mate* (224–310), alchemical and chemical symbols (311–28) and alchemical verses (329–37). For further information on Woodall, see Allen Debus, "John Woodall, Paracelsian Surgeon." For background on the sulfur-salt-mercury theory of alchemy, see Abraham, "Salt-Sulphur-Mercury" (176–77), in *Dictionary*; and Haeffner, "Mercury-Sulphur Theory" (175–77), "Paracelsus" (201–5), "Salt" (225–26), "Sulphur" (243–44), and *"Tria Prima"* (250–51).

16. Simeon Partlitz, *A New Method of Physick* (8, 9, 43).

17. *Pharmacopoeia Londinensis* (254). As F.N.L. Poynter observes in "Nicholas Culpeper and the Paracelsians, "Culpeper was certainly no whole-hearted Paracelsian, yet his writings are strongly flavored with the occult and mystical beliefs characteristic of those who were" (201). As the "narrative of the author's life" attached to *Culpeper's School of Physick* (1659) attests: "That he was not only for Galen and Hippocrates, but he knew how to correct and moderate the tyrranies of Paracelsus" (quoted in Poynter, 201). For more on Culpeper, see Allen Debus, *The English Paracelsians* (167, 182); and *Chemical Philosophy*, Vol. 2 (508).

18. In the very back of his copy of the *Pharmacopoeia* (369–426, Taylor's pagination), Taylor included a list of chemical and astrological symbols, all of which pertain to Paracelsian medicine. These symbols correlate with the chemical symbols found in Woodall (311–28). In addition, in Taylor's manuscript copy of *Metallographia* (upside down on 131, Taylor's pagination), there appears to be an iatrochemcial prescription (which includes sulfur and oxymol) for a headache or brain fever.

19. Debus, *Chemical Philosophy*, Vol. 2 (457).

20. J. Webster (11).

21. Ibid., "A Register of Chapters."

22. For more on the alkahest, see Haeffner (42–43).

23. Ruland (36). Compare this passage with Taylor's reference to Christ in 2.68[B] as "the Heavenly Alkahest" (*Poems* 207). For a further treatment of Taylor's use of *aqua vitae*, see Kathy Siebel and Thomas M. Davis, "Edward Taylor and the Cleansing of AQUA VITAE." For further background on *aqua vitae* and Mercury, see Abraham, "Aqua Vitae" (9) and "Mercurius" (124–28) in *Dictionary*; and J. Webster (193–98).

24. See also Abraham, "Bird of Hermes" (25–26), in *Dictionary*.

25. Alchemy was often referred to as the Royal or Divine Art. See Abraham, "Art and Nature" (11–12) and "Royal" (173–74), in *Dictionary*; and Ruland, "Great Work" (369–370).

26. De Jong (51); see also 106–7.

27. Taylor's source for the alkahest was probably John Webster:

By the help of that immortal and immutable liquor the *Alkahest*, by which (he declareth) that the body of Copper is totally destroyed, and the external Sulphur and salt (in which the medical Virtue lies) is separated, and the internal Sulphur that is inseparable from the Mercury, either by Art or Nature remaineth, by which it may be brought into a white metal.

But of this as far as by the *Alkahest* the medical Sulphur is separated from it, by which that universal medicine called by *Paracelsus* and *Helmont Mercurius Diaphoreticum*, and *Aurum Horizontale*, by mixing with Præcipitate prepared after *Vigo's* order is made. (253)

Taylor may have also been inspired by George Herbert's "The Elixir."

28. John Gatta, Jr., *Gracious Laughter* (154).

29. Oreovicz (33) has noted Taylor's comparison of Christ to Mercurius in *Meditation* 2.61.

30. Prime matter (*prima materia*) was the primary alchemical material from which the philosophers' stone was created. See Haeffner (208–11); and Abraham, *Dictionary* (153–56). Throughout the *Meditations*, Taylor's descriptions of his soul as impure "dross" suggests the despair that Donald Stanford ("Edward Taylor," 71) sees as being the first stage of emotional progression in Taylor's work.

31. This procedure is suggested by John Webster: "And in the first place, we shall find all the Philosophers as it were unanimously agreeing, that the transmutation of Metals is impossible, unless they be reduced *in materiam suam primam*: which we shall take to be granted as a certain truth" (166).

32. See Abraham, "Dross" (61), in *Dictionary*.

33. J. Webster (374).

34. Other references by Taylor to the transmutation of the soul are illustrated in passages from *Meditations* 1.30, 2.5, 2.12, 2.54, and 2.144.

35. Other examples of Taylor's vision of his soul as base metal or substance and its subsequent transmutation into golden objects reflecting spiritual perfection can be found in *Meditations* 2.54, where Taylor's "rusty Wires then shall / Bee fined gold" (*Poems* 178), and 2.144, where the poet writes, "And if thou makest mee to be thy mold / Though Clayey mould I bee, and run in mee / Thy Spirits Gold, thy Trumpet all of gold, / Though I be Clay Ist thy Gold-Trumpet bee" (*Poems* 344).

36. Whereas Rainwater has demonstrated the Galenic and Paracelsian themes in *Meditation* 1.4, I am focusing on the alchemical tropes as they relate to Taylor's alchemical paradigm.

37. Both rose and rose garden are illustrated in Emblem 27 of Michael Maier's *Atalanta Fugiens* (159) and by the title page of Joachim Frizius' (Robert Fludd's) *Summum bonum* (1629), reprinted in McIntosh, plate 4. Also see Stanislas Klossowski De Rola, *The Golden Game*, plate 22 (57), from Steffan Michelspacher's *Cabala* (1616). For further background, see Abraham, "Garden" (83–84) and "Rose" (173), in *Dictionary*.

38. The *cauda pavonis*, or peacock's tail, was the last stage in the opus before the appearance of the philosophers' stone. See Abraham, "Peacock's Tail" (141–42) and "Rainbow" (163), in *Dictionary*; and Haeffner, "Colours" (89) and "Peacock" (205). Heinrich Madathanas, in "The Golden Age Restored," attempts to show the relationship of "The Song of Solomon" to the alchemical work (*HM* 1: 50–67).

39. In "Truth's Golden Harrow," Robert Fludd claims that the alchemists' use of the rose and the lily derives from the Song of Songs. He speaks of "the rose of the field and the lilly of the vally, after the patterne wherof the Alkimists

have shaped their red and whit Elixir, or Stone" (quoted in Abraham, *Marvell and Alchemy*, 258–59). See also Abraham, "Lily" (117–18), in *Dictionary*.

40. Ashmole (320).

41. Ashmole (90). For more on the red man and white woman, see Abraham, *Dictionary* (167–68).

42. For further discussion of the conjunction of Sol and Luna, see De Jong's commentary (220–21) on Emblem 30 of Michael Maier's *Atalanta Fugiens*.

43. J. Webster (124).

44. See also Abraham, "Grave" (90–91), in *Dictionary* For alchemical illustrations of the grave, see Maier, Emblem 44 (193) and Emblem 50 (205). This image is not unique to Maier and can be found in many illustrated books on alchemy. Also see De Rola, plate 324 (174), from Johann Daniel Mylius' *Philosophia reformata* (1622).

45. For further background on the *citrinitas*, see Abraham, *Dictionary* (42); and Fabricius (14, 137, 140–69).

46. God's "gracious Chymistry" is also referred to in *Meditations* 2.4 and 2.32. Also see Abraham, "Chymist" (39), in *Dictionary*.

47. See Maier, Emblem 31 (167); for commentary on Emblem 31, see De Jong (224–25). See also Abraham, "Ablution" (1), in *Dictionary*.

48. Bonus (124–27). Jung (*Psychology and Alchemy*, 373) dates this work between 1330 and 1339. He also provides a stronger Christian translation (374–75).

49. The alchemists often noted a connection between Christ and the Stone in Luke 20:17, where Christ is "the stone that the builders rejected," which became "the head of the corner," and in 1 Corinthians 10:4 where Christ is called "the spiritual rock from which the water of life springs." In *The "Practica,"* Basilius Valentinus writes, "I promised to communicate to you a knowledge of our Corner Stone, or Rock, of the process" (*HM* 1: 315). See also Abraham, "Cornerstone" (47), in *Dictionary*.

50. For further background on the philosophers' son, see Abraham, *Dictionary* (148–50).

51. Paracelsus, Vol. 1 (22).

52. Quoted in Fabricius (190).

53. Quoted in Fabricius (208).

54. Philalethes, *Ripley Reviv'd* (278).

55. Since the Middle Ages the carbuncle has been a common name for the philosophers' stone. See Jung, *Alchemical Studies* (147); *Mysterium Coniunctionis* (423); and *Psychology and Alchemy* (469). According to the alchemist Heinrich Khunrath, the stone radiates a "shimmering carbuncle light" and "the carbuncle stone [shines] in the firelight" (quoted in Jung, *Psychology and Alchemy*, 469).

Chapter 3

Alchemical Spirits in Eighteenth-Century America

The zeitgeist of alchemy remained in the collective American psyche after Winthrop's death in 1676. Students at Harvard College used textbooks such as Charles Morton's *Compendium Physicae* (1687) long after 1714. While the *Compendium* focused on physical science, it also included a short discourse on alchemy from which the following is excerpted:

> The Artiface of Gold by Alchymy came from the last consideration, [for] hence they [the alchemists] took a Great Confidence of a transmutation of all mettals into Gold, by curing the Leprosities of them (as they Speak). This opperation is cal'd the finding of the Phylosophers stone; and tis affirm'd, that Some have done it, such are cal'd the Adepti; Sons of the Art, Sons of Hermes, etc.[1]

Here Morton alludes to the alchemical premise that the "seed" of gold is in every metal and it is the alchemist who, through various chemical operations, encourages the growth of gold from baser metals. Surprisingly, the alchemical interests of Harvard students did not end when the *Compendium* was discarded. Edward J. Young, in "Subjects for Master's Degree in Harvard College from 1655–1791," notes that a 1771 Harvard Master's Thesis gave a positive response to the question "Can real gold be made by the art of chemistry?"[2]

Later in the eighteenth century, the reverend Ezra Stiles (1727–1779), president of Yale College and, coincidentally, the grandson of Edward Taylor, corresponded with a number of New Englanders who were involved with alchemical experimentation. Stiles, however, was careful to note in his diary that he did not possess any practical knowledge of alchemy:

> I have no Knowledge of it at all; I never saw Transmutation, the aurific Powder, nor the Philosophers Stone; nor did I ever converse with an adept knowing him to be such. . . . I never had, or made an Exp[erimen]t with, a Furnace or Alembic in all my Life. . . . I never absorbed the extracted Sulpher of Gold in Terra. I have no practcal Knowl. of the Matter: the few Ideas I have about it are only imaginary, conjectural & speculative.[3]

Perhaps, in the words of Shakespeare, Stiles "doth protest too much." Although Stiles denied practical knowledge of the spagyric art, it appears that he was held in the same high esteem by would-be alchemists of eighteenth-century America as Winthrop was by his own philosophic circle in the seventeenth century.

One of Stiles' confidants, Samuel Danforth (1696–1777), practiced both medicine and alchemy in Boston. According to Stiles, Danforth "was deeply studied in the Writings of the Adepts, believed the Philosophers Stone a Reality and perhaps for Chemical knowledge might have passed among Chemists for [an adept]."[4] Although Danforth was a staunch Tory and a member of the Massachusetts governor's council, he appears to have had friends among the insurrectionists. Writing to his friend Benjamin Franklin in 1773, Danforth offered to give Franklin a sample of the philosophers' stone. Franklin, apparently with tongue in cheek, thanked Danforth for his "kind Intentions of including me in the Benefits of that inestimable Stone, which, curing all Diseases (even old Age itself) will enable us to see the future glorious State of our America," and then imagined "the jolly Conversation we and twenty more of our Friends may have 100 Years hence on this subject, over that well replenish'd Bowl at Cambridge Commencement."[5] Franklin, it seems, was well aware of the restorative powers associated with the *elixir vitae*.

It may very well have been an alchemist such as Danforth who suggested to Franklin one of Poor Richard's maxims in "The Way to Wealth" (1757):

> Get what you can, and what you get hold
> 'Tis the stone that will turn all your lead into gold,
> as Poor Richard says. And when you have got the Philosopher's Stone, sure you will no longer complain of bad times, or the difficulty of paying taxes.[6]

Offering a practical philosophy for a new land (soon to become a new nation), Franklin's essay emphasized secular regeneration. Although he presents a figurative equation of self-reliance (industry and frugality) with the philosophers' stone, Franklin's use of transmutation suggests that at least this aspect of alchemy was common knowledge among colonial Americans. On another occasion, Franklin was of a more philosophic state of mind: "Content is the Philosopher's Stone, that turns all it touches into Gold. He that's content, hath enough; He that complains, has too much."[7] While Franklin may have indeed appreciated the alchemical metaphor of regeneration, he was ever the empiricist and put no faith in alchemical experimentation. As he told Stiles on one occasion (ca. 1777), "there were several [alchemists] at Philad[elphia] & c. who were loosing their Time in chemical Experiments to no Effect."[8]

Besides Danforth, the *Literary Diary* of Stiles affords the reader an unusual list of names associated with the practice of the hermetic science in eighteenth-century America: Gosuinus Erkelens of East Haddam, Connecticut, Dr. Aeneas Munson (Stiles' former pupil at Yale), Dr. Ebenezer Cahoon of Wallingford, Connecticut, Samuel Woodruff, Captain Phipps of Savannah, Georgia, Dr. Prentice and son of New Haven, Connecticut, and Reverend Samuel West, a Massachusetts minister who helped to ratify the federal Constitution in 1788.[9] Although their names mean little (if anything) to us today, these figures were practitioners of the spagyric art and part of Stiles' hermetic circle.

In addition to Stiles and his company of alchemical investigators, America could boast of another alchemist, John William Gerar De Brahm (1718–1799). A Dutch engineer employed by the English crown to survey Georgia and Florida, De Brahm spent the second half of his life composing his own contribution to alchemical literature, "Hercules *ex Rore Rosatur*." Although De Brahm never published "Hercules," he did send a copy of the manuscript to Lord Dartmouth in 1769.[10] De Brahm's work would be the last alchemical manuscript to be produced in America until the 1857 publication of General Ethan Allen Hitchcock's *Remarks upon Alchemy and the Alchemists*.

Aside from Danforth, who was publicly known for his interest in alchemy,[11] the figure of the alchemist was probably a rare sight on the streets of eighteenth-century New England. However, allusions to alchemical science appeared in the most unlikely places. In *Letters from an American Farmer* (1782), Hector De Crèvecoeur evoked the image of America as an alembic, or melting pot, into which "individuals of all nations are melted into a new race of men, whose labours and posterity will one day cause great changes in the world."[12] Although De Crèvecoeur does not specifically refer to America in alchemical terms, his words recall the alchemically related science of metallurgy. More to the point, the subtext of this short passage (and of De Crèvecoeur's "Letter III") suggests that in America the European emigrant might be transformed/transmuted into a new, whole, golden being.[13] For De Crèvecoeur, America itself possessed qualities often associated with the philosophers' stone, for the transmuting powers of America could certainly, like the alchemical elixir, bring new life to the emigrant.

Although interest in alchemy had for all practical purposes disappeared in America by the end of the 1700s, references to Hermeticism, astrology, and other esoteric systems appeared occasionally in colonial almanacs.[14] Alchemy, however, was relegated to superstition and folk tales that illustrated the wages of gullibility. Thus, a writer such as James Fenimore Cooper could make passing reference to the philosophers' stone with regard to the pomposity of Richard Jones in *The Pioneers* (1823)—"His ingenuity will one day discover the philosopher's stone"[15]—and be sure that his satirical reference would not go unnoted by readers.

By the mid-nineteenth century, however, Poe, Hawthorne, and Fuller found an extraordinary application for hermetic science, especially its tropes and metaphors of transformation. Perhaps taking their cues from William Godwin's *St. Leon* (1799), Johann Goethe's *Faust* (1808), Robert Browning's *Paracelsus* (1835), and Edward Bulwer-Lytton's *Zanoni* (1842)—literary works that drew upon alchemical lore as material for romance—our writers exploited the tropes and metaphors of alchemy to illuminate their own visions of regeneration.[16]

America, as De Crèvecoeur asserted, was the land not only of opportunity but of transformation. The early Spanish explorers alluded to this possibility in the stories of riches and rejuvenating waters they sent back to Europe, and the Puritans certainly saw the potential of the new land in their vision of the New Jerusalem. As Viola Sachs suggests, "America conceived of itself as the world created anew."[17]

During the hundred odd years that passed between the death of Edward Taylor and the publication of Poe's first collection of poetry, *Tamerlane and Other Poems* (1827), the iatrochemical theories of medicine pioneered by Paracelsus and his followers became accepted treatment for the sick, and science and industrialization moved forward into the nineteenth century. The scientific materialism of Locke and Newton may indeed have prompted Poe to ask in "Sonnet—To Science" (1829):

> Hast thou [science] not dragged Diana from her car,
>   And driven the Hamadryad from the wood
> To seek a shelter in some happier star?
>   Hast thou not torn the Naiad from her flood,
> The Elfin from the green grass, and from me
> The summer dream beneath the tamarind tree? (*CW* 1:90)

Although the scientific community may have turned its back on alchemy, the three writers featured in the remaining chapters of this book adapted the metaphors and tropes of alchemy to express the process of the inner transformation of the self, a process that could lead to a perfect, ideal state of existence recalling the alchemists' marriage of heaven and earth.

While Poe, Hawthorne, and Fuller's exact sources for alchemical philosophy are difficult to pinpoint, they may have been familiar with stories surrounding the seventeenth- and eighteenth-century New England alchemists John Winthrop, Jr., George Starkey, Eirenaeus Philalethes, Robert Child, and Samuel Danforth. In addition to stories of American alchemists, encyclopedias of the nineteenth century and essays on "Alchymy" in the *Retrospective Review* (1826), Isaac Disraeli's *Curiosities of Literature* (1823), and Godwin's *Lives of the Necromancers* (1834) would have provided our writers with cursory background information on hermetic science.[18] More to the point, however, Hawthorne and Fuller may have also encountered books from the alchemical library of Danforth, donated to the Boston Athenaeum in 1812.[19] Included among the twenty-one annotated alchemical volumes in this collection are Elias Ashmole's *Theatrum Chemicum Britannicum* (London, 1652), George Starkey's *Pyrotechny Asserted and Illustrated* (London, 1658), and Eirenaeus Philalethes' *Secrets Reveal'd* and *Opus tripartum de philosophorum arcanis* (London, 1678).[20] While the works of Philalethes and Starkey are connected with the history of alchemy in seventeenth-century New England and thus may have been otherwise familiar to our authors, Ashmole's *Theatrum*, a massive compendium of alchemical tracts by British writers, would have been a particularly valuable find, providing abundant information about terms, symbols, and procedures.

Poe would have also found a virtual treasure trove consisting of hundreds of alchemical books and pamphlets that once belonged to John Winthrop, Jr., at the New York Hospital and the New York Society Library.[21] Our authors could also have found numerous treatises on alchemy in the bookstores of Boston, New York, Philadelphia, Baltimore, and Richmond. Interestingly, five years after Poe's death Ethan Allen Hitchcock began amassing an alchemical library of 318 volumes, many of which he obtained through antique bookstores in the New York and Philadelphia area.[22]

Indeed, Poe, Hawthorne, and Fuller not only had access to alchemical material but adapted the philosophy presented therein to shape the theme of regeneration that permeates their work. As we shall observe in the following chapters, the tropes and philosophy of the medieval alchemists found unique expression in the writings of these nineteenth-century American authors.

NOTES

1. Charles Morton, *Compendium Physicae* (121). The year 1714 marks the arrival at Yale of the New Learning, Jeremy Drummer's library gift. For more background on Morton's *Compendium*, see Leventhal (126–127); and Wilkinson ("New England's Last Alchemists" 128–129).

2. Edward J. Young, "Subjects for Master's Degree in Harvard College from 1655–1791" (131). A similar thesis was put forward in 1718 by a Yale student; see James J. Walsh, *Education of the Founding Fathers of the Republic* (20). Other related Master's subjects at Harvard include "Is there a stone that makes gold?" (Affirmative, 1687) and "Can metals be changed into one another?" (Affirmative, 1703)—see Young (130).

3. Stiles, Vol. 2 (173–74). For further discussion on Stiles, see Leventhal (129–31); and Wilkinson, "New England's Last Alchemists" (132–38).

4. Stiles, Vol. 2 (216).

5. Benjamin Franklin, *The Writings of Benjamin Franklin*, Vol. 6 (105–6).

6. Benjamin Franklin, *The Papers of Benjamin Franklin*, Vol. 7 (349). First printed in the Almanac of November 1756.

7. Franklin, *Papers*, Vol. 7 (353).

8. Stiles, Vol. 2 (173–74).

9. See Stiles, Vol. 2 (174) and Vol. 3 (267, 345, 471, 472).

10. For further discussion on De Brahm, see S. Foster Damon, "De Brahm: Alchemist." De Brahm retired to Philadelphia in 1783.

11. In 1754, Danforth was publicly ridiculed in the political pamphlet *The Monster of Monsters* (Boston, 1754) as "Madame CHEMIA (a very philosophical Lady) who some Years since (as is well known) discover'd that *precious Stone*, of which the Royal Society has been in quest a long Time, to no Purpose" (quoted in Wilkinson, "New England's Last Alchemists," 129).

12. Hector De Crèvecoeur, *Letters from an American Farmer* (43).

13. For further background on De Crèvecoeur and alchemy, see Werner Sollors, "A Defense of the Melting Pot" (184–89).

14. For background on the occult in colonial America, see Jon Butler, "Magic, Astrology, and the Early American Religious Heritage 1600–1960" (328–31, 338, 340).

15. James Fenimore Cooper, *The Pioneers* (303).

16. See Marie Roberts, *Gothic Immortals*, for discussions of Godwin (25–56) and Bulwer-Lytton (156–207). See also Ian Findlay, "Edward Bulwer-Lytton and the Rosicrucians"; and Gray.

17. Viola Sachs, "The occult, magic, and witchcraft in America culture" (942). See also "The occult language and scripture of the New World" (130).

18. Poe reviewed Godwin's *Lives of the Necromancers* (London, 1834) in 1835 (*Essays and Reviews*, 259–60). Poe was also familiar with Godwin's Rosicrucian novel *St. Leon* (*Essays and Reviews*, 259). "A Descent into the Maelström" and "The Fall of the House of Usher" reveal other sources from which Poe may have gleaned alchemical information. In "Maelström" Poe refers to Anthanasius Kircher (*CW* 2: 583), whose *Mundus Subteraneaus* (1678), a textbook on general science, includes sections on ocean currents and subterranean waters; it also

contains sections on alchemy and the Paracelsian ternary theory of the elements (J. Godwin, *Athanasius Kircher* 84–93). In "Usher" Poe includes a curious list of esoteric authors and titles contained in Roderick Usher's library; one of these authors, the English alchemist Robert Fludd, produced a voluminous amount of alchemical writing (*CW* 2: 409).

Disraeli's *Curiosities of Literature*, Vol. 1, contains essays on "Alchymy" (374–79); "Dr. [John] Dee" (285–312); and Robert Fludd (313–21). For background on Poe's reading of Disraeli, see Ruth Leigh Hudson, "Poe and Disraeli." Marion L. Kesselring, in "Hawthorne's Reading, 1828–1850" (179) notes Hawthorne's reading of Disraeli's *Curiosities* during 1833 and 1836. For references to Fuller's reading of Goethe and Godwin, see *EF* (192, 284, 315–19) and Margaret Fuller, "Goethe."

19. Hawthorne was in Boston for six months in 1836, as editor of the *American Magazine of Useful and Entertaining Knowledge* (Kesselring, 57), and again during the years 1839–1841, according to Danny Robinson in "Hawthorne in the Boston Athenaeum" (1–2).

20. For more on Danforth's library, see Wilkinson, "New England's Last Alchemists" (131–32).

21. See Wilkinson, *"Alchemical Library,"* Part 1 (35).

22. See I. Bernard Cohen, "Ethan Allen Hitchcock" (61–62). Coincidentally, Hitchcock was Poe's commander at West Point in 1830. It is, however, difficult to establish a link between Hitchcock and Poe's interests in occult science. See Barton Levi St. Armand, "Poe's Emblematic Raven" (209, n. 21).

Chapter 4

Poe's Alchemy and the Regeneration of Imagination

Edgar Allan Poe's most notable use of alchemical lore appears in "Von Kempelen and His Discovery" (1849).[1] In this, one of his last stories, Poe reveals his knowledge of the alchemical laboratory:

> Opening into the garret where they caught him, was a closet, ten feet by eight, fitted up with some chemical apparatus, of which the object has not yet been ascertained. In one corner of the closet was a very small furnace, with a glowing fire in it, and on the fire a kind of duplicate crucible—two crucibles connected by a tube. One of these crucibles was nearly full of *lead* in a state of fusion, but not reaching up to the aperture of the tube, which was close to the brim. The other crucible had some liquid in it, which, as the officers entered, seemed to be furiously dissipating in vapor. (*CW* 3: 1362)

Von Kempelen's laboratory is located in an "old house of seven stories" (*CW* 3: 1362)—an unimportant fact until we note that alchemical transmutation moved the *prima materia* through seven noble phases with seven planetary correspondences: lead and Saturn, tin and Jupiter, mercury and Mercury, iron and Mars, copper and Venus, silver and Moon, and gold and Sun. Finally, as to leave little doubt about Von Kempelen's means of producing the gold found in the scientist's quarters, Poe states,

> nothing unusual was found about him [Von Kempelen], excepting a paper parcel, in his coat-pocket, containing what was afterward

ascertained to be a mixture of antimony and some *unknown substance*, in nearly, but not quite, equal proportions. All attempts at analyzing the unknown substance have, so far, failed . . .

I need not go over the details of Von Kempelen's confession (as far as it went) and release, for these are familiar to the public. That he has actually realized, in spirit and in effect, if not to the letter, the old chimaera of the *philosopher's stone*, no sane person is at liberty to doubt. (*CW* 3: 1362–63; emphases mine)

Antimony, as Poe seems to be aware, was often considered a vital element in the creation of the philosophers' stone, as in Basilius Valentinus' *The Triumphal Chariot of Antimony* (1678).[2]

While "Von Kempelen" appears to be Poe's most explicit use of alchemical tropes, it is not his only reference to hermetic science. In his 1831 autobiographical poem "Romance," Poe writes the following:

> For, being an idle boy lang syne,
> Who read Anacreon, and drank wine,
> I early found Anacreon rhymes
> Were almost pasionate sometimes—
> And by strange alchemy of brain
> His pleasures always turn'd to pain—(*CW* 1: 157)

A seemingly innocuous passage, yet with the line "strange alchemy of brain" Poe alludes to the power of imagination to transform or transmute perceptions of reality. D. H. Lawrence was quick to note the darker implications of Poe's work and maintained that Poe was only concerned with the "disintegration process" of (the American) consciousness.[3] Yet Poe was concerned with more than disintegration.

In hermetic science, the alchemist brought the *prima materia* (or base metal) through a chemical process that was often likened to torture and annihilation. During this stage of chemical "torture," the impurities of the prime matter were stripped away (or dissolved) to allow the operator to recover the "seed of gold" that the alchemists believed to be the spirit of every metal. This hermetic process is summed up by the alchemical maxim "*Solve et coagula et habebis magisterium*"—"Dissolve and unite anew, and you will achieve mastery."[4] As William Bloomefield observes of the alchemical elements: "Dissolve and separate them, sublime, fix, and congeale, / Then has thou all."[5] In the context of Poe's stories, one must first dissolve the dross of the material world (perception) to experience the visionary, or spiritual, realm.

In the philosophy of the medieval alchemists Poe found a ready-made system of tropes and allegories that offered as its ultimate goal not merely the creation of the mythical philosophers' stone and the transmutation of base metal into gold, but intimations of a process that might transmute (through the power of imagination) his readers' mundane perceptions of the material world into visionary experiences of the supernal realm.[6] As Martin Ruland notes, imagination "is the Star *in* Man, the Celestial or Supercelestial Body."[7] In a hermetic context, imagination is tantamount to "the seed of gold" (the philosophers' stone) that the alchemists sought. In a sense, Poe was attempting no less than the regeneration of his readers' imagination.

THE *VAS HERMETICUM*

By the time Poe exploited the subject matter of alchemy for his hoax "Von Kempelen and His Discovery" (1849), he had already made use of alchemical color sequences and adapted alchemical tropes such as the *vas hermeticum* (hermetic vessel) in the settings of "The Assignation" (first published as "The Visionary" in 1834), "Ligeia" (1838), "The Fall of the House of Usher" (1839), and "The Colloquy of Monos and Unas" (1841) to afford his readers intimations of visionary experiences. Through the physical deaths of the main characters in these stories, Poe figuratively dissolves the dross of the material world in order to illustrate and facilitate visions of the supernal through the locus of imagination.

Although Richard P. Benton and G. R. Thompson have determined that Poe intended "The Assignation" as a hoax, this tale also demonstrates Poe's use of the alchemical theme of death and regeneration (*solve et coagula*).[8] The narrator's description of a drowning child in the opening immediately arrests the reader's attention:

> A child, slipping from the arms of its own mother, had fallen from an upper window of the lofty structure into the deep and dim canal. The quiet waters had closed placidly over their victim; and, although my own gondola was the only one in sight, many a stout swimmer, already in the stream, was seeking in vain upon the surface, *the treasure which was to be found, alas! only within the abyss*. (*CW* 2: 152; emphasis mine)

The Marchesa Aphrodite, the child's mother, then appears,

> She stood alone. Her small, bare and silvery feet gleamed in the black mirror of marble beneath her. Her hair, not as yet more than half loosened for the night from its ball-room array, clustered, amid a shower of diamonds, round and round her classical head,

in curls like those of the young hyacinth. A snowy-white and gauze-like drapery seemed to be nearly the sole covering to her delicate form. (*CW* 2: 152)

Although the name Aphrodite correlates to the planet Venus in alchemy,[9] Poe's description of the Marchesa's figure, clothed in "snowy-white . . . drapery," evokes the whiteness associated with the *albedo*.

With all efforts to save the drowning child proving vain, a dark figure (Poe's unnamed protagonist) emerges from the shadows of the Old Republican prison to dive into the canal's waters and save the child. Yet during all of this melodramatic action, one figure seems truly out of place—the husband of the Marchesa:

Many steps above the Marchesa, and within the arch or the watergate, stood, in full dress, the Satyr-like figure of Mentoni himself. He was occasionally occupied in thrumming a guitar, and seemed *ennuye* to the very death, as at intervals he gave directions for the recovery of his child. (*CW* 2: 153)

"Occasionally occupied in thrumming a guitar" while a child drowns! What nonsense, we may ask ourselves, is Poe up to now? Admittedly, the combination of music and alchemy may appear unusual, yet according to the English alchemist Robert Fludd, music helped to establish the harmony between microcosm and macrocosm.[10] As Peter J. Ammann notes, Fludd believed music to represent

an ascent from imperfection to perfection, from impurity to purity, from the depth to the summit, from crudeness to full maturity, from darkness to light, from earth to heaven, from evil to good, in fact from the devil to God. This is, according to Fludd, the secret and essential object of music. He evidently sees music in the same light as alchemy.[11]

Musical instruments also find their place in Heinrich Conrad Khunrath's engraving of the alchemical laboratory in *Amphitheatrum sapientiae aeternae* (1604) and suggest the strong connection between music and the alchemical opus with regard to the harmony of the microcosm (the material world) and macrocosm (the supernal).[12] On one side of Khunrath's laboratory is the alchemical furnace and still; on the other side is a sanctuary for prayer. Uniting these two important aspects of the alchemical work (i.e., the material and the spiritual) is a table covered with musical instruments (located in the middle of the laboratory). Thus, in Khunrath's illustration we may note the union of the chemical (material) and spiritual aspects of alchemy through music.[13]

We are now afforded an interesting perspective from which to view the incongruous image that Poe presents in the opening of "The Assignation": Mentoni as alchemist directing (and performing the music for) the alchemical drama in which the divine child ("the treasure") of Sol and Luna is born of the dark waters of the alchemical abyss. As Edward W. Pitcher notes, "the infant stands as the product and symbol of their [the protagonist and the Marchesa's] union, the offspring of a love sanctified by laws which transcend those of the marriage sacrament, sanctified by spiritual, not earthly bonds."[14]

The connection between Poe's protagonist of "The Assignation" and the alchemical king (Sol) is further strengthened by an examination of the protagonist's apartments that Poe includes in the second half of his story:

> In the architecture and embellishments of the chamber, the evident design had been to dazzle and astound. Little attention had been paid to the *decora* of what is technically called *keeping*, or to the proprieties of nationality. The eye wandered from object to object, and rested upon none—neither the *grotesques* of the Greek painters, nor the sculptures of the best Italian days, nor the huge carvings of untutored Egypt. Rich draperies in every part of the room trembled to the vibration of low, melancholy music, whose origin was not to be discovered. The senses were oppressed by mingled and conflicting perfumes, reeking up from strange convolute censers, together with multitudinous flaring and flickering tongues of emerald and violet fire. The rays of the newly risen sun poured in upon the whole, through windows, formed each of a single pane of crimson-tinted glass. Glancing to and fro, in a thousand reflections, from curtains which rolled from their cornices like cataracts of molten silver, the beams of natural glory mingled at length fitfully with the artificial light, and lay weltering in subdued masses upon a carpet of rich, liquid-looking cloth of Chili gold. (*CW* 2: 157–58).

As David Ketterer observes, the colors which Poe presents here are highly suggestive of alchemical transformation:

> The movement from night to day, "the tongues of emerald and violet fire," the "crimson-tinted glass," the curtains "like cataracts of molten silver," and the "liquid-looking cloth of Chili gold" suggest the colors associated with the seven stages of the alchemical

process: black (for primal matter), white (for the first transmutation into quicksilver), green, yellow, red (for sulphurous passion), silver, and finally gold."[15]

But what is the connection between the first and second parts of "The Assignation"? The common elements to both parts are the narrator, the protagonist, and the Marchesa (present in the second part of the story in both image—her painting—and spirit). We should set the narrator aside, for he is an unknowing witness to the events that occur, and focus on Poe's Byronic protagonist and the Marchesa, the alchemical couple in the first part of Poe's story. Both of these figures die during the first hour after sunrise (*aurora consurgens*), a propitious moment in the alchemical opus, for it not only represents dawning knowledge and the *conjunctio* (the chemical marriage of Sol and Luna), it also heralds the creation of the philosophers' stone in the alchemist's alembic.[16]

At the exact moment that a "cherub with a heavy golden hammer [makes] the apartment ring with the first hour after sunrise," Poe's protagonist states:

> To dream has been the business of my life. I have framed for myself, as you see, a bower of dreams. In the heart of Venice could I have erected a better? You behold around you, it is true, a medley of architectural embellishments. The chastity of Ionia is offended by antediluvian devices, and the sphynxes of Egypt are outstretched upon carpets of gold. Yet the effect is incongruous to the timid alone. Proprieties of place, and especially of time, are the bugbears which terrify mankind from the contemplation of the magnificent. Once I was myself a decorist; but that sublimation of folly has palled upon my soul. All this is now the fitter for my purpose. Like these arabesque censers, *my spirit is writhing in fire, and the delirium of this scene is fashioning me for the wilder visions of that land of real dreams whither I am now rapidly departing.* (*CW* 2: 165–66; emphasis mine)

In the protagonist's apartment, as in the *vas hermeticum* (the hermetic vessel, or alembic), the material elements of time and space collapse, and the spirit of Sol, awaiting conjunction with Luna, writhes in the alchemical fire.[17]

With the double suicide of the Marchesa and the protagonist at the end of "The Assignation," Poe intimates that through their deaths, the two lovers will be united in the afterlife (the "land of real dreams"). Indeed, material existence (time and space) is dissolved to facilitate the spiritual union of the Marchesa and the protagonist. In other words, earthly existence has been transmuted by visionary imagination into spiritual union. This idea seems to be what Poe foreshadows in the first half of "The Assignation." Just as the protagonist overcomes the watery abyss, so, Poe intimates, will he overcome the abyss of death.[18] Similarly, in alchemy the abyss of the *nigredo* (death) must be overcome before the conjunction can occur.

As a footnote to this reading of "The Assignation," Poe may have intended the child from the story's opening scene to evoke the characteristics of alchemical Mercury. Commenting upon the many qualities of this element, C. G. Jung notes,

> Mercurius stands at the beginning and end of the work: he is the *prima materia* . . . the *nigredo*. . . . He is the play of colours in the *cauda pavonis* and the division into four elements. He is the hermaphrodite that was in the beginning, that splits into the classical brother-sister duality and reunited in the *conjunctio*, to appear once again at the end in radiant form of the *lumen novum*, the stone. He is metallic yet liquid, matter yet spirit, cold yet fiery, poison and yet a healing draught—a symbol uniting all opposites.[19]

Jung's observations illuminate the opening image of "The Assignation," for the child is both agent and object of transmutation. Like alchemical Mercury, the child unites its mother (Luna) and the protagonist (Sol) and, like the philosophers' stone, represents the product of their union. Indeed, after the alchemical-like union of the protagonist and the Marchesa at the end of "The Assignation," Poe may have wanted his readers to contemplate the fate of the child. Perhaps Poe intended the child to fall heir to the visionary imagination of its mother and father.

Poe offers another variation on the alchemical theme *solve et coagula* in "Ligeia."[20] A close reading of this piece reveals an alchemical subtext to the story, which, Poe claimed in his letter to E. A. Duyckinck, was "the best story I have written" (*Letters* 2: 309).

At the beginning of "Ligeia" Poe emphasizes the connection between Ligeia and the esoteric feminine figure of wisdom:

> I have spoken of the learning of Ligeia: it was immense—such as I have never known in woman. . . . I said her knowledge was such as I have never known in woman—but where breathes the man who has traversed, and successfully, *all* the wide areas of moral, physical, and mathematical science? I saw not then what I now clearly perceive that the acquisitions of Ligeia were gigantic, were astounding; yet I was sufficiently aware of her infinite supremacy to resign myself, with a child like confidence, to her guidance

through the chaotic world of metaphysical investigation at which I was most busily occupied during the earlier years of our marriage. With how vast a triumph—with how vivid a delight—with how much of all that is ethereal in hope did I *feel*, as she bent over me in studies but little sought—but less known—that delicious vista by slow degrees expanding before me, down whose long, gorgeous, and all untrodden path, I might at length pass onward to the goal of a wisdom too divinely precious not to be forbidden! (*CW* 2: 315–16)

Clearly, Poe wants the reader to see that the figure of Ligeia is a personification of esoteric wisdom and knowledge itself.[21] Poe also intimates a connection between Ligeia and the philosophers' stone: "Wanting the radiant lustre of her eyes [her intellect], letters, lambent and golden, grew duller than Saturnian lead" (*CW* 2: 316). Thus, without the presence of Ligeia's illuminating and transmutating intellect (and here we might also add imagination), golden philosophy becomes drossy lead.

Ligeia, however, is stricken with a fatal illness. At high noon on the day of her death, Ligeia hands the narrator "certain verses composed by herself" (*CW* 2: 318) and bids the narrator to recite them. In this quasi-magical context Poe presents "The Conqueror Worm." While "The Conqueror Worm" evokes images of death (*nigredo*), the poem seems to end too soon, for there is no hint of resurrection or transmutation. This prompts Ligeia to state with her dying breath:

O God! . . . O God! O Divine Father!—shall these things be undeviatingly so?—shall this Conqueror be not once conquered? Are we not part and parcel in Thee? Who—who knoweth the mysteries of the will with its vigor? Man doth not yield him to the angels, *not unto death utterly*, save only through the weakness of his feeble will. (*CW* 2: 319)

It is significant that in the context of her imminent death Ligeia repeats Glanvill's words (which Poe also uses as the epigraph to this story), for the rest of Poe's tale completes the alchemical opus introduced by "The Conqueror Worm" and Ligeia's death. As Michael Maier intimates in *Atalanta Fugiens*, from the alchemical death of the lady (Luna) comes her rebirth in the form of the philosophers' stone.[22]

In the second part of the story (after Ligeia's death), Poe offers a description of the chambers in which the narrator resides with his new bride, the Lady Rowena Trevanion:

The room lay in a high turret of the castellated abbey, was pentagonal in shape, and of capacious size. Occupying the whole southern face of the pentagon was the sole window—an immense sheet of unbroken glass from Venice—a single pane, and tinted of a leaden hue, so that the rays of either the sun or moon passing through it, fell with a ghastly lustre on the objects within. Over the upper portion of this huge window, extended the trellis-work of an aged vine, which clambered up the massy walls of the turret. The ceiling of gloomy-looking oak, was excessively lofty, vaulted, and elaborately fretted with the wildest and most grotesque specimens of a semi-Gothic, semi-Druidical device. From the most central recess of this melancholy vaulting, depended, by a single chain of gold with long links, a huge censer of the same metals, Saracenic in pattern, and with many perforations so contrived that there writhed in and out of them, as if endued with a serpent vitality, a continual succession of parti-colored fires. (*CW* 2: 321)

Although we might speculate as to the meaning of the ancient symbols on the wall of the turret, the pentagon shape of the room evokes the pentacle of hermetic magic (and alchemy). To emphasize the hermetic atmosphere further, the turret containing the bridal chamber seems reminiscent of an alchemical furnace—the athanor—and the room an alchemical vessel recalling the interior setting of "The Assignation."

After Rowena's health fails due to a sudden illness, the narrator attempts to nurse her back to health. At the moment before the narrator offers a goblet of wine to Rowena, he notes "three or four large drops of a brilliant and ruby colored fluid" (*CW* 2: 325) magically falling into the goblet. After consuming this wine Rowena worsens, and on the third night after consuming the potion, she dies. The magical appearance of the ruby fluid is important to Poe's alchemical theme in "Ligeia," for this liquid is analogous to the alchemical *elixir vitae*—the Aurum Potabile Red.[23] While it may first seem ironic that the red tincture hastens Rowena's demise, from her death Ligeia is reborn.

As the narrator sits with Rowena's corpse on the fourth night (an evocation of the alchemical quaternity of air, earth, water, and fire) after she consumes the red elixir, the narrator notes signs of life returning to the corpse. After the corpse stirs for the fourth time, it rises and advances "boldly and palpably into the middle of the apartment." In a state of shock, the narrator notes:

> Could it, indeed, be the *living* Rowena who confronted me? Could it, indeed, be Rowena *at all*—the fair-haired, the blue-eyed Lady Rowena Trevanion of Tremaine? Why, *why* should I doubt it? . . . And the cheeks—there were the roses as in her noon of life—yes, these might indeed be the fair cheeks of the living Lady of Tremaine. . . . Shrinking from my touch, she let fall from her head, unloosened, the ghastly cerements which had confined it, and

there streamed forth into the rushing atmosphere of the chamber huge masses of long and dishevelled hair; *it was blacker than the raven wings of midnight*! And now slowly opened *the eyes* of the figure which stood before me. "Here then, at least," I shrieked aloud, "can I never—can I never be mistaken—these are the full, and the black, and the wild eyes—of my lost love—of the Lady—of the Lady Ligeia." (*CW* 2: 330)

The rose color of Ligeia's cheeks recalls the symbolic rose of the alchemical resurrection that the alchemists claimed would appear at the end of the opus. While the rose color on the fair (white) cheeks of the lady with raven hair combines the primary colors of the alchemical opus, this color combination also suggests the embodiment of the philosophers' stone in Ligeia herself.[24] Furthermore, this final scene evokes the royal marriage of Sol and Luna—the narrator and Ligeia—in the *vas hermeticum* of Poe's magical room.

Through the deaths of both Ligeia and Rowena, and Ligeia's subsequent rebirth, the reader witnesses Poe's literary adaptation of alchemical death and resurrection (*solve et coagula*). Indeed, Rowena is transmuted into Ligeia. Poe's final image of the resurrected Ligeia also recalls the alchemical marriage of heaven and earth, for the narrator's "lost love" has returned to the material realm.

It is interesting to note, however, that Poe's intention concerning "Ligeia" may not have been a successful transmutation after all. In a letter to P. Pendleton Cooke on September 21, 1839, Poe wrote the following:

Touching "Ligeia" you are right—all right—throughout. The *gradual* perception of the fact that Ligeia lives again in the person of Rowena is a far loftier and more thrilling idea than the one I have embodied. It offers, in my opinion, the widest possible scope to the imagination—it might be rendered even sublime. And this idea was mine—had I never written before I should have adopted it—but then there is "Morella." Do you remember there the *gradual* conviction on the part of the parent that the spirit of the first Morella tenants the person of the second? It was necessary, since "Morella" was written, to modify "Ligeia." I was forced to be content with a sudden half-consciousness, on the part of the narrator, that Ligeia stood before him. One point I have not fully carried out—I should have intimated that the *will* did not perfect its intention—there should have been a relapse—a final one—and Ligeia (who had only succeeded in so much as to convey an idea of truth to the narrator) should be at length entombed as Rowena—the bodily alterations having gradually faded away. (*Letters* 1: 118)[25]

Yet Poe never made the changes to "Ligeia" to which he alludes; he allowed the transmutation at the end to stand as he had written it.

One year after the publication of "Ligeia," Poe returned to the theme of alchemical death and resurrection in "The Fall of the House of Usher." In this, one of Poe's most famous stories, the reader witnesses the predeath entombment and resurrection of Madeline Usher, followed by the simultaneous deaths of both Roderick and Madeline. The grave and its related image of the coffin were frequently used in alchemical manuscripts to illustrate the contents of the alembic during the *nigredo*. Emblem 50 of Michael Maier's *Atalanta Fugiens* (1618) pictures Queen Luna (apparently dead) and lying in a freshly dug grave. However, as Maier intimates, from this death will come regeneration. While Madeline's tomb recalls the chemical death in an alchemist's alembic, her subsequent resurrection suggests a preparation for a more important event.

In his study of "Usher," Barton Levi St. Armand presents an enlightened reading of Poe's story that concentrates on the alchemical allegory presented in "The Mad Trist" and its correlation with the author's own use of alchemical tropes in the story. As St. Armand observes:

> the killing of the dragon by Ethelred is perfectly illustrated by the second figure of *The Book of Lambspring*. . . . In Poe's allegory, the dragon, which can be either Mercurius as "quicksilver" or as basematter, defends neither a fortress nor the golden garden . . . but rather "a palace of gold, with a floor of silver." And Ethelred, who is suggestive of the alchemist, Mars, and "sophic sulphur" (for his name can be construed as "red ether," and we remember that Roderick Usher's "ideality" threw "a sulphureous lustre over all"), will surely be an alchemical conqueror if he wins the shield of the *lapis*, the Philosopher's Stone.[26]

Indeed, "The Mad Trist" has all the trappings of an alchemical allegory, but then, so does Poe's story.

As the narrator finishes his reading of the story, the resurrected Madeline makes her entrance:

> there *did* stand the lofty and enshrouded figure of the lady Madeline of Usher. There was blood upon her white robes, and the evidence of some bitter struggle upon every portion of her emaciated frame. For a moment she remained trembling and reeling to and fro upon the threshold—then, with a low moaning cry, fell

heavily inward upon the person of her brother, and in her violent and now final death-agonies, bore him to the floor a corpse. (*CW* 2: 416–17)

Whereas the appearance of Usher's sister, clothed in white yet covered in blood, recalls the conjunction of alchemical white and red, the final death-embrace of Usher and his sister evokes an image of alchemical union between brother and sister (King Sol and Queen Luna). In Eirenaeus Philalethes' allegory of the alchemical process, the King, seeing the Queen in danger, "knew her to be his Sister, his Mother, and his Wife, and compassionating her estate, ran unto her, and took her in his Arms, and she feeling him, did so strongly embrace him, that he could not shake her off."[27] Later Philalethes writes, "The King is Brother to his Wife."[28] Philalethes' image of the brother-sister conjunction is not unique in alchemy, for the medieval alchemists often described the union of Sol and Luna in such terms to emphasize the close relationship between these mysterious alchemical elements.[29]

Finally, in the last paragraph of the story, the narrator offers a description of the conjunction of the four alchemical elements converging about Usher's house:

> Suddenly there shot along the path a *wild light*, and I turned to see whence a gleam so unusual could have issued; for the vast house and its shadows were alone behind me. The radiance was that of the full, setting, and blood-red moon, which now shone vividly through that once barely-discernible fissure, of which I have before spoken as extending from the roof of the building, in a zig-zag direction, to the base. While I gazed, this fissure rapidly widened—there came a fierce breath of the *whirlwind*—the entire orb of the satellite burst at once upon my sight—my brain reeled as I saw the mighty walls rushing asunder—there was a long tumultuous shouting sound like the voice of a thousand *waters*—and the deep and dank *tarn* at my feet closed sullenly and silently over the fragments of the *"House of Usher."* (*CW* 2: 417; emphases mine)

With the "wild [red] light" of the moon symbolizing fire, Poe's apocalyptic description recalls the conjunction of the four elements, thought by many alchemists to be the key to creating the philosophers' stone in the athanor (the house of Usher).[30] Poe's description here finds an interesting parallel with a passage from Paracelsus' "Tenth Book of the Archidoxies":

If, then, the predestinated element has to be separated, it is necessary that the house be broken up; and this breaking up or dissolution of the house is brought about in divers ways, as is clearly said in my Metamorphosis concerning the death of things. If the house is dissolved by strong waters, by calcinations, and the like, care must be taken that what is dissolved from that which is fixed must be separated by common distillations. For then the body of the quintessence passes over like phlegm, but the fixed element remains at the bottom.[31]

Previously in "Usher" (i.e., "The Haunted Palace"), Poe equates Usher's house with Roderick Usher himself.[32] At the climax of the story, the quintessence of Roderick and Madeline is produced from their conjunction as their physical bodies (the "house") are separated (dissolved) to facilitate the union of their spirits. With the collapse of the literal house in the final scene, Poe intimates that a transmutation of matter into spirit—"the seed of gold"—has taken place. Usher's house, like the athanor containing the philosophers' stone, becomes a signpost directing the reader's attention from the mundane world to the visionary realm of spirit. Furthermore, the appearance of the crimson moon that casts its light upon the fallen house combines, like Madeline's blood-stained gown, the alchemical white and red and announces the fifth element of hermetic science (the quintessence or the philosophers' stone) created by the union of Sol and Luna. Indeed, the unions of both Sol and Luna and Roderick and Madeline suggest an image reminiscent of the alchemical hermaphrodite.[33] As Philalethes notes of this hieroglyph, "our Hermaphrodite, [is] mighty in both Sexes."[34] Perhaps, as Poe intimates, a new spirit is created from the union of Roderick and Madeline.

THE CONJUNCTION IN THE GRAVE

The endings of "The Assignation" and "Usher" suggest that the male-female (Sol-Luna) couples in both stories unite in death. Yet in these stories death becomes a means to an end—part of a *process* that culminates with an alchemical-like conjunction in the afterlife, the supernal realm. But why does Poe go through such an elaborate process? Like the medieval alchemists, Poe realized that in order to experience the visionary realm, the dross of the material world had to be broken down, or dissolved, as in "The Colloquy of Monos and Una."

In "The Colloquy," Poe's angelic spirit of Monos discourses on "the majestic novelty of the Life Eternal" (*CW* 2: 608) following his alchemical-like experience of death during the "corrosive hours" (*CW* 2: 617) in the grave. Poe's primary theme in "The Colloquy" suggests the regeneration of the soul, but this theme also has a broader application. As Monos states,

> for the infected world at large I could anticipate no regeneration save in death. That man, as a race, should not become extinct, I saw that he must be *"born again."*
>
> And now it was, fairest and dearest [Una], that we wrapped our spirits, daily, in dreams. Now it was that, in twilight, we discoursed of the days to come, when the Art-scarred surface of the Earth, having undergone that purification which alone could efface its rectangular obscenities, should clothe itself anew in the verdure and the mountain-slopes and the smiling waters of Paradise, and be rendered at length a fit dwelling-place for man:— for man the Death-purged—for man to whose now exalted intellect there should be poison in knowledge no more—for the redeemed, regenerated, blissful, and now immortal, but still for the *material*, man. (*CW* 2: 611–12)

In this passage death becomes the means to purge "the general turmoil and decay" (*CW* 2: 612), the dross of civilization, from the human race. In addition, by focusing his attention on the after-death experience of Monos, Poe is afforded the opportunity to speculate on both the annihilation of time and space and existence beyond the material realm:

> And now, from the wreck and the chaos of the usual senses, there appeared to have arisen within me a sixth, all perfect. In its exercise I found a wild delight—yet a delight still physical, inasmuch as the understanding had in it no part. Motion in the animal frame had fully ceased. No muscle quivered; no nerve thrilled; no artery throbbed. But there seemed to have sprung up in the brain, *that* of which no words could convey to the merely human intelligence even an indistinct conception. Let me term it a mental pendulous pulsation. It was the moral embodiment of man's abstract idea of *Time*. By the absolute equalization of this movement—or such as this—had the cycles of the firmamental orbs themselves, been adjusted.... And this—this keen, perfect, self-existing sentiment of *duration*—this sentiment existing (as man could not possibly have conceived it to exist) independently of any succession of events—this idea—this sixth sense, upspringing from the ashes of the rest, was the first obvious and certain step of the intemporal soul upon the threshold of the temporal Eternity. (*CW* 2: 614–15)

Poe's words evoke an image of the alchemical phoenix (an emblem for the philosophers' stone), "uprising from [its] ashes," as both a mystical sixth-sense and a bridge to eternity.[35] As Robert Fludd notes in his "Clavis": "To die is simply the falling asunder and disintegration of the mechanism of the senses."[36] Yet from death, a sixth sense (the "seed of gold") emerges.

The body of Monos is "at length stricken with the hand of deadly Decay" (*CW* 2: 615) and interned into its "prison house" (*CW* 2: 616). Here again, Poe's images recall alchemical death. During the *nigredo* the alchemists often referred to the alembic as a dungeon or prison.[37] Martin Ruland, in his *Lexicon*, notes, "The Philosophers use this term [*prison*] in several senses. They apply it firstly to the more gross and heterogeneous matters, in which their Mercury and their Gold are shut up as in a Prison, and from which it is necessary to set them free. They apply it, secondly, to the Vase, in which the Matter of the Work is placed, in order to work upon it with a view to the Magisterium."[38]

Following the internment, a year passes and Monos notes the following:

> The consciousness of *being* had grown hourly more indistinct, and that of mere *locality* had, in great measure, usurped its position. The idea of entity was becoming merged in that of *place*. The narrow space immediately surrounding what had been the body, was now growing to be the body itself. At length, as often happens to the sleeper (by sleep and its world alone is *Death* imaged)—at length, as sometimes happened on Earth to the deep slumberer, when some flitting light half startled him into awaking, yet left him half enveloped in dreams—so to me, in strict embrace of the *Shadow*, came *that* light which alone might have had power to startle—the light of enduring *Love*. Men toiled at the grave in which I lay darkling. They upthrew the damp earth. Upon my mouldering bones there descended the coffin of Una. (*CW* 2: 616)

In this passage Poe intimates the need to dissolve the material (senses) in order to discover intimations of the visionary realm. Moreover, with the final union of spirit (Monus and Una in the grave), Poe's description recalls the words of Philalethes: "Join heaven to earth in the fire of love, and you will see in the middle of the firmament the bird of Hermes [the philosophers' stone]." Indeed, through "the light of enduring love," the two lovers are united in and for eternity. The grave itself, like the alchemist's alembic, directs the reader to the visionary realm.[39] Thus, in "The Colloquy," we find that heaven and earth, spirit and matter, unite in the grave through what might best be referred to as "the fire [power] of love."

Poe's use of the alchemical conjunction at the grave also recalls the imagery in one of the author's final and most powerful poems, "Annabel Lee" (1849). After the first five stanzas in which the speaker describes his love for and his loss of his lover, the poem concludes:

> For the moon never beams without bringing me dreams
>   Of the beautiful Annabel Lee;
> And the stars never rise but I see the bright eyes
>   Of the beautiful Annabel Lee;
> And so, all the night-tide, I lie down by the side
> Of my darling, my darling, my life and my bride,
>   In her sepulchre there by the sea—
>   In her tomb by the side of the sea. (*CW* 1: 478)

Here the conjunction of the two lovers at and in the grave suggests not merely necrophilia, but an alchemical conjunction (through love) that forms a bridge to the realm of spirit.

Although Andrew Marvell noted, "The grave's a fine and private place, / But none, I think, do there embrace,"[40] in alchemy Sol and Luna do embrace in the crypt. It is just such an image that Poe incorporates into his work to illustrate his visions of existence beyond the material realm. Love, for Poe, is a synonym for the philosophers' stone, the magic of which could illuminate the way to the supernal realm.

POE'S HERMETIC GARDEN AND THE MARRIAGE OF HEAVEN AND EARTH

In this section we will explore Poe's ongoing interest in the alchemists' garden (along with the alchemical color sequences connected with this hermetic space) as a signpost illuminating the way to the supernal. Poe's knowledge of alchemical lore may have (ironically) suggested to the author that although Newtonian science had demythologized the universe, the hermetic science of alchemy might offer a way back to a vision of nature (e.g., the philosophers' garden) that would provide a solution to the cultural decay Poe saw around him.[41] Indeed, the mystic undercurrent of alchemy proposed the possibility of spiritual renewal through a reconciliation of heaven and earth. Whereas examples of Poe's early use of the tropes associated with the alchemical garden can be found in the landscape settings of "Eleonora" (1841) and "The Gold-Bug" (1843), his treatment of the philosophers' garden culminates in "The Domain of Arnheim" (1846), where the alchemists' marriage of heaven and earth informs Poe's twofold vision of art and the artist as mediators between the material world and the supernal.

In his essay on "The Gold-Bug," St. Armand notes that alchemy "masked an incredibly complex and profound philosophy, basically Neoplatonic in content, in which the search for the 'philosopher's stone' was not just the quest for a catalytic agent which could turn base metals into gold, but a long rite of initiation which conducted the neophyte through various disciplinary types of experience toward an ideal state of soul."[42] In "Usher Unveiled," St. Armand observes that Poe combined the tropes of alchemy with the philosophy of Gnosticism to articulate his vision of the soul's struggle toward the supernal (the liberation of spirit from matter).[43] As we shall observe with regard to "The Domain of Arnheim," Poe's familiarity with the alchemists' garden allowed him to speculate upon the reconciliation of spirit and matter by using both art and the artist as mediators in the process.

On the more mystical and spiritual level of alchemical philosophy, once spirit was liberated from matter, it was then joined (once again) with matter.[44] Thus, the ultimate goal of alchemy was not merely the transmutation of lead into gold (sometimes described as the liberation of golden spirit from leaden matter),[45] but the marriage (or conjunction) of spirit and matter, heaven and earth. According to Johann Daniel Mylius, in *Philosophia reformata* (1622), "So many times must the heaven above the earth be reproduced until the earth becomes heavenly and spiritual, and heaven becomes earthly, and is joined to the earth; then the work will be finished."[46]

Mylius suggests that with the creation of the philosophers' stone, heaven and earth are joined in a mystical marriage reflecting the chemical marriage in the alchemist's alembic.[47] The spiritual implications here are quite extraordinary, for just as the philosophers' stone is said to transmute lead into gold, so the fallen (material) world is once again linked with heaven—a new Eden is generated—and the alchemist, the mediator and operator of this process, is spiritually transformed. Among the many diverse images onto which the alchemists encoded this procedure, the hieroglyph of the philosophers' garden clearly portrays this conjunction of heaven and earth.[48] The garden of the philosophers, cognate with the Garden of Eden, recapitulates "the wholeness of paradise," and its centerpiece, the *arbor philosophica* (the philosophers' tree), symbolically links heaven and earth.[49] Thus, the philosophers' garden represents the *vas hermeticum*, and the *arbor philosophica* recalls the properties of the philosophers' stone.

The reconciliation of heaven and earth appears to have preoccupied Poe in 1846 (the year he published "Arnheim"), for he writes the following in his "Marginalia":

> I regard the visions, even as they arise, with an awe which, in some measure, moderates or tranquilizes the ecstasy—I so regard them, through a conviction (which seems a portion of the ecstasy

> itself) that this ecstasy, in itself, is of a character supernal to the Human Nature—is a glimpse of the spirit's outer world...
>   Now, so entire is my faith in the *power of words*, that, at times, I have believed it possible to embody even the evanescence of fancies such as I have attempted to describe. In experiments with this end in view, I have proceeded so far as, first, to control (when the bodily and mental health are good) the existence of the condition:—that is to say, I can now (unless when ill) be sure that the condition will supervene, if I so wish it, at the point of time already described:—of its supervention, until lately, I could never be certain, even under the most favorable circumstances. I mean to say, merely, that now I can be sure, when all circumstances are favorable, of the supervention of the condition, and feel even the capacity of inducing or compelling it:—the favorable circumstances, however, are not the less rare—else had I compelled, already, the Heaven into the Earth. (*ER* 1383–84)

Although describing a hypnotic (dreamlike) state in this passage, Poe's words also suggest the role of the artist as alchemical mediator compelling "the Heaven [supernal] into the Earth" through the "*power of words.*"

While Poe first alluded to the "mystic or undercurrent" of literature in his 1839 review of *Undine*, it was not until his 1842 review of Longfellow's *Ballads and Other Poems* that Poe articulated the intended destination to which the "undercurrent" was to carry his readers:

> An important condition of man's immortal nature is thus, plainly, the sense of the Beautiful.... This burning thirst belongs to the *immortal* essence of man's nature.... It is a wild effort to reach the beauty above.... Inspired with a prescient ecstasy of the beauty beyond the grave, it struggles by multiform novelty of combination among the things and thoughts of Time, to anticipate some portion of that loveliness whose very elements, perhaps, appertain solely to Eternity.... Its [Poesy's] first element is the thirst for supernal BEAUTY–a beauty which is not afforded the soul by any existing collocation of earth's forms–a beauty which, perhaps, *no possible* combination of these forms would fully produce. (*ER* 685–87)

Here Poe suggests that the poetic (creative) imagination might provide a link between earth and the supernal. In his "Chapter of Suggestions" (1845), Poe clarifies this connection between the poetic imagination and the supernal:

That the imagination has not been unjustly ranked as supreme among the mental faculties, appears, from the intense consciousness, on the part of the imaginative man, that the faculty in question brings his soul often to a glimpse of things supernal and eternal—to the very verge of the *great secrets*. There are moments, indeed, in which he perceives the faint perfumes, and hears the melodies of a happier world. Some of the most profound knowledge—perhaps all *very* profound knowledge—has originated from a highly stimulated imagination. (*ER* 1293)

"To the very verge of the *great secrets*": the emphasis is Poe's, and he suggests that through the artistic imagination a poem can become a vehicle into *the unknown* (the visionary realm) for both the poet and the reader. As Poe notes in "The Poetic Principle" (1850):

Thus, although in a very cursory and imperfect manner, I have endeavoured to convey to you my conception of the Poetic Principle. It has been my purpose to suggest that, while this Principle itself is, strictly and simply, the Human Aspiration for Supernal Beauty, the manifestation of the Principle is always found in *an elevating excitement of the Soul*—quite independent of that passion which is the intoxication of the Heart—or of that Truth which is the satisfaction of the Reason. (*ER* 92–93)

In addition to the artistic vision as a way to access the supernal, Poe intimates a connection between the dreamworld (the supernal) and alchemical philosophy in "Dream-land" (1844). Although most scholars concentrate solely on Poe's phrase "Supernal Beauty," beauty is indeed in the eye of the beholder, and in the second stanza of "Dream-land" Poe offers a unique description of a landscape reflecting the sublime (if not wild) aspect of what he may have envisioned as the supernal: "*Mountains* toppling evermore / Into *seas* without a shore;/ Seas that restlessly aspire,/ Surging, unto *skies* of *fire*" (*CW* 1: 344, lines 13–16; emphasis mine). In these lines Poe conflates the conjunction of the four classical elements (earth/"Mountains," water/"seas," air/"skies," and fire) that the alchemists believed would form the philosophers' stone with the dreamscape or landscape of this poem. In the context of "Dream-land" (and the reflection of the supernal and the imagination that the poem evokes), the juxtaposed images reflected in this conjunction suggest Poe's conscious equation of his sublime world of dreams (accessed through poetic imagination) with the philosophy of the alchemists. Poe further emphasizes this connection in the sixth stanza of the poem where he equates his dream-land with the mythical city of gold: "For the heart whose woes are legion / 'Tis a peaceful, soothing region—/ For the spirit that walks in shadow / O! it is an Eldorado!" (*CW* 1: 345, lines 39–42). Here "Eldorado" evokes a place of rest and riches, eternity and perfection.[50] Thus, Poe's "Dream-land," located "Out of Space—out of Time" (*CW* 1: 344, line 8), becomes a place accessible through the visionary's imagination.

According to Poe, art could indeed provide a link (or bridge) for the reader from the material world to the supernal, or spiritual realm; thus, art, and by extension the artist, might mediate between the supernal (heaven) and earth. As Robert Jacobs notes, "Poe had difficulty in reconciling the Newtonian universe of perfect order with the phenomenal disorder he observed on every side. His characteristic solution was to bring in the artist as mediator, which of course was in keeping with the romantic tendency to regard the artist as the transcendental hero who would save us all."[51] The idea of the artist-as-mediator suggests that Poe's artistic stance (his vision of the artist) is metaphorically situated between earth and heaven, between the material world and the supernal. This idea is also suggested by the vision of Poe's landscape artist Ellison in "The Domain of Arnheim":

> A poet, having very unusual pecuniary resources, might, while retaining the necessary idea of art, or culture, or, as our author expresses it, of interest, so imbue his designs at once with extent and novelty of beauty, as to convey the sentiment of spiritual interference. It will be seen that, in bringing about such result, he secures all the advantages of interest or *design*, while relieving his work of the harshness or technicality of the worldly *art*. In the most rugged of wildernesses—in the most savage of the scenes of pure nature—there is apparent the *art* of a creator; yet this art is apparent to reflection only; in no respect has it the obvious force of a feeling. Now let us suppose this sense of the Almighty design to be *one step depressed*—to be brought into something like harmony or consistency with the sense of human art—to form an intermedium between the two:—let us imagine, for example, a landscape whose combined vastness and definitiveness—whose united beauty, magnificence, and *strangeness*, shall convey the idea of care, or culture, or superintendence, on the part of beings superior, yet akin to humanity—then the sentiment of *interest* is preserved, while the art intervolved is made to assume the air of an intermediate or secondary nature—a nature which is not God, nor an emanation from God, but which still is nature in the sense of the handiwork of the angels that hover between man and God. (*CW* 3: 1276)

In this passage Ellison envisions a work of art that would function as a bridge between the material world and the spiritual realm, and the image of the "handiwork of the angels that hover between man and God" emphasizes the role of the artist as alchemical mediator reconciling heaven and earth. While Alice Chandler observes that Ellison, as landscape artist, mediates "between the ideal [world] and the real,"[52] Ellison's garden of Arnheim also produces an effect capable of elevating the soul of the reader or viewer toward a visionary experience of the supernal and offers the opportunity of spiritual renewal for those fortunate enough to visit.

As we shall observe, the alchemical marriage of heaven and earth illuminates the synthesis of the spiritual (supernal) and material in the "undercurrent" of "Arnheim" and helps demonstrate Poe's ongoing interest in alchemical metaphors and tropes as signposts leading the reader toward possible visionary experiences. Poe, in fact, may have known that alchemy was referred to as "The Great Art," a phrase that suggests further affinities between the artist and the alchemist.[53] Poe alludes to this connection, noting in his *Marginalia* of May 1849, "as often analogously happens in physical chemistry, so not unfrequently does it occur in this chemistry of the intellect, that the admixture of two elements results in something that has nothing of the qualities of one of them, or even nothing of the qualities of either" (*ER* 1451). As Poe intimates, the artist, like the alchemist who combines the four classical elements to produce the philosophers' stone, can at times combine images ("elements") to create a work of art that evokes visions of the supernal. Thus, by drawing on the tropes and metaphors of alchemy (especially those associated with the philosophers' garden) Poe offered his readers intimations of cosmic harmony, the alchemical marriage of heaven and earth.

An early example of Poe's use of the alchemical garden is found in "Eleonora." While Poe's epigraph attributed to Raymond Lull, the thirteenth-century Catalan philosopher (and reputed alchemist), is an interesting starting point,[54] the imagery that Poe employs in the garden scenes of this tale evokes the tropes of alchemical transmutation. At the beginning of "Eleonora," the garden "beneath a tropical sun" (*CW* 2: 639) reflects the innocence of its two occupants, but as the couple realizes the passion associated with their love (a loss of innocence), a transformation takes place in the valley garden:

A change fell upon all things. Strange brilliant flowers, star-shaped, burst out upon the trees where no flowers had been known before. The tents of the green carpet deepened; and when, one by one, the white daisies shrank away, there sprang up, in place of

> them, ten by ten of the ruby-red asphodel. And life arose in our paths; for the tall flamingo, hitherto unseen, with all gay glowing birds, flaunted his scarlet plumage before us. The golden and silver fish haunted the river, out of the bosom of which issued, little by little, a murmur that swelled, at length, into a lulling melody more divine than that of the harp of Æolus—sweeter than all save the voice of Eleonora. And now, too, a voluminous cloud, which we had long watched in the regions of Hesper, floated out thence, all gorgeous in crimson and gold, and settling in peace above us, sank, day by day, lower and lower, until its edges rested upon the tops of the mountains, turning all their dimness into magnificence, and shutting us up, as if forever, within a magic prison-house of grandeur and of glory. (*CW* 2: 640–41)

Here we see the transmutation of the valley as it mirrors the change of emotions in the lovers: the white daisies recall the *albedo* (the white-silver phase of the opus that proceeds the *rubedo*) yet give way to images evoking the *rubedo* (the red-gold color that often heralds the creation of the philosophers' stone in the alchemist's alembic)—the ruby red asphodels, the bird with scarlet plumage, and a crimson and gold cloud that settles over the valley. While the trees with star-shaped flowers recall the alchemical tree found in Mylius's *Anatomia auri sive tvrocinium medico-chymicum* (1620), Poe's phrase "magic prison-house" evokes the *vas hermeticum*.[55] On one level, Poe's use of colors in the Valley of the Many-Colored Grass reflects the change from innocence to experience (awakening passion); however, the maturing experience of love and desire in the two young lovers also recalls the conjunction of the alchemical King and Queen (suggested by the golden and silver fish).[56] Thus, the colors of this garden suggest the alchemical conjunction of heaven and earth, the supernal and material realm, realized through an alchemy of love.

With the death of Eleonora, however, we note the failure of the lovers to maintain the magic they discovered (Poe's pun on the dying "lulling melody" seems to suggest this fact), and the signs of transmutation fade from the garden:

> The star-shaped flowers shrank into the stems of the trees, and appeared no more. The tints of the green carpet faded; and, one by one, the ruby-red asphodel withered away; and there sprang up, in place of them, ten by ten, dark eye-like violets that writhed uneasily and were ever encumbered with dew. And Life departed from our paths; for the tall flamingo flaunted no longer his scarlet plumage before us, but flew sadly from the vale into the hills, with

all the gay glowing birds that had arrived in his company. And the golden and silver fish swam down through the gorge at the lower end of our domain and bedecked the sweet river never again. And the lulling melody that had been softer than the wind-harp of Æolus and more divine than all save the voice of Eleonora, it died little by little away, in murmurs growing lower and lower, until the stream returned, at length, utterly, into the solemnity of its original silence. And then, lastly the voluminous cloud uprose, and, abandoning the tops of the mountains to the dimness of old, fell back into the regions of Hesper, and took away all its manifold golden and gorgeous glories from the Valley of the Many-Colored Grass. (*CW* 2: 643)

As Poe intimates, love may indeed reflect the qualities of the philosophers' stone and thus offer intimations of the supernal, but a human being is a fragile container for such a wonder-working quintessence.[57] Although the transmutation in the garden does not last, what we glimpse in the first part of "Eleonora" suggests Poe's interest in the alchemical garden's hermetic space as a meeting point of earth and heaven (the material and the supernal) capable of evoking visions of paradise.

Another example of Poe's adaptation of the philosophers' garden is located in "The Gold-Bug," and although this story does not immediately recall the conjunction of heaven and earth, it does illustrate Poe's ongoing treatment of the philosophers' garden. In his study of "The Gold-Bug," St. Armand provides a provocative analysis that focuses on the figure of William Legrand as alchemist and the alchemical metal and color imagery that permeates the story.[58] But it is Poe's use of the tulip tree as *arbor philosophica* that illuminates the alchemical garden of "The Gold-Bug."

Midway through "The Gold-Bug" Poe offers a description of a tulip tree with the slave Jupiter—the symbolic name for tin in alchemy—clinging to it:

In youth, the tulip-tree, or *Liriodendron Tulipiferum*, the most magnificent of American foresters, has a trunk peculiarly smooth, and often rises to a great height without lateral branches; but, in its riper age, the bark becomes gnarled and uneven, while many short limbs make their appearance on the stem. Thus the difficulty of ascension, in the present case, lay more in semblance than in reality. Embracing the huge cylinder, as closely as possible, with his arms and knees, seizing with his hands some projections, and resting his naked toes upon others, Jupiter, after one or two narrow escapes from falling, at length wriggled himself into the first great fork, and seemed to consider the whole business as virtually accomplished. (*CW* 3: 818–19)[59]

As Legrand orders Jupiter to the seventh limb of the tree—where a human skull is secured and from where the slave will suspend the gold bug attached to a cord—Poe presents his readers with an image that recalls the alchemical analogy between the seven limbs of the tulip tree (the *arbor philosophica*) and the seven alchemical metals and their corresponding planets.[60] The alchemical text *Theatrum Chemicum* (1660) offers an interesting description of the seven-branched alchemical tree by which we may further glean alchemical meaning of Poe's seven-limbed tree: "On account of likeness alone, and not substance, the philosophers compare their material to a golden tree with seven branches, thinking that it encloses in its seed the seven metals, and that these are hidden in it, for which reason they call it a living thing."[61]

The tulip tree occupies a central place not only in Poe's story but in Poe's alchemical garden of Sullivan's Island as well, for underneath the tree, Legrand and company discover Captain Kidd's treasure:

As the rays of the lanterns fell within the pit, there flashed upwards from a confused heap of gold and of jewels, a glow and a glare that absolutely dazzled our eyes.... There was not a particle of silver. All was gold of antique date and of great variety. ... There were diamonds ... eighteen rubies ... three hundred and ten emeralds ... sapphires ... an opal.... We estimated the entire contents of the chest, that night, at a million and a half of dollars; and, upon the subsequent disposal of the trinkets and jewels ... it was found that we had greatly undervalued the treasure. (*CW* 3: 826–28)

Here we see the play of colors and light associated with the *cauda pavonis*—the peacock's tail—that signals the arrival of the philosophers' stone.[62] With the equation of the gold bug with the philosophers' stone, the treasure becomes a symbol for the *multiplicatio* of the alchemical process.[63] Not only has the gold of the bug been multiplied, but the family wealth of Legrand's past is restored and the financial security of his future assured. Thus, Legrand becomes renewed (materially, at least) when he discovers the treasure of Poe's alchemical garden.

Perhaps Poe's most telling use of the alchemical garden, however, is in "The Domain of Arnheim," for here Poe most graphically depicts the synthesis of the material and the supernal through art. Whereas scholars such as Robert Jacobs and Jeffrey A. Hess have examined this tale in terms of Poe's effort to re-create the lost Eden and to reproduce in prose the landscape murals of Thomas Cole, a close look at "Arnheim" with recourse to the tropes and metaphors of alchemy reveals Poe's use of the philosophers' garden as a primary analogue for his vision of art and illuminates his vision of the artist as mediator between earth and the supernal.[64]

While emphasizing that the garden of Arnheim, like its precursors in "Eleonora" and "The Gold-Bug," is a magical, hermetically enclosed space, separated from the outside world (reality),[65] Poe asserts that its creator (Ellison) possesses the poetic sentiment:

> In the widest and noblest sense he [Ellison] was a poet. He comprehended, moreover, the true character, the august aims, the supreme majesty and dignity of the poetic sentiment. The fullest, if not the sole proper satisfaction of this sentiment he instinctively felt to lie in the creation of novel forms of beauty. Some peculiarities, either in his early education, or in the nature of his intellect, had tinged with what is termed materialism all his ethical speculations; and it was this bias, perhaps, which led him to believe that the most advantageous at least, if not the sole legitimate field for the poetic exercise, lies in the creation of novel moods of purely *physical* loveliness. (*CW* 3: 1271)

Indeed, the landscape garden becomes Ellison's vehicle for creativity and as such it functions as a bridge between the material world and the supernal:

> Ellison maintained that the richest, the truest and most natural, if not altogether the most extensive province, had been unaccountably neglected. No definition had spoken of the landscape-gardener as of the poet; yet it seemed to my friend that the creation of the landscape-garden offered to the proper Muse the most magnificent of opportunities. Here, indeed, was the fairest field for the display of imagination in the endless combining of forms of novel beauty; the elements to enter into combination being, by a vast superiority, the most glorious which the earth could afford. In the multiform and multicolor of the flower and the trees, he recognized the most direct and energetic efforts of Nature at physical loveliness. And in the direction or concentration of this effort—or, more properly, in its adaptation to the eyes which were to behold it on earth—he perceived that he should be employing the best means—laboring to the greatest advantage—in the fulfillment, not only of his own destiny as poet, but of the august purposes for which the Deity had implanted the poetic sentiment in man. (*CW* 3: 1272)[66]

The idea of art as the "creation" and "combination" of "novel forms of beauty" leading toward "the [purpose] for which the Deity had implanted the poetic sentiment in man"—"The Human Aspiration for Supernal Beauty"—recalls Poe's metaphor of (al)chemical imagination as well as his vision that art might indeed function as a bridge from the material to the supernal.

The connection between the artist and the alchemist is further strengthened when we examine Poe's description of Ellison's garden domain. In the second half of Poe's tale, the narrator describes his journey toward Arnheim:

> The stream took a thousand turns, so that at no moment could its gleaming surface be seen for a greater distance than a furlong. At every instant the vessel seemed imprisoned within an enchanted circle, having insuperable and impenetrable walls of foliage, a roof of ultra-marine satin, and *no* floor.... The channel now became a *gorge*—although the term is somewhat inapplicable, and I employ it merely because the language has no word which better represents the most striking—not the most distinctive—feature of the scene. The character of gorge was maintained only in the height and parallelism of the shores; it was lost altogether in their other traits. The walls of the ravine (through which the clear water still tranquilly flowed) arose to an elevation of a hundred and occasionally of a hundred and fifty feet, and inclined so much toward each other as, in a great measure, to shut out the light of day. (*CW* 3: 1279)

Poe's suggestion that the passenger vessel seems "imprisoned within an enchanted circle" as it floats down the channel recalls the alchemists' analogy of the *vas hermeticum* as prison house, and as the channel opens into a gorge, Poe again evokes the image of the *vas*, equating the gorge with the alchemical vessel.

Continuing the journey, the narrator observes, "The windings became more frequent and intricate, and seemed often as if returning in upon themselves, so that the voyager had long lost all idea of direction. He was, moreover, enwrapt in an exquisite sense of the strange" (*CW* 3: 1279). Whereas the windings of the boat's course suggests the image of a coiled distillation apparatus, Poe's observation of the landscape— "The thought of nature still remained, but her character seemed to have undergone modification; there was a weird symmetry, a thrilling uniformity, a wizard propriety in these her works" (*CW* 3: 1279)—alludes to the alchemists' objective of perfecting nature (i.e., extracting the golden spirit or seed from a base element). Indeed, it appears that Ellison has brought the elements of nature to their perfected end, for "Not a dead branch—not a withered leaf—not a stray pebble—not a patch of the brown earth was anywhere visible. The crystal water welled up against the clean granite, or the unblemished moss, with a sharpness of outline that delighted while it bewildered the eye" (*CW* 3: 1279).

At this instant the passenger vessel enters a great basin, suggestive of yet another alchemical vessel:

> Having threaded the mazes of this channel for some hours, the gloom deepening every moment, a sharp and unexpected turn of the vessel brought it suddenly, as if dropped from heaven, into a circular basin of very considerable extent when compared with the width of the gorge. It was about two hundred yards in diameter, and girt in at all points but one—that immediately fronting the vessel as it entered—by hills equal in general height to the wall of the chasm, although of a thoroughly different character. Their sides sloped from the water's edge at an angle of some forty-five degrees, and they were clothed from base to summit—not a perceptible point escaping—in a drapery of the most gorgeous flower-blossoms; scarcely a green leaf being visible among the sea of odorous and fluctuating color. This basin was of great depth, but so transparent was the water that the bottom, which seemed to consist of a thick mass of small round alabaster pebbles, was distinctly visible by glimpses—that is to say, whenever the eye could permit itself *not* to see, far down in the inverted heaven, the duplicate blooming of the hills. (*CW* 3: 1279–80)[67]

The last sentence of this passage is especially telling when compared to the following passage from the alchemical text *Tractatus Aureus Hermetis Trismegisti* (1600):

> Circulation of spirits, or circular distillation, that is, the outside to the inside, the inside to the outside, likewise the lower to the upper; and when they meet together in one circle, you could no longer recognize what was outside or inside, or lower or upper; but all would be one thing in one circle or vessel. For this vessel is the true philosophical Pelican [alchemical vessel], and there is no other to be sought for in all the world.[68]

"Inside to the outside ... lower to the upper," Poe's "inverted heaven"—these phrases suggest the conjunction of heaven and earth, a reconciliation of opposites, and the synthesis of the material and the supernal.

As the narrator of the story transfers vessels, Poe's description recalls the alchemical imagery of the *albedo*:

> But here the voyager quits the vessel which has borne him so far, and descends into a light canoe of ivory, stained with arabesque

devices in vivid scarlet, both within and without. The poop and beak of this boat arise high above the water, with sharp points, so that the general form is that of an irregular crescent. It lies on the surface of the bay with the proud grace of a swan. On its ermined floor reposes a single feathery paddle of satin-wood; but no oarsman or attendant is to be seen. The guest is bidden to be of good cheer—that the fates will take care of him. (*CW* 3: 1280–81)

As David Fideler points out, the language of alchemy is hieroglyphic by nature,[69] and Poe appears to borrow heavily from alchemical hieroglyphs in this passage. The canoe of (white) ivory is in a crescent shape, evoking the alchemical image of the moon (Luna), and it floats with the grace of a (white) swan—an alchemical emblem of the *albedo*, illustrated in Andreas Libavius' *Commentariorum Alchymiae* (1606).[70] As Philalethes notes in *Ripley Reviv'd*, "When . . . the colour changeth to white, they [the alchemists] then call it their Swan."[71] Furthermore, the scarlet devices on the canoe announce the coming of the *rubedo*, the culmination of the opus. Thus, we are prepared for the crescent-shaped canoe to move—"slowly swing[ing] itself around until its prow points toward the sun" (*CW* 3: 1281)—and the alchemical conjunction of Sol and Luna begins.

There is but one alchemical stage left for Poe's narrator (and the reader) to experience—the red-gold of the *rubedo*. In alchemy the red of the *rubedo* represents the luminous redness of pure gold, and at this stage the *prima materia* reaches celestial, or spiritual, perfection. Symbolized by the philosophers' stone, the phoenix, or the creation of the homunculus (new man),[72] the final stage of the alchemical work represents the synthesis of earth and heaven, matter and spirit. As the narrator notes:

Floating gently onward, but with a velocity slightly augmented, the voyager, after many short turns, finds his progress apparently barred by a gigantic gate or rather door of burnished gold, elaborately carved and fretted, and reflecting the direct rays of the now fast-sinking sun with an effulgence that seems to wreath the whole surrounding forest in flames. This gate is inserted in the lofty wall; which here appears to cross the river at right angles. In a few moments, however, it is seen that the main body of the water still sweeps in a gentle and extensive curve to the left, the wall following it as before, while a stream of considerable volume, diverging from the principle one, makes its way, with a slight ripple, under the door, and is thus hidden from sight. The canoe falls into the lesser channel and approaches the gate. Its ponderous wings are slowly and musically expanded. The boat glides between them, and commences a rapid descent into a vast amphitheatre entirely begirt with purple mountains, whose bases are laved by a gleaming river throughout the full extent of their circuit. (*CW* 3: 1282–83)

In this passage, the red-gold of alchemy is clearly present in both the golden gate and the flame-like color of the setting sun. Here Poe's description of the amphitheatre recalls both the title of Khunrath's *Ampitheatrum sapientiae aeternae* (1602) and its illustrations of a boat winding along a river passage leading to what appears to be the palace of wisdom.[73] Finally, as the golden doors magically open for the narrator,

the whole Paradise of Arnheim bursts upon the view. There is a gush of entrancing melody; there is an oppressive sense of strange sweet odor;—there is a dream-like intermingling to the eye of tall slender Eastern trees—bosky shrubberies—flocks of golden and crimson birds—lily-fringed lakes—meadows of violets, tulips, poppies, hyacinths, and tuberoses—long intertangled lines of silver streamlets—and, upspringing confusedly from amid all, a mass of semi-Gothic, semi-Saracenic architecture sustaining itself as if by miracle in mid-air; glittering in the red sunlight with a hundred oriels, minarets, and pinnacles. (*CW* 3: 1283)

The image here evokes the full majesty of the alchemical garden: the medley of flowers recalls the colors of the *cauda pavonis* (peacock's tail); the flocks of "golden and crimson birds" evoke the *multiplicatio* of the alchemical phoenix;[74] and the architecture, suspended in mid-air, suggests the meeting-point (conjunction) of heaven and earth.

In "Arnheim" Poe conflates tropes from the philosophers' garden with an allegory for creative (artistic) imagination, and the result is indeed golden. The artist-alchemist Ellison becomes a mediator (reconciling matter with spirit) between earth and heaven, and his creation of Arnheim appears to the narrator to be "the phantom handiwork, conjointly, of the Sylphs, of the Fairies, of the Genii, and of the Gnomes" (*CW* 3: 1283)—Rosicrucian elemental beings.[75] These figures evoke the four elements (earth, fire, water, and air), the alchemical combination of which was often believed to form the philosophers' stone. As the philosophers' stone is the bridge between heaven and earth, so Arnheim represents an artistic bridge between the material and spiritual (supernal) realms. In "Arnheim," Poe suggests that this marriage or conjunction is possible through the artistic imagination, and Ellison not only succeeds in re-ordering nature (we might even say perfecting it), he brings the supernal and earth into a conjunction reflecting the alchemists' marriage of heaven and earth.

As we have observed with regard to "The Domain of Arnheim," Poe viewed the artist as a mediator—at once both the alchemist-operator *and* the mercurial spirit (*Spiritus Mercurius*, the guide)—between the reader (the microcosm of the material world) and the supernal (visionary) realm. While he drew on the tropes and metaphors of alchemy throughout his career, in "The Domain of Arnheim" Poe adapted alchemical philosophy into a symbolic paradigm for his vision of the creative imagination, and the hermetic garden became a signpost illuminating the way to the visionary experience of the supernal.

When Vachel Lindsay referred to Poe as the "wizard in the street,"[76] he was closer to the truth than he imagined. However, Poe's alchemy was certainly not for the masses, as he reminds us in "The Colloquy" and Arnheim"; it was for those individuals who had the vision to perceive the transmutative and regenerative power of imagination. Like his images of ships, castles, and gardens, the stories and poems themselves are intended to stimulate the reader's imagination through the experience(s) of extraordinary individuals. Indeed, such experiences are capable (if understood correctly) of transmuting the mundane perceptions of the material world to the visionary perceptions of the supernal realm—a figurative wedding of heaven and earth through "the power of words."

NOTES

1. See Burton R. Pollin, "Poe's 'Von Kempelen and His Discovery.' " Pollin's essay identifies the work of Sir Humphry Davy, Isaac Disraeli, and Edward Bulwer-Lytton as sources for Poe's literary hoax aimed at the California Gold Rush of the 1840s.

2. For further background on antimony, see Abraham, *Dictionary* (8); and Haeffner (46–47).

3. D. H. Lawrence, *Studies in Classic American Literature* (70).

4. Joscelyn Godwin, Introduction to *Atalanta Fugiens* (60). As the alchemical tract "The Glory of the World" suggests, in alchemy only separate things can unite (*HM* 1: 238). See also Abraham, "*Solve et Coagula*" (186–87), in *Dictionary*.

5. William Bloomfield, "Bloomfields Blossoms" (315).

6. Alchemy was only one of many esoteric philosophies from which Poe borrowed. Throughout Poe's work there are references to the Jewish Kabbalah, Gnosticism, and hermetic magic.

7. Ruland (182).

8. See Richard P. Benton, "Is Poe's 'The Assignation' a Hoax?"; and G. R. Thompson, "Poe's Flawed Gothic."

9. For more on the alchemical significance of Venus, see Abraham, *Dictionary* (208–9). Abraham notes that copper (Venus) is close to alchemical perfection.

10. Joscelyn Godwin, *Robert Fludd* (18). Most readers of Poe will recognize Fludd's name as one of the authors in Usher's library.

11. Peter J. Ammann, "The Musical Theory and Philosophy of Robert Fludd" (212). See also Debus, *The Chemical Philosophy* Vol. 1: (218, 231).

12. See De Rola, plate 5 (33), from Khunrath's *Amphitheatrum*.

13. For further commentary on Khunrath's engraving, see Nicholl (53). See Maier for further examples of the combination of alchemy and music.

14. Edward W. Pitcher, "Poe's 'The Assignation': A Reconsideration" (3).

15. David Ketterer, "The Sexual Abyss" (8).

16. See Fabricius (153). See also Abraham, "Chemical Wedding" (35–39), "King" (110–12), "Luna" (119–20), "Queen" (161–62), and "Sol" (185–86), in *Dictionary*.

17. As in "The Assignation," and to a lesser degree in "Ligeia," the colors crimson and gold are prominent in Poe's "Philosophy of Furniture" (1840; *CW* 2: 501–3). In this sketch we find Poe's description of the ideal room. On a couch in the center of the room is a sleeper (a dreamer), and of the room itself, Poe writes:

> [The window] panes are of a crimson-tinted glass, set in rose-wood framings. . . . Without the recess are curtains of an exceedingly rich crimson silk, fringed with a deep network of gold, and lined with the silver tissue. . . . The colors of the curtains and their fringe—the tints of crimson and gold—appear everywhere in profusion, and determine the *character* of the room. The carpet . . . is of the same crimson ground, relieved simply by the appearance of a gold cord. . . . Two large low sofas of rose-wood and crimson silk, gold-flowered, form the only seats. (*CW* 2: 501–2)

Poe's use of the colors crimson and gold suggest the attainment of the philosophers' stone in the form of the supernal dreamworld. And the room itself evokes the image of an alchemical container or vessel—the *vas hermeticum*. As Poe notes, the crimson lamp, suspended from a golden chain, "throws a tranquil but *magical radiance* over all" (*CW* 2: 503; emphasis mine).

18. For more on the alchemical abyss, see Abraham, *Dictionary* (2).

19. Jung, *Psychology and Alchemy* (294–95).

20. Claude Richard, in "Ou L'Indicibilité de Dieu, offers a reading of "Ligeia" exploring an alchemical sequence that moves the dark figure of Ligeia to the light (golden) figure of Rowena and then back to Ligeia as a version of the failed opus.

21. Alice Chandler, " 'The Visionary Race' " (76) and Daniel Hoffman, *Poe Poe Poe Poe Poe Poe Poe* (247, 249) view Ligeia as the personification of wisdom.

22. Poe may have seen Emblem 50 from Maier (205)—an illustration of Queen Luna lying in a grave with the alchemical serpent coiled around her. For commentary on Emblem 50, see De Jong (313).

23. Muriel West notes this in passing in "Poe's 'Ligeia' " (16) and "Poe's 'Ligeia' and Isaac D'Israeli" (25). Poe may have run across references to the red elixir (*elixir vitae*) in William Godwin's *Lives of the Necromancers* (18).

24. For a discussion on Poe's possible use of the raven and the *nigredo* in "The Raven," see St. Armand, "Poe's Emblematic Raven" (196–99).

25. In *Poe's Fiction*, G. R. Thompson suggests that Poe's letter to Cooke is indeed more hoaxing on Poe's part (77–80, especial 80). Thompson's observations in no way detract from my reading of "Ligeia."

80   The Marriage of Heaven and Earth

26. Barton Levi St. Armand, "Usher Unveiled" (5).
27. Philalethes, *Ripley Reviv'd* (116).
28. Ibid. (187).
29. The alchemical figure of the brother-sister conjunction may be found in almost every illustrated alchemical text. For example, see Maier, Emblem 4 (113), Emblem 25 (155), Emblem 30 (165), and Emblem 34 (173). See also Abraham, Alchemical "Incest" (106–7), in *Dictionary*; and De Jong (73–75).
30. See Haeffner, "Elements" (114–16).
31. Paracelsus, Vol. 2 (84).
32. See Darrel Abel, "A Key to the House of Usher" (48–50).
33. For an illustration of the alchemical hermaphrodite, see Maier, Emblem 33 (171); for commentary on Emblem 33, see De Jong (232–34). For more on the alchemical hermaphrodite, see Abraham, *Dictionary* (98–99); Fabricius (41, 50, 61, 66, 90–95, passim); and Haeffner (140–42).
34. Philalethes, *Secrets Reveal'd* (2). See De Rola, plate 84 (109), from Michael Maier's *Symbola aureae mensae* (1617); and plate 343 (179), from Johann Daniel Mylius' *Philosophia reformata* (1622).
35. For further background on the alchemical phoenix, see Abraham, *Dictionary* (152); De Jong (93); Fabricius (207, 209); and Haeffner (207–8).
36. Quoted in J. B. Craven, *Dr. Robert Fludd* (146).
37. For more on the alchemical prison (alembic) see Abraham, *Dictionary* (156–57). The alchemical prison may help to account for Poe's image of the dungeon in "The Pit and the Pendulum" (*CW* 2: 678–97) as well. Poe uses the images of the dungeon-as-vessel and the presiding alchemical figure of Saturn (alchemical lead or Time) (*CW* 2: 689) in "The Pit" to suggest the rebirth of the prisoner from the death that the Inquisition prepared for him. See Abraham, "Saturn" (178–79) *Dictionary*. The alchemical prison also suggests an interesting gloss to the first half of "The Assignation," which opens by "the old Republican prison."
38. Ruland (413).
39. See De Rola, plate 324 (174), from Daniel Mylius' *Philosophia reformata*.
40. Andrew Marvell, "To His Coy Mistress" (107, lines 31–32).
41. In Poe's aesthetic vision, articulated in "The Colloquy of Monos and Una," the alchemical *nigredo* (black-death) is reflected in the decline (and subsequent decay) of culture (*CW* 2: 609–11); art, however, becomes a means to redemption and regeneration for culture (*CW* 2 : 611–12).
42. Barton Levi St. Armand, "Poe's 'Sober Mystification' " (1).
43. St. Armand argues that Poe was intrigued with the liberation of spirit from matter ("Usher Unveiled," 7).
44. See Haeffner, "Spirit" (232–35).
45. See Haeffner, "Gnosticism" (127–28); and "Redemption " (217–18).
46. Quoted in Jung, *Psychology and Alchemy* (381).
47. According to Section 8 of the *Emerald Tablet*: "It [the philosophers' stone] ascends from the earth to heaven, and descends again to the earth, and receives the power of the higher and lower things. So shall you have the glory of the world" (quoted in Fabricius, 214).
48. See Fabricius, plate 237 (128), from Maier's *Symbola aureae mensae* (1617).

49. See David Fideler, "The Rose Garden of the Philosophers" (41); also see Abraham. "Garden" (83–84) and "Philosopher's Tree" (150–51), in *Dictionary*. The frontispiece to "The Glory of the World" (*HM* 1: 166) offers a fine illustration of the philosophers' tree. This figure also appears in Mylius' *Philosophia reformata*, reprinted in De Rola, plate 339 (177). For further illustrations of the philosophers' tree, see De Rola, plate 378 (206), from Mylius' *Anatomia auri* (1628); plate 18 (50), from Andreas Libavius' *Alchemia* (1606); and plate 85 (110), from Maier's *Symbola aureae mensae*.

50. Compare this stanza to Poe's "Eldorado" (1849, *CW* 1: 463).

51. Robert Jacobs, *Poe* (405). See "Poe's Earthly Paradise" (413).

52. Chandler (80).

53. St. Armand suggests that the name Legrand in "The Gold Bug" is a reference to the "Great Work," the magnum opus of the alchemists ("Poe's 'Sober Mystification,' " 3).

54. Poe's use of Lull's name is especially curious in light of a spurious alchemical tract attributed to Lull—"Liber ad Reginam Eleanoram" (1355); see Arthur Edward Waite, *Raymond Lully* (53). Poe's epigraph reads: "*Sub conservatione formae specificae salva anima*—Raymond Lully" (*CW* 2: 638). Thomas Ollive Mabbott translates the motto thus: "Under the protection of a specific form, the soul is safe" (*CW* 2: 645). Although both Pollin (*Discoveries in Poe*, 38–53) and Mabbott (*CW* 2: 645) conclude that Poe's source for his epigraph was Victor Hugo's *Notre-Dame*, it seems a very odd coincidence that Poe's title choice echoes that of Lull's book of Queen Eleanora. Poe also makes reference to Lull in "Fifty Suggestions" (1849; *ER* 1297). For more on Lull, see Haeffner (160–62); and Waite, *Raymund Lully*.

55. For a superlative example of the alchemical tree with star-shaped flowers, see De Rola, plate 376 (204), from Mylius' *Anatomia auri sive tvrocinium medico-chymicum*.

56. With regard to Sol and Luna, see Haeffner (230–31). Emblem 30 from Maier (165) offers a fine illustration of the alchemical marriage of Sol (Sun/gold/male) and Luna (Moon/silver/female).

57. Poe may have been influenced by the stories of Nathaniel Hawthorne; see Randall A. Clack, "The Alchemy of Love." The plot of "Eleanora" may also have been inspired by John Donne's "Love's Alchemy." Thus, Poe may have included the reference to Lull to emphasize the mystical (alchemical) "undercurrent" in the first part of the tale. In the second part of the story, Eleanora may represent the mercurial spirit (of love) that leads the narrator to a final conjunction with Ermagarde. For a fine illustration of the Spiritus Mercury as the quintessence of love, see De Rola, plate 307 (171), from Mylius' *Philosophia reformata*.

58. St. Armand, "Poe's 'Sober Mystification' " (3–6).

59. According to St. Armand, Poe's apparent misspelling of *Liriodendron Tulipifera*—"*Liriodendron Tulipiferum*" (*CW* 3: 818)—was "for the sake of a pun on *ferrum*, which denotes the metal iron, a sword, or any iron implement" ("Poe's 'Sober Mystification,' " 2).

60. St. Armand, "Poe's 'Sober Mystification' " (2).

61. *Theatrum Chemicum* (1: 513; quoted in Fabricius, 87). Also see John Read, *The Alchemist in Life, Literature, and Art* (59).

62. St. Armand, "Poe's 'Sober Mystification,' " (4).

63. As St. Armand notes, the lead shot is metaphorically transmuted into the gold bug ("Poe's 'Sober Mystification,' " 4, 5). For further discussion on alchemical multiplication and projection, see Abraham, "Multiplication" (132) and "Projection" (157–58) in *Dictionary*; Fabricius (174–87, 190–95, 209, passim); and Haeffner (185–86). Poe's image of multiplication also evokes the rebirth of the alchemical phoenix—one of the many symbols for the philosophers' stone, related to the metaphor of the sun and the mystery of death and resurrection; it is the symbol of augmentation and multiplication of alchemical gold by the agency of the philosophers' stone.

64. Jacobs, "Poe's Earthly Paradise" (404, 407–409); and Jeffrey A. Hess, "Sources and Aesthetics of Poe's Landscape Fiction." In addition to Jacobs and Hess, John Robert Moore, in "Poe's Reading of *Anne of Geierstein*" (496), suggests that Poe's primary source for "Arnheim" was Walter Scott's *Anne of Geierstein*.

65. In "Eleanora" the Valley of the Many-Colored Grass is cut off from the outside world; in "The Gold-Bug" Sullivan's Island is isolated from the mainland; and in "Arnheim" the visitor is navigated through many twists and turns along a flowing river. To this list we might also include Usher's mansion, the abbey in "Ligeia," and the protagonist's apartment in "The Assignation."

66. See also "The Poetic Principle" (*ER* 77).

67. The image of twin alembics (alchemical vessels) also appears in "Von Kempelen and His Discovery" (*CW* 3: 1362).

68. *Tractus Aureus* (262; quoted in Nicholl, 148).

69. Fideler (41).

70. For illustrations of the alchemical swan, see De Rola, plate 15 (47) and plate 17 (49), from Libavius' *Alchymia*. For further information on the alchemical swan, see Adam McLean, *The Alchemical Mandala* (66, 69); Abraham, *Dictionary* (196–97); Fabricius (136–37, 146, 209, passim).

71. Philalethes, *Ripley Reviv'd* (178).

72. For more on the homunculus, see Abraham, *Dictionary* (102–3).

73. See De Rola, plate 6 (34) and plate 8 (36), from Khrunrath's *Ampitheatrum*.

74. For illustrations of the marriage of Sol and Luna and the *multiplicatio* of the alchemical phoenix, see De Rola, plate 15 (47) and plate 17 (49), from Libavius' *Alchymia*.

75. Poe's possible sources for these Rosicrucian elementals include W. Godwin (22–24) and Alexander Pope's "The Rape of the Lock" (1712/1714).

76. Vachel Lindsay, "The Wizard in the Street (Concerning Edgar Allan Poe)" (101).

Chapter 5

Hawthorne's Alchemy of Love

The wealth of twentieth-century critical responses to Nathaniel Hawthorne includes no fewer than seventeen essays concerned with the use of alchemical metaphors and tropes in his tales and romances.[1] These explorations of the alchemical themes found in such works as "The Birth-mark," "The Great Carbuncle," *The Scarlet Letter*, and the "Septimius" stories generally corroborate the judgment of Raymona E. Hull: "By the time Hawthorne reached the climax of his writing career . . . he had made use of several phases of alchemy—the alchemist and his experiments, the various magic effects of elixirs, the idea of renewed youth, and the search for the unattainable. In almost every work the alchemist, whether approached humorously or seriously, is treated unfavorably."[2]

Hawthorne's first mention of the alchemist occurs in "Sir William Pepperell" (1833):

> Another pale and emaciated person, in neglected and scarcely decent attire, and distinguished by the abstract fervor of his manner, presses through the crowd and attempts to lay hold of Pepperell's skirt. He has spent years in wild and shadowy studies, and has searched the crucible of the alchemist for gold, and wasted the life allotted him in a weary effort to render it immortal; the din of warlike preparation has broken in upon his solitude, and he comes forth with a fancy of his half maddened brain, the model of a flying bridge, by which the army is to be transported into the heart of the hostile fortress with the celerity of magic. (*CE* 23: 87–88)

Hawthorne's description of this figure recalls the entry in Stiles' *Diary* that "there were several [alchemists] at Philad[elphia] ... who were loosing [sic] their Time in chemical Experiments to no Effect." Indeed, the alchemist in "Pepperell" is little more than a hopeless dreamer who has devoted his life to the search of chimeras.[3]

As a student of Puritan and colonial history, Hawthorne was undoubtedly familiar with some of the stories surrounding the seventeenth- and eighteenth-century New England alchemists. In a journal entry of 1838, he notes that the Boston-Salem area had its own hermetic tradition:

> The house on the eastern corner of North and Essex Streets, supposed to have been built about 1640, had, say, sixty years later, a brick turret erected, wherein one of the ancestors of the present occupants used to practice alchemy. He was the operative of a scientific person in Boston, the director. There have been other alchemists of old in this town,—one who kept his fire burning seven weeks, and then lost the elixir by letting it go out. (*CE* 8: 181)[4]

In "The Great Carbuncle" Hawthorne introduces the figure of Doctor Cacaphodel, "who had wilted and dried himself into a mummy, by continually stooping over charcoal furnaces, and inhaling unwholesome fumes, during his researches in chemistry and alchymy" (*CE* 9: 151). One of Hawthorne's most famous scientists, Aylmer in "The Birthmark," is studied in the philosophy of the medieval alchemists, "who spent so many ages in quest of the universal solvent, by which the Golden Principle might be elicited from all things vile and base" (*CE* 10: 46). In *The Scarlet Letter*, Hawthorne informs his readers that Roger Chillingworth has "sought gold in alchemy" (*CE* 1: 75) and studied the chemical work of both Paracelsus and Kenelm Digby (*CE* 1: 72 and 121). Finally, in the "Septimius" stories and *The Dolliver Romance*, Septimius Felton, Septimius Norton, and Dr. Dolliver, like the old alchemist in "Pepperell," are obsessed with discovering the *elixir vitae*. The one trait that all of these characters have in common is that they are failures. Not one of Hawthorne's alchemists succeeds in attaining either the philosophers' stone or the *elixir vitae*.[5]

HAWTHORNE'S HERMETIC MYTHOLOGY

While Hawthorne may have culled limited background information on alchemy from reference books, he also was aware of the metaphorical connection between Greek and Roman mythology and alchemy. As Septimius Norton notes of the *elixir vitae*:

> Who could tell what far antiquity it came down from? With some changes, losing ingredients of power by the way, here might be the spell, the concoction of natural drugs, which Medea brewed into her cauldron, and so renewed her from age to rosy youth. Myths have their truth, and why not this, since the heart of man (ever dying just as he begins to live) so imperatively demands that it should be true, reaching old age and decrepitude with the burning spark of youth torturing him still, when it can no longer vivify him. (*CE* 13: 408–9)[6]

The possible connection between myth and the alchemical elixir of life seems to have been on Hawthorne's mind in the years between 1862 and 1864, yet what of the years preceding the "Septimius" manuscripts?

Hawthorne first juxtaposed the images of myth and alchemy—both products of fantasy, or the imagination—in "A Virtuoso's Collection" (1842). According to Hawthorne's narrator, in one particular alcove of the exhibition hall

> we saw the golden thigh of Pythagoras, which had so divine a meaning.... Here was a remnant of the Golden Fleece; and a sprig of yellow leaves that resembled the foliage of a frost-bitten elm, but was duly authenticated as a portion of the golden branch by which Æneas gained admittance to the realm of Pluto. Atalanta's golden apple, and one of the apples of discord, were wrapt in the napkin of gold which Rampsinitus brought from Hades; and the whole were deposited in the golden vase of Bias, with its inscription: "To The Wisest." (*CE* 10: 484–85)

Later in the sketch Hawthorne's narrator notes the following:

> The Virtuoso pointed out to me a crystalline stone, which hung by a gold chain against the wall.
> "That is the Philosopher's Stone," he said.
> "And have you the Elixir Vitae, which generally accompanies it?" inquired I.
> "Even so,—this urn is filled with it," he replied. "A draught would refresh you. Here is Hebe's cup,—will you quaff a health from it?" (*CE* 10: 489)

In these passages Hawthorne underscores the idea that both myth and alchemy are products of the imagination. Curiously enough, Ben Jonson noted the connection between some of these same mythic elements and alchemy in *The Alchemist* (1610), where the greedy and deluded Mammon tells Surly the following:

> I have a piece of Jason's fleece, too,
> Which was no other than a book of alchemy,
> Writ in large sheepskin, a good fat ram-vellum.
> Such was Pythagoras' thigh, Pandora's tub,
> And, all that fable of Medea's charms,
> The manner of our work [alchemy]; the bulls, our furnace,
> Still breathing fire; our argent-vive, the dragon:
> The dragon's teeth, mercury sublimate,
> That keeps the whiteness, hardness, and the biting;
> And they are gathered into Jason's helmet,
> The alembic, and then sowed in Mars his field,
> And thence sublimed so often, till they're fixed.
> Both this, the Hesperian garden, Cadmus' story,
> Jove's shower, the boon of Midas, Argus' eyes,
> Boccace his Demogorgon, thousands more,
> All abstract riddles of our [philosophers'] stone.[7]

Although Hawthorne noted in a journal entry of 1855 that Jonson's *Alchemist* "is certainly a great play" (*CE* 22 pt. 1: 275), Hawthorne's own juxtaposition of Pythagoras' golden thigh and Jason's Golden Fleece with the alchemical images of the philosophers' stone and the *elixir vitae* in "A Virtuoso's Collection" suggests his reading of Jonson's *Alchemist* before 1842. In fact, Jonson's alchemical explication of Jason's quest for the golden fleece and the "boon of Midas" as alchemical riddles, or hieroglyphs, suggests a source of inspiration for Hawthorne's own stories of "The Golden Touch," in *The Wonder Book* (1851) and "The Golden Fleece," in *Tanglewood Tales* (1853).

By the time Jonson wrote *The Alchemist*, alchemical allegories based on myth had been a popular technique among hermetic writers. The connection of the seven alchemical metals and their corresponding planets to the Greek and Roman gods illustrates this point, for alchemical transmutation moved the *prima materia* through seven noble phases with seven planetary correspondences.

Among the many chroniclers of myth and alchemy, the Rosicrucian alchemist Michael Maier suggests in *Arcana arcanissima* (1614) that Egyptian and classical mythology could be interpreted as an allegorical expression of the alchemical process. Among the six areas of myth identified by Maier as allegories of alchemy are Grecian myths, the Golden Fleece and Jason, the Apples of the Hesperides, which all have reference to the Golden Medicine, and the Labors of Hercules and their meanings. Maier claimed that the quests of Jason and Hercules, like the alchemical opus itself, were spiritual quests that were rewarded with the attainment of the golden object(s).[8] Maier further developed this theme in *Atalanta Fugiens*, where the image of three golden apples of the Hesperides also plays a significant role in the alchemical quest for enlightenment. As Joscelyn Godwin notes, "The Golden Apple, as a symbol of the immortal power of love, is the one that succeeds in bringing about a balance of powers; it stands by the alchemist who helps to complete the work through his love of wisdom and through his sheer effort to fathom the great mysteries of God, the cosmos and the human spirit, and to work towards their unification."[9]

While Hawthorne may have drawn his inspiration from Jonson or Maier, he may also have found other sources that led him to explore the expression of alchemical allegories in classical mythology.[10] Even so slight a reference as Hawthorne's renaming Mercury-Hermes "Quicksilver"—a chemical term for the element mercury—suggests that Hawthorne, like the alchemists, knew that philosophic (alchemical) Mercury had, as Quicksilver himself tells Perseus in "The Gorgon's Head," "more names than one; but the name of Quicksilver suits me as well as any other" (*CE* 7: 15).[11]

In addition to Hawthorne's reference to alchemical Mercury in "The Gorgon's Head," Hawthorne takes particular liberty in describing the gorgons of his story:

> They were three sisters, and seem to have borne some distant resemblance to women, but were really a very frightful and mischievous species of dragon. It is indeed difficult to imagine what hideous beings these three sisters were. Why, instead of locks of hair, if you can believe me, they had each of them a hundred enormous snakes growing on their heads, all alive, twisting, wriggling, curling, and thrusting out their venomous tongues, with forked stings at the end! (*CE* 7: 12–13)

In Ovid's *Metamorphosis*, only Medusa has snake hair, and none of the gorgons are equated with dragons. Yet these are not the only liberties Hawthorne takes, as seen in his embellished description of the gorgons:

> The teeth of the Gorgons were terribly long tusks; their hands were made of brass, and their bodies were all over scales, which, if not iron, were something as hard and impenetrable. They had wings, too, and exceedingly splendid ones, I can assure you; for every feather in them was pure, bright, glittering, burnished gold, and they looked very dazzlingly, no doubt, when the Gorgons were flying about in the sunshine.
>
> But when people happened to catch a glimpse of their glittering brightness, aloft in the air, they seldom stopt to gaze, but ran and hid themselves as speedily as they could. . . . For the worst thing about these abominable Gorgons was, that, if once a poor mortal

fixed his eyes full upon one of their faces, he was certain, that very instant, to be changed from warm flesh and blood into cold and lifeless stone! (*CE* 7: 13)

The conjunction of brass, iron, and gold in this description illustrates how Hawthorne plays with the theme of metal and stone in connection with the gorgons. As a "species of dragon," the gorgon reflects the alchemical dragon that Perseus slays with the help of Quicksilver. The gaze of the gorgon also provokes comparison with the philosophers' stone, for as an agent of transmutation, it can change the physical nature of human beings. Thus the gorgon's head suggests a symbol for alchemical victory, for once Perseus obtains the (stone) head of Medusa, he becomes a(n) (alchemist) king, as Maier noted in his own explication of the myth.[12]

In this same light, the dragons found in Hawthorne's stories of Hercules ("The Golden Apple") and Jason ("The Golden Fleece") recall the mercurial dragon of alchemy. To slay or subdue the mercurial dragon and to obtain the golden object of the quest in these stories of Jason and Hercules may have suggested for Hawthorne, as it did for Maier, an allegorical retelling of the *opus magnum*.

THE HEART OF THE STONE

Although Hawthorne does suggest in *The Marble Faun* that the goal of the medieval alchemists, the literal transmutation of lead into gold, was a "glorified dream" (*CE* 4: 266), in a more favorable light he artistically adapts the philosophy of alchemy into an allegory of human nature where the human heart corresponds to the *prima materia* (base matter, or the philosophers' stone *in potentia*) that can be transmuted through the alchemy of love. For Hawthorne, love, like the philosophers' stone, can bring heaven and earth into conjunction, transmuting our mundane existence and allowing us to live "once for all in Eternity, to find the perfect Future in the present," as he observes at the end of "The Birth-mark" (*CE* 10: 56). In the following pages, we will examine the uses to which Hawthorne applies the metaphors and tropes of alchemy in his investigations of human love. Whereas such tales as "The Man of Adamant," "Ethan Brand," "The Birth-mark," and "Rappaccini's Daughter" demonstrate the consequences of rejecting the transmutative qualities of love, "The May-Pole of Merry Mount," "The Great Carbuncle," "Peter Goldthwaite's Treasure," "Egotism; or, The Bosom-Serpent," "The Artist of the Beautiful," and "The Golden Touch" illustrate the marvelous effects of love's alchemy. Finally, *The Scarlet Letter* and *The House of the Seven Gables*, which we will consider briefly, reveal that Hawthorne's interest in the hermetic allegory of the heart extends to his romances.

Curiously enough, at the end of Hawthorne's career, as he struggled to shape his theme of the elixir of life in the unfinished romances "Septimius Felton," "Septimius Norton," and "The Dolliver Romance" (The Elixir of Life Manuscripts), his reputation inspired a visit from the American hermeticist General Ethan Allen Hitchcock to "The Tower" at the Wayside.[13] Hitchcock sought out Hawthorne in 1862, five years after publishing his magnum opus, *Remarks on Alchemy and the Alchemists*, and though no record exists of their conversations, it seems likely that he recognized a kindred spirit in the author.[14] Prefiguring the work of C. G. Jung, Hitchcock's twofold thesis proposes that the hermetic science is concerned with the inner (or psychic) transformation of the alchemist and that love, at once physical and spiritual, is the true philosophers' stone. According to Hitchcock:

> *Man* was the *subject* of Alchemy and . . . the *object* of the Art was the perfection, or at least the improvement, of Man.
>   The salvation of man—his transformation from evil to good, or his passage from a state of nature to a state of grace—was symbolized under the figure of the transmutation of metals.
>
> The [philosophers'] Stone is Man, of one nature,—of body, soul, and spirit.
>
> Philosophical [alchemical] Gold, which is sometimes called Venus . . . is Love.[15]

Anticipating Hitchcock's observations, Hawthorne notes in "Earth's Holocaust" (1844) that the heart, like alchemical lead, is corrupt, base matter, but it also carries the potential for transmutation:

> [U]nless they hit upon some method of purifying that foul cavern [the human heart], forth from it will re-issue all the shapes of wrong and misery—the same old shapes, or worse ones—which they have taken such a vast deal of trouble to consume to ashes. I have stood by, this live-long night, and laughed in my sleeve at the whole business. . . .
>   How sad a truth—if true it were—that Man's age-long endeavor for perfection had served only to render him the mockery of the Evil Principle, from the fatal circumstance of an error at the very root of the matter! The Heart—the Heart—there was the little, yet boundless sphere, wherein existed the original wrong, of which

the crime and misery of this outward world were merely types. Purify that inner sphere; and the many shapes of evil that haunt the outward, and which now seem almost our only realities will turn to shadowy phantoms, and vanish of their own accord. (*CE* 10: 403–4)

If the inner world (the microcosm of the heart) could be purified or transmuted, Hawthorne here contends, the outer world (the macrocosm) would also be redeemed. In the alchemical allegory he elaborates in a number of tales and romances, Hawthorne proposes that the human heart might indeed be transmuted from its base nature to reflect a golden ideal through the agency of "love or sympathy" (*CE* 9: 48).[16]

But Hawthorne's vision of the alchemy of love was not limited to his literary life, as his love letters to Sophia demonstrate. In 1841 he wrote to her, "Thou art my reality; and nothing else is real for me, unless thou give it that golden quality by thy touch."[17] And writing from Brook Farm on 18 October 1841, he cautioned his fiancée to avoid the practitioners of the occultlike science of magnetism or mesmerism and then proclaimed, "Love is the true magnetism" (*CE* 15: 589–90). The conclusion that I suggest we draw here echoes a passage from Hitchcock: "Love is of a transmuting and transforming nature. The great effect of Love is to turn all things into its own nature, which is all goodness, sweetness, and perfection. . . . [Love is the] Divine Elixir, whose transforming power and efficacy nothing can withstand."[18] Both Hitchcock and Hawthorne affirm that love, like the philosophers' stone, can transmute our base existence into a golden conjunction of male and female reflecting the alchemical marriage of the sun and moon.

Hawthorne's first treatment of the alchemy of love is found in "The May-Pole of Merry Mount" (1836).[19] While the images of the central scene of "The May-Pole" may have been borrowed from Milton's *Comus*, as Hawthorne alludes (*CE* 9: 56), a close examination of this scene reveals Hawthorne's use of alchemical tropes to suggest a type of hermetic garden:

> But what was the wild throng that stood hand in hand about the May-Pole? It could not be, that the Fauns and Nymphs, when driven from their classic groves and homes of ancient fable, had sought refuge, as all persecuted did, in the fresh woods of the West. These were Gothic monsters, though perhaps of Grecian ancestry. On the shoulders of a comely youth, uprose the head and antlers of a stag . . .
>
> Within the ring of monsters, appeared the two airiest forms, that had ever trodden on any more solid footing than a purple and golden cloud. One was a youth, in glistening apparel, with a scarf

of the rainbow pattern crosswise on his breast. His right hand held a gilded staff, the ensign of high dignity among the revellers, and his left grasped the slender fingers of a fair maiden, not less gaily decorated than himself. Bright roses glowed in contrast with the dark and glossy curls of each, and were scattered round their feet, or had sprung up spontaneously there. Behind this lightsome couple, so close to the May-Pole that its boughs shaded his jovial face, stood the figure of an English priest, canonically dressed, yet decked with flowers. (*CE* 9: 55–57)[20]

In this passage Hawthorne evokes conjunction of Sol and Luna—Edgar (the youth) and Edith (the fair maiden)—in the alchemist's (priest's) chemical marriage. Furthermore, the May-Pole recalls the image of the *arbor philosophica* (the philosophers' tree) symbolically uniting heaven and earth:

Down nearly to the ground, the pole was dressed with birchen boughs, and others of the liveliest green, and some with silvery leaves, fastened by ribbons that fluttered in fantastic knots of twenty different colors, but no sad ones. Garden flowers, and blossoms of the wilderness, laughed gladly forth amid the verdure, so fresh and dewy, that they must have grown by magic on that happy pine tree. Where this green and flowery splendor terminated, the shaft of the May-Pole was stained with the seven brilliant hues of the banner at its top. On the lowest green bough hung an abundant wreath of roses, some that had been gathered in the sunniest spots of the forest, and others, of still richer blush, which the colonists had reared from English seed. (*CE* 9: 55)

Hawthorne intimates that the settlers of Merry Mount will initiate a symbolic marriage of the old and new worlds (symbolized by the roses from both England and America). The "seven brilliant hues" of the May-Pole's streamers suggest the seven metals (and the corresponding colors) of alchemy and recall the colors of the *cauda pavonis*, or peacock's tail (the alchemical stage said to announce the creation of the philosophers' stone in the alchemist's alembic). To further emphasize this alchemical allusion, Edgar tells his betrothed that "this is our golden time!" (*CE* 9: 58). In this context the May-Pole scene recalls the reconciliation of opposites that the alchemists believed would generate a new earth.

Hawthorne, ever true to the historical plot, brings forth Puritans led by John Endicott to shatter the golden age of Merry Mount. Hawthorne emphasizes the iron—base, yet strong and tempered—resolve of the Puritans, and despite their "moral gloom" (*CE* 9: 66), Endicott and company appear to possess the metal to tame the new world.[21] After the Puritans end the revelers' celebration, Endicott

> lifted the wreath of roses from the ruin of the May-Pole, and threw it, with his own gauntleted hand, over the heads of the Lord and Lady of the May. It was a deed of prophecy. As the moral gloom of the world overpowers all systematic gaiety, even so was their home of wild mirth made desolate amid the sad forest. They returned to it no more. But, as their flowery garland was wreathed of the brightest roses that had grown there, so, in the tie that united them, were intertwined all the purest and best of their early joys. They went heavenward, supporting each other along the difficult path which it was their lot to tread, and never wasted one regretful thought on the vanities of Merry Mount. (*CE* 9: 66–67)

Here the roses ironically recall the union of Edgar and Edith begun earlier in the story. Although this couple abandons the golden dream of Merry Mount, Hawthorne intimates the golden spirit of their love will rise above the base constitutions (the "moral gloom") of Endicott and the Puritans.

While "The May-Pole of Merry Mount" illustrates Hawthorne's first use of alchemical tropes to illustrate an allegory of the heart, Hawthorne would later turn his attention to the heart itself. The idea of the heart as both *prima materia* and philosophers' stone at once calls to mind Hawthorne's "Man of Adamant" (1837) and "Ethan Brand" (1850).[22] Since these stories were written thirteen years apart, the characters of Digby (in "Adamant") and Brand reflect Hawthorne's ongoing interest in the heart of stone. In "Adamant" we learn not only of Digby's separatist religious convictions but also of his heart:

> Richard Digby, before he withdrew himself from the world, was supposed by skillful physicians to have contracted a disease, for which no remedy was written in the medical books. It was a deposition of calculous particles within his heart, caused by an obstructed circulation of the blood, and unless a miracle should be wrought for him, there was danger that the malady might act on the entire substance of the organ, and change his fleshly heart to stone. (*CE* 11: 163–64)

Although Digby cuts himself off from humanity, he is offered redemption from his isolated life through the love and fellowship of Mary Goffe. Hawthorne's story evokes the alchemical theme of *solve et coagula* (dissolve and make whole), for Mary's love has the potential to dissolve the cold hardness of Digby's heart. Although Mary is first rejected by Digby, she later brings him a cup of water with which her tears have mingled:

> "Richard," she said, with passionate fervor, yet a gentleness in all her passion, "I pray thee, by thy hope of Heaven, and as thou wouldst not dwell in this tomb forever, drink of this hallowed water, be it but a single drop! Then, make room for me by thy side, and let us read together one page of that blessed volume—and, lastly, kneel down with me and pray! Do this; and thy stony heart shall become softer than a babe's, and all be well." (*CE* 11: 167)

The healing draft that Mary offers recalls the universal solvent of alchemy; able to break down and purify the elements in their corrupt state (what the alchemists refer to as the *massa confusa*), the universal solvent is said to transform "corruption" into a refined form of the *prima materia*, as it was in the beginning (in Hawthorne's allegory, the heart of a baby).[23]

Digby, however, again refuses Mary, his only link with humanity and chance for salvation:

> "Tempt me no more, accursed woman," exclaimed he, still with his marble frown, "least I smite thee down also! What hast thou to do with my Bible?—what with my prayers?—what with my Heaven?"
>
> No sooner had he spoken these dreadful words, than Richard's [*sic*] Digby's heart ceased to beat. (*CE* 11: 167)

Digby's final denial of Mary suggests a repudiation of both love and humanity, yet his story also functions as an alchemical allegory. As potential object of transmutation, Digby is afforded a chance for redemption from pride and isolation; when he rejects this opportunity, his heart, instead of being renewed and transmuted, hardens further and becomes like the stone of death—a dark counterpoint to the philosophers' stone.

Hawthorne presents a similar image of the stone heart in "Ethan Brand." Mark Hennelly asserts that the unpardonable sin for which Brand searches is "a symbolic Philosopher's Stone" and that he finds it within his own heart;[24] Klaus Stich also suggests that Brand can be viewed as an alchemist, but an abortive one.[25] Yet perhaps we should not view Brand as an alchemist at all, for Hawthorne intimates that Brand himself is the object of transmutation, at the center of another alchemical allegory of the heart. Like Digby, Brand denies the connection between himself and humanity, rejecting any bond of fellowship offered to him. Once his flesh has been purged away in the limeburner's kiln (a symbolic athanor, or alchemical furnace), his heart turns to stone. Although Hennelly suggests that Brand's heart has been transmuted by the refining fire, the transformation is superficial.[26] While the physical organ has indeed changed composition, the soul has not been purified: Brand, like Digby, rejects the true values of the heart. Once again Hawthorne's stone heart leaves a wake of death and destruction.

In "The Great Carbuncle" (1837), Hawthorne's allegory takes on the mythic dimensions of the alchemical opus as eight individuals attempt to attain possession of the mythic gem that gives forth "a gleam of red splendor" (*CE* 9: 157).[27] The color of the stone is an important signal that Hawthorne intends to conflate the legend of the Great Carbuncle of the Crystal Hills with the philosophers' stone, for the gem's red gleam reflects the alchemical *rubedo*, the red-gold color that often heralds the creation of the philosophers' stone in the alchemist's alembic.

It is fitting that the newlyweds, Matthew and Hannah, first recognize the carbuncle, for their union exemplifies true love; thus they are the rightful heirs to Hawthorne's stone of transmutation. In the context of Hawthorne's allegory, however, Matthew and Hannah have already experienced love's transmutation in their own hearts and have no need for the physical stone. Instead of the "ruddy blaze of the Great Carbuncle" illuminating their home, Matthew avers, "[t]he blessed sunshine, and the quiet moonlight, shall come through [their] window." They will "kindle the cheerful glow of [the] hearth, at eventide, and be happy in its light" (*CE* 9: 163). As Stich observes, Matthew's words picture a conjunction of Sol (Sun and gold) with Luna (Moon and silver) that will light their home (a symbolic athanor).[28] Hawthorne also emphasizes the newlyweds' connection with the rest of humanity when Matthew vows, "[N]ever again will we desire more light than all the world may share with us" (*CE* 9: 163). Although the Cynic, the only other seeker to reach the carbuncle and live, fails to recognize the stone when he sees it, the love radiated by the union of Matthew and Hannah momentarily clears his vision.

Hawthorne further strengthens the connection between alchemy and the values of the heart in "Peter Goldthwaite's Treasure" (1838).[29] In this story, Goldthwaite believes an alchemist's treasure is hidden in his ancestral home: "Reports were various, as to the nature of [Goldthwaite's] fortunate speculation; one intimating, that the ancient Peter had made gold by alchemy. . . . Peter himself chose to consider the legend as an indisputable truth, and, amid his many troubles, had this one consolation, that, should all other resources fail, he might build up his fortunes by tearing his house down" (*CE* 9: 388). To "tear down the house" is an alchemical metaphor for the creation of the philosophers' stone,[30] represented in the story by the treasure Goldthwaite hopes to find. In Goldthwaite's dreams his house resembles an alembic, the vessel in which the alchemist's treasure is concocted:

> Anon, he had returned to the old house, as poor as ever, and was received at the door, by the gaunt and grizzled figure of a man, whom he might have mistaken for himself, only that his garments were of a much older fashion. But the house, without losing its former aspect, had been changed into a palace of the precious metals. The floors, walls, and ceilings, were of burnished silver; the doors, the window frames, the cornices, the balustrades, and the steps of the staircase, of pure gold; and silver, with gold bottoms, were the chairs, and gold, standing on silver legs, the highest chests of drawers, and silver the bedsteads, with blankets of woven gold, and sheets of silver tissue. The house had evidently been transmuted by a single touch. . . . A happy man would have been Peter Goldthwaite, except for a certain ocular deception, which, whenever he glanced backward, caused the house to darken from its glittering magnificence into the sordid gloom of yesterday. (*CE* 9: 390)

Although Hawthorne draws heavily upon the alchemical conjunction of gold and silver in this passage, he later undercuts this symbolism by emphasizing that it is part of Goldthwaite's fantasy, his "golden dream" (*CE* 9: 402).

When the deluded Goldthwaite discovers an old parchment with figures "denoting the amount of the treasure" and a lamp, he offers an interpretation that is reminiscent of an alchemist deciphering an alchemical hieroglyph: "A lamp! . . . That indicates light on my researches" (*CE* 9: 397). Later, on the verge of finding his ancient relative's gold, Goldthwaite prepares to drink from a bottle of wine he has discovered while searching; as Goldthwaite and his maid Tabitha drink from teacups, Hawthorne notes, "So clear and brilliant was this aged wine, that it shone within the cups, and rendered the sprig of scarlet flowers, at the bottom of each, more distinctly visible, than when there had been no wine there" (*CE* 9: 403). Although the scarlet flowers suggest the alchemical *rubedo* that signals the coming of the philosophers' stone, it is not Goldthwaite who discovers the alchemical treasure.[31]

Hawthorne's philosophers' stone, the transmuted heart, is concocted in the character of Goldthwaite's former business partner, John Brown. As Goldthwaite and Tabitha finish the bottle of wine, the thoughts of the absent Brown are dwelling on Goldthwaite:

It so chanced, that, on this stormy night, Mr. John Brown found himself ill at ease, in his wire-cushioned arm-chair, by the glowing grate of anthracite, which heated his handsome parlour. He was naturally a good sort of man, and kind and pitiful, whenever the misfortunes of others happened to reach his heart through the padded vest of his own prosperity. This evening, he had thought much about his old partner, Peter Goldthwaite, his strange vagaries, and continual ill luck, the poverty of his dwelling, at Mr. Brown's last visit, and Peter's crazed and haggard aspect, when he had talked with him at the window.

"Poor fellow!" thought Mr. John Brown. "Poor, crack-brained Peter Goldthwaite! For old acquaintance' sake, I ought to have taken care that he was comfortable, this rough winter."

These feelings grew so powerful, that, in spite of the inclement weather, he resolved to visit Peter Goldthwaite immediately. The strength of the impulse was really singular. (*CE* 9: 403–4)

Brown braves a late-winter snowstorm (the color of the *albedo*, the white-silver phase of the opus that precedes the *rubedo*) and arrives at Goldthwaite's house in time for the discovery of a "treasure" of worthless provincial currency. Yet Brown's feelings of fellowship for Goldthwaite represent the true "gold" of Hawthorne's story. Although Hawthorne uses alchemical imagery to parody Goldthwaite's failed quest, the real transformation occurs in the heart of Brown, as he tells his old partner: "I have house-room for you and Tabby, and a safe vault for the chest of treasure. Tomorrow we will try to come to an agreement about the sale of this old house. Real estate is well up, and I could afford you a pretty handsome price" (*CE* 9: 406). The true treasure of the story lies in the benevolent heart of Brown.

The alchemical allegory of the heart also informs two stories that Hawthorne published in 1843, "Egotism; or, The Bosom-Serpent" and "The Birth-mark." In "Egotism," Hawthorne adopts the alchemical serpent as an emblem of "diseased self-contemplation" (*CE* 10: 283).[32] When Roderick Elliston's friend, George Herkimer, asks if there is a cure for the bosom-serpent said to coil around the heart of Elliston, the latter replies, "Could I, for one instant, forget myself, the serpent might not abide within me" (*CE* 10: 282). At this critical moment, Elliston's estranged wife Rosina emerges,

"Then forget yourself, my husband," said a gentle voice above him—"forget yourself in the idea of another!"

Rosina had emerged from the arbor, and was bending over him, with the shadow of his anguish reflected in her contenance, yet so mingled with hope and unselfish love, that all anguish seemed but an earthly shadow and a dream. She touched Roderick with her hand. A tremor shivered through his frame. At that moment, if report be trustworthy, the sculptor beheld a waving motion through the grass, and heard a tinkling sound, as if something had plunged into the fountain. Be the truth as it might, it is certain that Roderick Elliston sat up like a man renewed, restored to his right mind, and rescued from the fiend, which had so miserably overcome him in the battle-field of his own breast. (*CE* 10: 283)

Hawthorne draws heavily upon the biblical theme of Eden and the eternal war between good and evil in this passage, yet the allegory carried in the undercurrent of this climactic scene also suggests the alchemy of love: Rosina's name connotes the alchemical rose of the *rubedo* that signals the end of the alchemist's great work, when the philosophers' stone (the human heart) is liberated from the darkness (*nigredo*) of the alchemical serpent. In addition, Rosina's action recalls Hawthorne's words to Sophia, written two years before "Egotism": "[N]othing else is real to me, unless thou give it that golden quality by thy touch." Thus, Elliston's heart, once held captive by his bosom-serpent, is freed at the moment that his thoughts turn to Rosina, who brings with her touch the means for Elliston's transmutation.

In contrast to "Egotism," "The Birth-mark" illustrates the consequences of rejecting love's transmutative power. While Hawthorne's alchemical imagery in this tale has been the focal point of a number of scholarly studies,[33] a reading focused specifically on the alchemy of love helps to further illuminate the hermetic allegory. Ironically, Hawthorne's alchemist, Aylmer, fails to comprehend that alchemy offers a metaphor for redemption as well as transmutation. As Aylmer goes about the business of transforming his wife into an image of perfection by removing her red, hand-shaped birthmark, he rejects, as Georgiana later tells him, "the best that earth could offer" (*CE* 10: 55). Hawthorne's emphasis here is not only on Georgiana's beauty but on her love for Aylmer as well.

Taking into account Hawthorne's copious use of hermetic tropes in "The Birth-mark," Shannon Burns suggests that Aylmer subjects Georgiana to the whitening (purifying) process of the *albedo*, yet as John Gatta observes, the conjunction of the white and the red, the final stage of perfection, is already present in Georgiana's character.[34] The crimson hand on her cheek recalls the alchemical *rubedo*; as Gatta notes, Aylmer "misreads the crucial signs of color, and destroys the very quintessence he is seeking to discover."[35] The name Georgiana itself suggests the alchemical marriage of male and female, often represented by the alchemical hermaphrodite, and the birthmark in the shape of a hand evokes the fifth element (the quintessence reflected by the five digits), a synonym for the philosophers' stone.[36] Ironically, the perfection that Aylmer labors to bring forth in Georgiana is already present in her love for him, a love that allows her to give herself willingly over to his experiments. Yet as in many stories of failure in the course of the alchemical opus, Aylmer unwittingly destroys the vessel of containment (Georgiana's body), and the spirit of love embodied there escapes his grasp.

The year after Hawthorne penned "The Birth-mark," he returned to his hermetic allegory of the heart as a subtext in "Rappaccini's Daughter" (1844). In this tale, the strange garden of Rappaccini recalls the image of the philosophers' garden, for both gardens are isolated (hermetically sealed) from the outside world. Furthermore, Rappaccini is closely connected with the philosophy, if not the character, of the German alchemist Paracelsus. As Dame Lisabetta tells Giovanni, "It is said that he [Rappaccini] distills these plants into medicines that are as potent as a charm" (*CE* 10: 94). Baglioni comes to a similar conclusion with regard to Rappaccini: "he is as true a man of science as ever distilled his own heart in an alembic" (*CE* 10: 119).[37]

As alchemist, Rappaccini attempts a literal chemical union of Giovanni and Beatrice through the poison he has introduced into both of their systems. Toward the end of the story, as Beatrice consumes the contents of a silver vial containing the supposed antidote for her poisoned nature, Hawthorne presents the transmutation of Beatrice herself, a transmutation of matter to spirit. "Farewell, Giovanni! Thy words of hatred are like lead within my heart—but they, too, will fall away as I ascend. Oh, was there not, from the first, more poison in thy nature than in mine" (*CE* 10: 127), Beatrice tells Giovanni. With her dying words we glimpse the image of *Spiritus Mercurius* (love as embodied by Beatrice) bursting out of the vessel (the alchemical garden) and ascending to heaven. Beatrice's words to Giovanni suggest that her soul has become golden—purified of the poison that permeated her essential being. Giovanni, however, remains with poison still in his "nature," and like Aylmer in "The Birth-mark," beyond love's promise of transmutation.

In contrast to Giovanni's failure to recognize the redemptive quality of love, Owen Warland, in "The Artist of the Beautiful" (1844), embodies Hawthorne's vision of the soul transformed by love. Through his artistic labor of "converting what was earthly [the springs and gears of base metal] to spiritual gold" (*CE* 10: 472), Warland recalls the alchemist's attempt to accomplish the spiritualization of matter. Even though Warland's golden butterfly, his mechanical masterpiece, is destroyed at the end of the story, the reader is cognizant of a spiritual change that has occurred within the soul of the artist:

And as for Owen Warland, he looked placidly at what seemed the ruin of his life's labor, and which was yet no ruin. He had caught a far other butterfly than this. When the artist rose high enough to achieve the Beautiful, the symbol by which he made it perceptible to mortal senses became of little value in his eyes, while his spirit possessed itself in the enjoyment of the Reality. (*CE* 10: 475)

Here, as Hawthorne intimates, Warland's soul (or heart) has been transmuted. Not only has Warland "won the Beautiful into his handiwork" (*CE* 10: 472), he has "won the Beautiful" into his heart as well. The artistic work (the butterfly) is no longer important, for it is merely the reflection of the inner work of art (a symbolic lapiz) that has been created in the artist's soul.[38] Hawthorne's hermetic allegory in "The Artist of the Beautiful" anticipates the thesis that Hitchcock would publish thirteen years later: "*Man* was the *subject* of Alchemy and . . . the *object* of the Art was the perfection, or at least the improvement, of Man." Indeed, Warland's selfless experience of love for the "Beautiful" transmutes his heart.

Perhaps the most telling of Hawthorne's hermetic allegories, however, is "The Golden Touch," the story of King Midas in *A Wonder Book*, for here Hawthorne most graphically depicts the alchemy of love and the transmutation of the human heart. In the familiar myth, Midas is so consumed by his lust for gold that he requests from Bacchus the ability to change all he touches into the precious element. Significantly, as Hawthorne retells this story he uses the verb "transmute" seven times.[39]

Although Hawthorne emphasizes Midas's lust for gold in the opening of the story, there does exist one thing that Midas might value more highly: "This King Midas was fonder of gold than of any thing else in the world. He valued his royal crown chiefly because it was composed of that precious metal. If he loved anything better, or half so well, it was the one little maiden who played so merrily around her father's footstool. But, the more Midas loved his daughter, the more did he desire and seek for wealth" (*CE* 7: 40). The name of the king's daughter, Marygold, evokes the marriage of the alchemical king and queen, Sol and Luna, as well as the brilliance of alchemical gold. It is a mysterious stranger (Bacchus), however, who grants Midas his desire: " 'Be it as you wish, then,' replied the stranger, waving his hand in token of farewell. 'Tomorrow, at sunrise, you will find yourself gifted with the Golden Touch!' " (*CE* 7: 45). Sunrise, or *aurora consurgens*—the golden dawn of the alchemists—is a most propitious moment in alchemy, for it represents the dawning of spiritual knowledge. Yet instead of acquiring knowledge, Midas, as Hugo McPherson asserts, experiences a "progressive loss of those values to which [he] has become blind."[40] Hawthorne's narrator, Eustace Bright, relates that Midas

> took up a book from the table. At his first touch, it assumed the appearance of such a splendidly bound and gilt-edged volume, as one often meets with, now-a-days; but, on running his fingers through the leaves, behold! it was a bundle of thin golden plates, in which all the wisdom of the book had grown illegible. . . .
> But it was not worth while to vex himself about a trifle. Midas now took his spectacles from his pocket, and put them on his nose, in order that he might see more distinctly what he was about. . . . To his great perplexity, however, excellent as the glasses were, he discovered that he could not possibly see through them. But this was the most natural thing in the world; for, on taking them off, the transparent crystals turned out to be plates of yellow metal, and, of course, were worthless as spectacles, though valuable as gold. It struck Midas as rather inconvenient, that, with all his wealth, he could never again be rich enough to own a pair of serviceable spectacles! (*CE* 7: 46–47)

As McPherson observes, in these two episodes Midas loses touch with the "wisdom of books" and becomes metaphorically blind.[41] In alchemical terms, Midas descends into the spiritual darkness of the *nigredo*.

Still undaunted, however, the alchemist king continues to "transmute" the physical reality around him:

> He lifted the door-latch, (it was brass, only a moment ago, but golden, when his fingers quitted it,) and emerged into the garden. Here, as it happened, he found a great number of beautiful roses in full bloom, and others in all the stages of lovely bud and blossom. Very delicious was their fragrance in the morning breeze! Their delicate blush was one of the fairest sights in the world; so gentle, so modest, and so full of sweet tranquillity, did these roses seem to be. But Midas knew a way to make them far more precious, according to his way of thinking, than roses had ever been before. So he took great pains in going from bush to bush, and exercised his magic touch most indefatigably; until every individual flower and bud, and even the worms at the heart of some of them, were changed to gold. (*CE* 7: 47)

To be noted first in this passage is the alchemical-like transmutation of brass to gold. In addition, the golden roses hint at what Hawthorne is doing with alchemy and myth of Midas, for the rose, found in the philosophers' garden, symbolizes God's grace and love, the philosophers' stone, and the human heart.[42] As McPherson notes, at this point Midas, through his "crass materialism," has lost touch with divinity, wisdom, and human love.[43]

After a comic scene at the breakfast table where Midas finds he cannot touch his food without transmuting it to gold, the king unintentionally transforms Marygold: "Her soft and tender little form grew hard and inflexible within her father's encircling arms. Oh, terrible misfortune! The victim of his insatiable desire for wealth, little Marygold was a human child no longer, but a golden statue!" (*CE* 7: 53). At this moment of crisis the mercurial stranger, the agent of change, reappears to the king:

> The stranger's countenance still wore a smile, which seemed to shed a yellow lustre all about the room, and gleamed on little Marygold's image, and on the other objects that had been transmuted by the touch of Midas.
> "Well, friend Midas," said the stranger, "pray how do you succeed with the Golden Touch?"
> Midas shook his head.
> "I am very miserable!" said he.
> "Very miserable, indeed?" exclaimed the stranger. "And how happens that? Have I not faithfully kept my promise with you? Have you not everything that your heart desired?"
> "Gold is not everything," answered Midas. "And I have lost all that my heart really cared for!"
> "Ah! So you have made a discovery, since yesterday!" observed the stranger. "Let us see, then! Which of these two things do you think is really worth the most . . . ?"
> "The Golden Touch," asked the stranger, "or your own little Marygold, warm, soft, and loving, as she was an hour ago?"
> "Oh, my child, my dear child!" cried poor Midas, wringing his hands. "I would not have given that one small dimple in her chin, for the power of changing this whole big earth into a solid lump of gold!" (*CE* 7: 54–55)

In this exchange we glimpse the epiphany manifested in the alchemist king's love for his daughter. With Midas's rejection of material wealth, Hawthorne affirms the values of the heart, where love reigns supreme. Bacchus remarks of Midas, "You are wiser than you were, King Midas! . . . Your own heart, I perceive, has not been entirely changed from flesh to gold. Were it so, your case would indeed be desperate. But you appear to be still capable of understanding that the commonest things, such as lie within everybody's grasp, are more valuable than the riches which so many mortals sigh and struggle after"

(*CE* 7: 55). A transmutation, as the god implies, has worked internally on Midas; the king has grown wise. As Midas undergoes a final purification, an alchemical *ablutio* or cleansing, Hawthorne fully discloses his alchemical theme:

> As [Midas] dipt the pitcher into the water, it gladdened his very heart to see it change from gold into the same good, honest earthen vessel which it had been, before he touched it. He was conscious, also, of a change within himself. A cold, hard, and heavy weight seemed to have gone out of his bosom. No doubt, his heart had been gradually losing its human substance, and transmuting itself into insensible metal, but had now softened back again into flesh. (*CE* 7: 56)

Thus "The Golden Touch" dramatizes how the heart, the heart of the matter, or the heart of the stone, is transmuted through the alchemy of love, for it is Midas's heart that is transmuted from cold, unfeeling metal to warm flesh and blood.

His heart transmuted, Midas is enabled to feel a sympathetic connection with others. In this context, Marygold serves not only as a symbolic alembic, or vessel that contains the philosophers' stone, she also releases the king from the bonds of his base existence. Thus it is fitting that at the end of Hawthorne's story Marygold's hair retains a "golden tinge" that further manifests her connection to the philosophers' stone. Moreover, the final scene, in which Midas plays with his golden-haired grandchildren, images the alchemical *multiplicatio*—the multiplication of gold through the agency of the philosophers' stone—and suggests that Midas has become, according to Hawthorne, a true alchemical philosopher: "[T]o tell you the truth," the king proclaims, "ever since that morning, I have hated the very sight of all other gold, save this!" (*CE* 7: 57). Once again, Hawthorne's emphasis is on the "golden touch" of love.

In the tales we have considered thus far, Hawthorne uses the female figure as a vessel for the essence of love and its transmuting (and salvific) qualities. This figure, whether Mary Goffe, Rosina Elliston, Georgiana, Beatrice Rappaccini, or Marygold, represents one half of the alchemical conjunction of Sol and Luna (male and female); as Hawthorne explores the failure of this conjunction (the rejection of love), he focuses on the outcome with regard to such male characters as Digby, Brand, Aylmer, and Giovanni. From Hawthorne's point of view, the female is exalted in these tales, for she carries the promise of transmutation in the alchemical allegory of the heart.[44] This hermetic allegory is not limited to Hawthorne's tales, however; a brief look at *The*

Scarlet Letter (1850) and *The House of the Seven Gables* (1851) will illustrate his maturing vision of the alchemy of love.

Luther H. Martin proposes in his study of *The Scarlet Letter* that Hawthorne embodies in Pearl's character the qualities of the alchemical mediator (Mercury), symbolically uniting Hester Prynne and Arthur Dimmesdale in an alchemical marriage.[45] However, Pearl's actions at the end of the romance also cast her as agent of transmutation, the philosophers' stone. As Martin remarks, the scarlet letter itself, embroidered with gold, bears the colors associated with the philosophers' stone,[46] and Pearl, as the embodiment of Hester's sin, is also a reflection of the letter: "The mother's impassioned state had been the medium through which were transmitted to the unborn infant the rays of its mortal life; and, however white and clear originally, they had taken the deep stains of crimson and gold, the fiery luster, the black shadow, and the untempered light, of the intervening substance" (*CE* 1: 91). Hawthorne's description of Pearl mirrors the alchemical colors black, white, red, and gold as they appear in her inward nature, and Reverend Wilson later notes of her name and appearance: "Pearl?—Ruby rather!—or Coral!—or Red Rose, at the very least, judging from thy hue!" (*CE* 1: 110). During Pearl's brief encounter with Wilson, Hawthorne emphasizes the alchemical conjunction of white (Pearl) and red (Pearl's dress), the *albedo* and *rubedo*, in her physical appearance; furthermore, pearl, ruby, coral, and the red rose are synonyms for the philosophers' stone.[47]

It is in the climactic chapter, "The Revelation of the Scarlet Letter," however, that Pearl, wrapped in a golden chain, fully assumes her role as philosophers' stone. After Dimmesdale confesses his sin on the scaffold and collapses, Pearl kisses him. In the context of Hawthorne's alchemy of love, the kiss suggests a golden touch, and the tears that fall on her father, though they do not prolong his life, evoke the redeeming elixir of life and suggest sympathy and love. To underscore the importance of Pearl's action, Hawthorne notes that "[a] spell was broken." This moment also marks a change in Pearl's character, for Hawthorne notes, "[her tears] were the pledge that she would grow up amid human joy and sorrow, nor for ever do battle with the world, but be a woman in it" (*CE* 1: 256). Thus Hawthorne emphasizes that Pearl has also undergone a transmutation. No longer an indifferent elf-child, she discovers her own capacity for love and sympathy, Hawthorne's values of the heart. Although there are other alchemical references in *The Scarlet Letter* (the most obvious relating to the alchemist Roger Chillingworth), it is notable that Hawthorne embodies the redeeming quality of love in Pearl, and in so doing adds a further dimension to the alchemy of love, for the child is at once both agent and object of transmutation.

At the beginning of *The House of the Seven Gables*, his last full-length treatment of the alchemy of love, Hawthorne indicates that the Pyncheon house is emblematic of the human heart (*CE* 2: 27). Having previously equated the heart with the philosophers' stone, Hawthorne here uses a variation of this paradigm: the heart of the house, the spirit of the Pyncheon family itself, becomes the *prima materia*. The physical house (like the story itself) is but the alembic in which the transmutation and redemption of the corrupt past, symbolized by the legend of the Pyncheon curse, occurs through the union of Phoebe and Holgrave.[48]

The corruption (or imperfect nature) of the past is given form by Hawthorne in the legend of the Pyncheon curse; as a blight upon the Pyncheon family, the curse manifests in the bloody (and mysterious) deaths of Colonel Pyncheon and his descendants. A once prosperous family, the Pyncheons, during the timeframe of the story, consist of Clifford and Hepzibah, Judge Pyncheon, and Phoebe. Clifford and Hepzibah, as characters who reflect the impotence of the past, seem little more than caricatures of the alchemical marriage of Sol and Luna.[49] Judge Pyncheon, in searching for a lost treasure (the Pyncheon fortune), is, as Edward Kleiman observes, a type of false alchemist, who in his lust for gold (and power) reveals a heart of lead.[50] Hawthorne notes, "One perceived him [Judge Pyncheon] to be a personage of mark, influence, and authority; and especially, you could feel just as certain that he was opulent, as if he had exhibited his bank account—or as if you had seen him touching the twigs of the Pyncheon-elm, and, Midas-like, transmuting them to gold" (*CE* 2: 57). However, what we observe in the character of the Judge is a figure who reflects Midas before his change of heart in "The Golden Touch."

Phoebe Pyncheon, on the other hand, embodies the alchemical qualities of Sol—the light-bringer—and the philosophers' stone.[51] Her character "Betoken[s] the cheeriness of an active temperament, finding joy in its activity, and therefore rendering it beautiful; it was a New England trait—the stern old stuff of Puritanism, with a gold thread in the web" (*CE* 2: 76). As an embodiment of the transmuting and redeeming qualities of the alchemists' stone, Phoebe's very essence (and her dreams) seems to banish the ghosts of the past, and even tincture (relieve) the gloom that surrounds Clifford and Hepzibah:

> [Phoebe's room] was now a maiden's bed-chamber, and had been purified of all former evil and sorrow by her sweet breath and happy thoughts. Her dreams of the past night, being such cheerful ones, had exorcised the gloom, and now haunted the chamber in its stead. (*CE* 2: 72)

... the purifying influence, scattered throughout the atmosphere of the household by the presence of one, youthful, fresh, and thoroughly wholesome heart.... so did all the thoughts and emotions of Hepzibah and Clifford, sombre as they might seem, acquire a subtle attribute of happiness from Phoebe's intermixture with them. (*CE* 2: 137)

The union of Phoebe and Holgrave redeems the past through a reconciliation of the Maules and Pyncheons—a transformation of the past through the alchemy of love. While Matthew Maule's curse and the lost Pyncheon fortune reflect the decay and corruption of the past, Hawthorne suggests as a remedy, "The moss-grown and rotten Past ... be torn down, and lifeless institutions ... be thrust out of the way, and their dead corpses buried, and everything ... begin anew" (*CE* 2: 179). To this Holgrave adds the following:

Shall we never, never get rid of this Past! ... It lies upon the Present like a giant's dead body! In fact, the case is just as if a young giant were compelled to waste all his strength in carrying about the corpse of the old giant, his grandfather, who died a long while ago, and only needs to be decently buried. Just think a moment; and it will startle you to see what slaves we are to by-gone times— to Death, if we give the matter the right word! ... if each generation were allowed and expected to build its own houses, that single change, comparatively unimportant in itself, would imply almost every reform which society is now suffering for. I doubt whether even our public edifices—our capitols, state-houses, court-houses, city-halls, and churches—ought to be built of such permanent materials as stone or brick. It were better that they should crumble to ruin, once in twenty years, or thereabouts, as a hint to the people to examine into and reform the institutions which they symbolize....
Now this old Pyncheon-house! Is it a wholesome place to live in, with its black shingles, and the green moss that shows how damp they are?—its dark, low-studded rooms?—its grime and sordidness, which are the crystallization on its walls of the human breath, that has been drawn and exhaled here, in discontent and anguish? The house ought to be purified with fire—purified till only its ashes remain! (*CE* 2: 182–84)

Holgrave's statement recalls Hawthorne's final observation in "Earth's Holocaust," yet in the context of *Seven Gables* we are presented with the anguished cry of a character who is just as much a victim of the past (as Maule's descendant) as any Pyncheon ever was. Yet instead of tearing down the past (and the house), Holgrave undergoes a transmutation of spirit.

At the moment of Holgrave's confession of love for Phoebe, a transmutation takes place within him:

> Could you but know, Phoebe, how it was with me, the hour before you came! ... A dark, cold, miserable hour! The presence of yonder dead man threw a great black shadow over everything; he made the universe, so far as my perception could reach, a scene of guilt, and of retribution more dreadful than the guilt. The sense of it took away my youth. I never hoped to feel young again! The world looked strange, wild, evil, hostile;—past life, so lonesome and dreary; my future, a shapeless gloom, which I must mould into gloomy shapes! But, Phoebe, you crossed the threshold; and hope, warmth, and joy, came in with you! The black moment became at once a blissful one. It must not pass without the spoken word. I love you! (*CE* 2: 306)

Here, imaged obliquely in the alchemical phoenix reborn, Holgrave finds his lost youth, and even the "black moment" of Judge Pyncheon's death is transformed for him by the presence of Phoebe.

As Phoebe in turn confesses her love for Holgrave, the moment of conjunction, the symbolic alchemical marriage, occurs:

> And it was in this hour, so full of doubt and awe, that the one miracle was wrought, without which every human existence is a blank. The bliss, which makes all things true, beautiful, and holy, shone around this youth and maiden. They were conscious of nothing sad nor old. They transfigured the earth, and made it Eden again, and themselves the two first dwellers in it. The dead man, so close beside them, was forgotten. At such a crisis, there is no Death; for Immortality is revealed anew, and embraces everything in its hallowed atmosphere. (*CE* 2: 307)

Here the reconciliation of opposites (the Maules and the Pyncheons) comes about through the (female) agency of Hawthorne's philosophers' stone, the transmuting and redeeming essence of love that effects the alchemical marriage of heaven and earth and creates a new Eden.

Hawthorne further emphasizes this transformation in his description of the Pyncheon elm:

> The Pyncheon-elm, throughout its great circumference, was all alive, and full of the morning sun and a sweetly tempered little

breeze, which lingered within this verdant sphere, and set a thousand leafy tongues a-whispering all at once. This aged tree appeared to have suffered nothing from the gale. It had kept its boughs unshattered, and its full complement of leaves, and the whole in perfect verdure, except a single branch, that, by the earlier change with which the elm-tree sometimes prophesies the autumn, had been transmuted to bright gold. It was like the golden branch, that gained Æneas and the Sibil's admittance into Hades. (*CE* 2: 284–85)

While the Pyncheon elm recalls the *arbor philosophica*,[52] the reference to Æneas and the Sibil's descent into the underworld evokes not only the House of Death (i.e., Hades), but also the alchemical promise of rebirth and transmutation at the culmination of the opus.

The union of opposites through the agency of love leads to the climactic act of redemption in the final paragraph of *Seven Gables*:

Maule's Well, all this time, though left in solitude, was throwing up a succession of kaleidoscopic pictures, in which a gifted eye might have seen fore-shadowed through the coming fortunes of Hepzibaph, and Clifford, and the descendant of the legendary wizard, and the village-maiden, over whom he had thrown love's web of sorcery. The Pyncheon-elm moreover, with what foliage the September gale had spared to it, whispered unintelligible prophecies. And wise Uncle Venner, passing slowly from the ruinous porch, seemed to hear a strain of music, and fancied that sweet Alice Pyncheon—after witnessing these deeds, this by-gone woe, and this present happiness, of her kindred mortals—had given one farewell touch of a spirit's joy upon her harpsichord, as she floated heavenward from the HOUSE OF THE SEVEN GABLES! (*CE* 2: 319)

The colors in the well evoke the *cauda pavonis* or peacock's tail, the "multi-coloured flowering and blossoming of the opus,"[53] heralding the conclusion of Hawthorne's opus—for the philosophers' stone (love) has indeed been created through a joining of opposites. In addition, the freed spirit of Alice Pyncheon suggests that not only has the age-old curse of Matthew Maule been lifted from the house, but (a) spirit has been redeemed from fallen (base) matter.

In many of Hawthorne's stories the conjunction of male and female reflects the royal marriage in alchemy, and his alchemy of love offers the possibility of transmuting the *prima materia* of the heart into a golden reflection of the philosophers' stone. We can observe in Hawthorne's characters successful alchemical transformations and conjunctions as well as emotionally crippled failures, yet even in the failures Hawthorne's alchemy of love offers the potential to bring heaven and earth into conjunction and transmute our mundane existence into an earthly paradise. Even in "Septimius Felton," written at the end of his career, Hawthorne employs a variation of this theme when Sybil drinks the elixir of death to prevent Septimius from poisoning himself through his failed attempt at creating the *elixir vitae*. Although Sybil originally sets out to poison Septimius, she experiences a change of heart through her newfound love for him: "I thought I loved that youth in the grave yonder; but it was you I loved;—and I am dying" (*CE* 13: 190). Hawthorne never completed a final draft of this story; however, what we glimpse in "Septimius Felton" intimates that Hawthorne was working toward an ending along the same lines as the hermetic allegories of "The Birth-mark" and "Rappaccini's Daughter."

From what we have noted of Hawthorne's explorations of the alchemy of love and the transmutation of the heart, we may indeed suspect that Hawthorne viewed himself as a literary alchemist—transmuting his imaginations into golden words upon the page, as he notes in "The Custom-House." Although "The Artist of the Beautiful" presents an idealistic view of the artist-alchemist as ruler of both his inner and outer worlds, we may indeed wonder if Hawthorne experienced difficulty in sustaining this view with regard to his own life. Moving into the public eye as a writer of romances, Hawthorne achieved success with *The Scarlet Letter*, *The House of the Seven Gables*, and *The Marble Faun*. In these stories Hawthorne left his mark, so to speak. In a sense, Hawthorne's tales and romances became his way to immortality. However, in his last unfinished works, specifically "Etherege" and the "Septimius" stories, the golden words eluded his grasp.

In an effort to perform his artistic alchemy once again, Hawthorne turned to the image of the *elixir vitae* to rejuvenate his creative imagination. First in "Etherege," then in the "Septimius" stories, and finally in "The Dolliver Romance," Hawthorne tried to find the right plot, the right symbols, the right theme. He tried, and he failed. But our final assessment of Hawthorne's alchemy should not be based on his inability to complete one final romance. His legacy of tales, sketches, and romances are truly his *elixir vitae*, for like the medieval alchemists, his work still speaks to us out of the past, and his alchemy of love offers the promise for the future.

NOTES

1. See Shannon Burns, "Alchemy and 'The Birth-mark' "; Clack, "The Alchemy of Love"; Janine Dove-Rume, "Hawthorne, l'alchimiste, et son Grande' Oeuvre, *The Scarlet Letter*"; John Gatta, Jr., "Aylmer's Alchemy in 'The Birth-

mark' "; Mark Hennelly, "Hawthorne's *Opus Alchmicum*"; Raymona E. Hull, "Hawthorne and the Magic Elixir of Life"; David Ketterer, " 'Circle of Acquaintance' "; Edward Kleiman, "The Wizardry of Nathaniel Hawthorne"; Luther Martin, "Hawthorne's *The Scarlet Letter*"; Jeffrey L. Meikle, "Hawthorne's Alembic"; Alfred S. Reid, "Hawthorne's Humanism"; Liz Rosenberg, " 'The Best That Earth Could Offer' "; Klaus P. Stich, "Hawthorne's Intimations of Alchemy"; Charles Swann, "Alchemy and Hawthorne's *Elixir of Life Manuscripts*"; David M. Van Leer, "Aylmer's Library"; Itala Vivan, "An Eye into the Occult in Hawthorne's Text"; and Elémire Zolla, "Septimius Felton e la letteratura alchemica inglese e americana."

2. Hull (103).

3. In "Pepperell," we have reference to both alchemical gold and the *elixir vitae* of the alchemist. In addition, the "model of a flying bridge" recalls the winged "Invisible College" of the Rosicrucians illustrated in Theophilus Schweighardt's *Speculum Sophicum Rhodo-Stauroticum* (1618), reprinted in Yates (Frontispiece).

4. Hawthorne's approximate date of 1700 suggests that he may be referring to Wait Still Winthrop (1642–1717), who, like his father, John Winthrop, Jr., was interested in alchemy (Wilkinson, "Alchemical Library," Part 1, 49). Hawthorne's reference to the alchemist's fire burning for seven weeks would indicate that he was familiar with the alchemical significance of the number 7.

5. To this list we might also add the mysterious mathematician in "A Select Party" (*CE* 10: 61) who has been successful at "squaring the circle"—an alchemical metaphor for creating the philosophers' stone. See Maier, Emblem 21 (147). For commentary on Emblem 21, see De Jong (166–76). For further information on squaring the circle, see "Alchymy" (100, 131); John Mitchell, "Michael Maier's Alchemical Quadrature of the Circle" (72–75); Read, *Prelude to Chemistry* (239); and Abraham, "Square and Circle" (189–90), in *Dictionary*.

6. For more on Jason and Medea and alchemy see Abraham, "Aeson" (4), in *Dictionary*, and De Jong (61). Also see Hawthorne's "Dr. Heidigger's Experiment" (1837; *CE* 9: 227–38) for a further treatment of the *elixir vitae*.

7. Ben Jonson, *The Alchemist* (Act 2, Scene 1, lines 89–104).

8. For more on Maier's *Arcana arcanissima*, see De Jong (7–8, 307–9); H. J. Sheppard, "The Mythological Tradition and Seventeenth Century Alchemy" (52–53); and Read, *Alchemist* (234).

9. J. Godwin, "Introduction" (77).

10. For background on Jonson's sources, see Supriya Chaudhuri, "Jason's Fleece" (71–73). For background on Maier's sources, see De Jong.

11. Ruland (229–30) lists thirty-six separate names for alchemical mercury—the catalyst of the alchemical opus—yet Hawthorne again may be borrowing from Jonson, for in *Eastward Ho!* (1605) we find Jonson's mercurial character of Quicksilver. See also Abraham, "Quicksilver" (162), in *Dictionary*.

12. See Read, *Alchemist* (161).

13. See Ethan Allen Hitchcock, *Fifty Years in Camp and Field* (444); see also Cohen (54, 90).

14. There are letters documenting the correspondence between Hitchcock and Sophia Hawthorne. See Edwin Haviland Miller, *Salem Is My Dwelling Place* (476, 478–80, 482, 524). Although the connection between Hitchcock and

Hawthorne is obscure at best, Sophia does note in a letter to her daughter Una that Hitchcock sent her "a catalogue of his Hermetic Library," a collection of more than 300 volumes (letter of December 11, 1862, Concord, reprinted in Julian Hawthorne, *Nathaniel Hawthorne and His Wife*, Vol. 2, 326).

15. Ethan Allen Hitchcock, *Remarks upon Alchemy and the Alchemists* (iv–v, 39, 71).

16. On the significance of the microcosm-macrocosm dichotomy, see Abraham, "Microcosm" (129–30), in *Dictionary*; and Haeffner, "The Emerald Tablet" (118) and "Microcosm-Macrocosm" (180–82). See also the alchemical illustrations of the heart and athanor in Daniel Cramer's *The Rosicrucian Emblems of Daniel Cramer* (51, 62).

17. Nathaniel Hawthorne, *The Love Letters of Nathaniel Hawthorne* (231).

18. Hitchcock, *Remarks* (134–35).

19. Whether or not the historical Thomas Morton, leader of Merry Mount, had any connection with British alchemists is a matter of speculation; however, as Hawthorne notes of the Merry Mount settlement: "All the hereditary pastimes of Old England were transplanted hither" (*CE* 9: 60). Hermetic science was sometimes included among these "pastimes."

20. This scene recalls an illustration from Johann Daniel Mylius' *Opus medico-chymicum* (1618), reprinted in De Rola, plate 119 (138). The figure of the stag in both the hieroglyph and the May-Pole scene suggests the presence of the mercurial spirit in the alchemical drama. See Abraham, "Cervus Fugitivus" (32–33), in *Dictionary*; and Jung, *Psychology and Alchemy* (65–66).

21. According to Stephan A. Hoeller in *Freedom* (176–80), it was the iron Puritan resolve that displaced the political utopia of the Rosicrucians in America.

22. See also "The Threefold Destiny" (1838), where the stone, a white quartz brooch, is "in the shape of a Heart" (*CE* 9: 481).

23. Haeffner, "Prime Matter" (208–11). See also Abraham, *Dictionary*, for background on *massa confusa*, or chaos (33–34), and tears as "mercurial waters" (198).

24. Hennelly (104).

25. Stich (25).

26. See Hennelly (99–100, 102).

27. Stich (25).

28. Ibid. (17–18).

29. The publication date of "Peter Goldthwaite's Treasure" coincides, curiously enough, with Hawthorne's journal entry of 1838 concerning the alchemist's house.

30. For more on the alchemical metaphor "tear down the house," see Abraham, "House" (104), in *Dictionary*; Fabricius (128); and Paracelsus, Vol. 2 (84).

31. The connection between the scarlet flowers and the *rubedo* may also allude to the alchemical rose of the Rosicrucians; see Fabricius (160–61, 176–79, 201–2, passim); and Yates (30, 65, passim).

32. A possible source for this image is "The Book of Lambspring" (*HM* 1: 287; see also 1: 279). Hawthorne had access to this work in the collection of Danforth at the Boston Athenaeum (Wilkinson, "New England's Last Alchemists" 131–32). Another possible source is Maier, Emblem 25 (155); for commentary on

Emblem 25, see De Jong (191–95). See also Abraham, "Dragon" (59), "Serpent" (181), and "Uroboros" (207), in *Dictionary* and Haeffner, "Uroboros-Serpent" (254–55).

33. Gatta ("Aylmer's Alchemy") and Van Leer, for example, offer historical approaches to the alchemy in "The Birth-mark." Burns, on the other hand, views Hawthorne's alchemy from a Jungian perspective, and Rosenberg explores the concept of marriage in the context of matter and spirit.

34. Burns (154); Gatta, "Aylmer's Alchemy" (408).

35. Gatta, "Aylmer's Alchemy" (408).

36. See De Rola, plate 343 (178), from Mylius' *Philosophia reformata*.

37. Through his work of distilling poisons (of nature) into medical compounds, Rappaccini follows Paracelsian medical theory. See Carol Marie Bensick, *La Nouvelle Beatrice* (59, 60).

38. Among the ancients, the butterfly was an emblem of the soul. See J. E. Cirlot, *A Dictionary of Symbols* (35).

39. The number 7 is itself significant, indicating the seven alchemical metals and their corresponding planets. See Haeffner, "Metals and Planets" (179–80). Meikle (175) makes a similar observation with regard to the seven gables of the Pyncheon house.

40. Hugo McPherson, *Hawthrone as Myth-Maker* (57).

41. Ibid.

42. Cirlot (275). See also Abraham, "Rose" (173), in *Dictionary*.

43. McPherson (110).

44. The implication here is that the female is closer to redemption than the male, for the quality of love is stronger in her character. Although this may seem to be a sexist perspective to some people, the alchemical conjunction (synthesis) of Sol and Luna seeks to equalize the roles of the sexes in a perfect and balanced union.

45. Martin aligns Dimmesdale with the white spirituality of alchemy and Hester with its red passion and argues that Pearl, as Mercurius, effects their "spiritual union ... in Chillingworth's [alchemical] art" (35, 37). For further discussion of *The Scarlet Letter* and alchemy, see Dove-Rume; Ketterer, " 'Circle of Acquaintance' " (300, 304); Stich (15, 22–25); and Vivan.

46. Martin (34).

47. Paracelsus, Vol. 1 (17) and Vol. 2 (52), and Maier (169) suggest that the pearl, the ruby, and coral possess qualities of the philosophers' stone. In Jonson (Act 2, Scene 1, lines 47–48), Mammon refers to the liquid form of the philosophers' stone as "the flower of the sun, / The perfect ruby, which we call elixir." In Bonus, *pearl* is a synonym for the philosophers' stone. See also Abraham, "Coral" (47), "Pearls" (142–43), and "Ruby" (175), in *Dictionary*; and De Jong (226–29).

48. Meikle (175). Whereas Meikle focuses on the conjunction of Phoebe and Holgrave, my reading goes one step further to illustrate the redemption of the Pyncheon family spirit (embodied in Alice Pyncheon).

49. Compare this with the alchemical marriage of brother and sister (Sol and Luna) in Poe's "The Fall of the House of Usher."

50. Kleiman (295–96).

51. Kleiman (292) notes Phoebe's relationship with the alchemical sun, or

Sol; Meikle (177–78), on the other hand, sees Phoebe as containing the seed of gold within her nature.
   52. See Kleiman (293) and Meikle (175).
   53. Haeffner (89)

Chapter 6

Fuller and the Golden Seed

Thus far we have observed how, in the nineteenth century, Poe and Hawthorne made use of alchemical tropes to underscore their visions of regeneration. Interestingly, the Sage of Concord was also intrigued with the promise of transformation offered by hermetic science.[1] The equation of alchemy and power appears to have interested Ralph Waldo Emerson, for in a journal entry of 1848 he notes:

> Power. There must be a relation between power & probity. We have, no doubt, as much power as we can be trusted with. *We seem to be on the eve of wonderful additions through alchemy* & mesmerism, and yet [it will not be given,] our hands will not be unbound, until our sanity is quite secure (emphasis mine).[2]

Clearly, Emerson saw a relationship between power and alchemy; like Poe, Hawthorne, and many of the medieval alchemists who preceded them, Emerson saw alchemy as a metaphor for the power of self-transformation and self-transmutation inherent in each individual. The metaphor of alchemy continued to interest Emerson for some time, and in "Beauty" (1860) he writes:

> Astrology interested us, for it tied man to the system. Instead of an isolated beggar, the farthest star felt him and he felt the star. However rash and however falsified by pretenders and traders in it, the hint was true and divine, the soul's avowal of its large relations, and that climate, century, remote natures as well as near, are part of its biography. Chemistry takes to pieces, but it does

not construct. *Alchemy*, which sought to transmute one element into another, to prolong life, to arm with power,—*that was in the right direction* (emphasis mine).[3]

Emerson, however, never fully explored the metaphor of alchemy and its connection to regeneration. Instead, he drew upon the Neoplatonists and German philosophers to formulate his philosophy of New England self-reliance.

Like Emerson, Hawthorne, and Poe, Margaret Fuller too explored the connection between alchemy and regeneration. John Gatta observes that Fuller's

> aspiration to regenerate herself—and, by extension, her nineteenth-century sisters stillborn into that fixed domain of cultural identity defined as "true womanhood"—often expressed itself symbolically through mythology. Fuller's eclectic mythologizing drew mainly from ancient Greek, Roman, Egyptian, Hebrew, and Christian paradigms. She enriched it further through her extensive reading in German romanticism. But the archetypal Goddess, bearing her sundry names from this vast span of cultures, remains a pervasive presence throughout Fuller's prose and poetic writings.[4]

Whereas the figure of the archetypal goddess recurs throughout Fuller's work, an exploration of the alchemical tropes Fuller employs in her writing affords a unique and rewarding perspective from which to view Fuller's themes of regeneration and gender equality. In both her prose and poetry (specifically, those writings of 1840 through 1844), we can discern Fuller's maturing vision of alchemical regeneration. As she stated in "Summer on the Lakes" (1844), "Of all dreams, that of the alchymist is the most poetical, for he looked at the finest symbol. Gold, says one of our friends, is the hidden light of the earth, it crowns the mineral, as wine the vegetable order, being the last expression of vital energy" (*EF* 78).[5] Like many of the alchemists, Fuller understood that alchemical gold, unlike the yellow metal sought by greedy individuals, was a symbol for spiritual perfection. Drawing on tropes of the alchemical *hieros gamos*, Fuller envisioned a mystical union of male and female that would effect a marriage of heaven and earth.

Although Fuller had ample opportunity to locate the same alchemical source material in the Boston and New York libraries that intrigued Poe and Hawthorne, in all probability she came to her appreciation of alchemical tropes through the writings of Jacob Boehme, Louis Claude de Saint Martin, William Godwin, and Johann Wolfgang Von Goethe.[6] In the writings of Boehme and his follower Saint Martin, Fuller observed the tropes and metaphors of alchemy illustrating spiritual regeneration.[7] Additionally, Godwin's *St. Leon* and Goethe's *Märchen* (Fairy Tale) and *Faust*, with their copious references to alchemy, provided Fuller with examples of alchemical themes adapted to literary convention.[8]

Possibly Fuller's first reference to alchemy appears in a letter of 1840 to Caroline Sturgis. During the years 1839 and 1840, Fuller experienced an emotional crisis of sorts precipitated by the marriage of her friends Anna Barker and Samuel Ward and Fuller's inevitable separation from the two. Fuller seems to have emerged from this crisis with new creative energy, for in the Sturgis letter she writes, "I live, I am— *The carbuncle is found* [sic] And at present the mere sight of my talisman is enough. The hour may come when I wish to charm with it, but not yet" (*EF* 13). Fuller's declaration that she lives and "The carbuncle is found" recalls the metaphor of alchemical death and rebirth and suggests the difficult (and often perilous) search for and the attainment of the stone of transmutation or regeneration.[9] Fuller also intimates that she may "wish to charm with it [the stone]," much like the *projectio* and *multiplicatio* of the opus when the alchemists would transmute base metals to gold through the agency of the philosophers' stone. Indeed, for Fuller, the stone of power she claims to possess appears analogous with imagination and inspiration, and it foreshadows Fuller's mystic vision of "Leila" published one year later.[10]

While Jeffrey Steele and Gatta have identified Fuller's figure of Leila with the archetypal goddess, a close look at the language Fuller uses in "Leila" (1841) reveals the figure's strong affinity with the philosophers' stone.[11] Like the stone of transmutation, Leila is elemental, linked with water, air, fire, and earth:

> Leila is *the vast deep.* . . . At night I look into the *lake* for Leila. . . .
> I have seen her among the Sylphs' [elemental spirits of the air] faint florescent forms that hang in the edges of life's rainbows. . . .
> Then glows through her whole being the *fire* that so baffles men, as she walks upon the surface of the *earth.* . . . There in these secret veins of *earth* she thinks herself into fine gold, or aspires for her purest self, till she interlaces the soil with veins of silver. She disdains not to retire upon herself in the iron ore. (*EF* 54–55; emphases mine)

It is especially interesting to note that while Fuller links Leila with the four elements the alchemists believed to compose the philosophers' stone, Leila's link with the earth's metals recalls the alchemical theory of the "seed of gold." The metals associated with Leila further emphasize this mysterious figure's connection to the philosophers' stone, for like the seed of gold believed by the alchemists to be common to (present in) all metals, Leila's nature manifests in gold, silver, and iron. According to Eirenaeus Philalethes, "Mercury, then, is the common seed of gold, silver, copper, tin, iron, lead, etc.; their difference is only to be sought in the degree of their digestion" ("Metamorphosis of Metals" *HM* 2: 236). While this alchemical theory maintained that all metals could be transformed, or perfected (given time), into gold by virtue of the seed of gold that each metal possessed, the alchemist could facilitate this process through specific chemical actions involving alchemical Mercury. Thus, alchemical Mercury was the key, or seed, to discovering the philosophers' stone. Fuller seems to be familiar with this alchemical theory, for she emphasizes Leila's connection with both the higher forms of metal (gold and silver) and the base metal iron.

To further emphasize Leila's likeness to the philosophers' stone, Fuller adds that "the blood-red, heart's-blood-red of the carbuncle. She is, like it, her own light" (*EF* 55). While the deep red of the carbuncle corresponds to the alchemical *rubedo*, the connection between Leila and the carbuncle or philosophers' stone also recalls Fuller's reference to the carbuncle in her 1840 letter to Sturgis and accents the writer's discovery of Leila as a source of inspiration.[12]

There is, however, more than just Fuller's image of the carbuncle that links Leila with the philosophers' stone. Through her vision of Leila, Fuller experiences a symbolic union with the infinite: "But I, Leila, could look on thee;—to my restless spirit thou didst bring a kind of peace, for thou wert a bridge between me and the infinite; thou didst arrest the step, and the eye as the veil hanging before the Isis" (*EF* 54). Just as the philosophers' stone was believed by the alchemists to initiate the marriage of heaven and earth, Fuller intimates that Leila possesses this same quality: Leila is a bridge between the material world (Fuller) and heaven ("the infinite").

While (most) males, being bound to the material world, do not comprehend Leila's power, Fuller does. Thus, at the moment of Leila's touch Fuller experiences a transmutation or transformation: "At her touch all became fluid, and the prison walls grew into Edens. Each ray of particolored light grew populous with beings struggling into divinity. The redemption of matter was interwoven into the coronal of thought, and each serpent form soared into a Phenix [*sic*]" (*EF* 57). Here Fuller's words recall the alchemical admonition *solve et coagula* (dissolve and make whole), for at Leila's touch "prison walls" (matter) become "fluid" (dissolves) and then transform into Eden (the transfiguration of earth), signaling "the redemption of mater."[13] Fuller's image of the prison walls transformed into Eden suggests the alchemical alembic (or prison house) bursting open to reveal the stone of transmutation and the alchemical marriage of earth and heaven. Fuller underscores her alchemical theme by the use of the (alchemical) serpent, the uroboros, transformed by Leila into a phoenix, a symbol for the philosophers' stone.[14]

The images of uroboros and phoenix, both signaling alchemical death and rebirth, lead to a cryptic passage evoking further imagery of regeneration:

> And I heard her voice, which sang, "I shrink not from the baptism, from slavery let freedom, from parricide piety, from death let birth be known."
>
> *COULD I* but write this into the words of earth [Fuller claims], the secret of moral and mental alchymy would be discovered, and all Bibles have passed into one Apocalypse; but not till it has all been lived can it be written. (*EF* 57)

Aside from Fuller's literal reference to alchemical transformation in this passage, Leila becomes for Fuller the "wondrous circle" (*EF* 57) of wholeness, the alchemical uroboros of transmutation underscored by Leila's own creed of regeneration.

Fuller discovered a source of inspiration in the figure of Leila. As both mercurial guide and alchemical solvent to dissolve the prison(s) of the past, Leila possesses regenerative powers similar to the philosophers' stone. In discovering this power, imagined as Leila, Fuller symbolically discovered the power in herself—a power she would later focus, or "charm with," in *Woman in the Nineteenth Century*, where she would present the "secret of moral and metal alchemy." In a psychological sense, Leila is a projection of Fuller's psyche—what C. G. Jung might call the "wise old woman." But Fuller incorporates the tropes of alchemy into her spiritual essay in order to emphasize the process of inner, self-transmutation that she has experienced. In this context, "Leila" represents for Fuller a figurative *aurora consurgens* (the dawning of knowledge associated with the philosophers' stone). Curiously enough, Fuller's final words in the above passage, "not till it has all been lived can it be written," intimate a spiritual journey that Fuller had yet to complete at the time she composed "Leila."

Fuller returned to the carbuncle and Leila in her poems of 1844, the year that she was readying her opus of gender roles and regeneration, *Woman in the Nineteenth Century*, for publication. Although Steele notes that many of Fuller's poems (especially those of 1844) take on the dimensions of spiritual diaries in which the reader may trace the poet's emotional and intellectual development, we might further observe that Fuller's poems of 1844 are similar to Edward Taylor's *Meditations*.[15] Just as Taylor's poems were personal reflections on the sacrament, Fuller's poems may be viewed as meditations on her themes in *Woman*. In poems such as "Boding raven of the breast," "Leila in the Arabian zone," "Double Triangle, Serpent and Rays," "Winged Sphynx," "Lead, lunar ray," and "To the Face Seen in the Moon," we can observe the poet's maturing use of alchemical tropes as signposts pointing the way toward spiritual regeneration and union with the divine.

In addition to her poems of regeneration, Fuller returned to her image of the glowing carbuncle in two early poems of 1844. In "Now wandering on a tangled way, " the lost child of Fuller's poem is protected by the diamond by day and the carbuncle by night (*EF* 226). The carbuncle is again evoked in "With equal sweetness the commissioned hours" where Fuller concludes:

> The heart of stone in me renew
> A heart of marble pure and white,
> Sculptured with characters of light
> For when all souls all love may know,
> And their true core time's falseness show
> Then hard and soft together flow
> And Marble melting like the snow
> With sunset rays shall roseate glow.[16]

In this passage, Fuller's white heart of marble, transformed ("melting like the snow") by what might be called love's alchemy, gives off a "roseate glow."[17] While these final lines recall the reconciliation of opposites ("hard and soft together flow") that transpires in the heart that is transformed by love, they also anticipate Fuller's observation in *Woman* that "Male and female represent the two sides of the great radical dualism. But, in fact, they are perpetually passing into one another. Fluid hardens to solid, solid rushes to fluid. There is no wholly masculine man, no purely feminine woman" (*EF* 310). In other poems of 1844 and in *Woman*, Fuller further develops her theme of the reconciliation of opposites as it pertains to the transmutation or regeneration of self.

In "Boding raven of the breast," Fuller's images of baptism, burial, and marriage suggest a cycle of death and rebirth reminiscent of the coded language of the alchemists. Fuller begins this poem with the images of the raven and vulture, alchemical symbols of death and putrefaction associated with the *nigredo*.[18] These dark images of the spirit are then transformed by love into the dove:

> Boding raven of the breast
> Dost call the vulture to thy nest
> Through broken hearted trusting love
> That vulture may become a Dove. (*EF* 227–28)

In this passage the discerning reader may be reminded of Hawthorne's own alchemy of love.[19] For Fuller, love transmutes the images of the *nigredo* into the dove, a symbol for the white phase of the alchemical opus, the *albedo*.[20] Fuller then abruptly changes her imagery to that of baptism (recalling the alchemical *ablutio*) and burial (the grave as alchemical vessel), suggesting a preparation for rebirth or regeneration: "While I baptize in the pure wave, / Then prepare a deep safe grave" (*EF* 228). As if taking her cue from the texts of the alchemists, Fuller moves her imagery from the grave to a flower of rebirth, the violet:

> Where the plighted hand may bring
> Violets from that other spring.
> Whence the soul may take its flight
> Lark-like spiral seeking light
> Seeking secure the source of light. (*EF* 228)[21]

Fuller's use of the violet is especially interesting when we recall the deep blue or purple color often associated with this flower. According to H.M.E. De Jong, the alchemists often associated purple with the deep red of the *rubedo*, the royal color of the philosophers' stone.[22] In the context of the alchemical opus, Fuller's color sequence of black, white, and purple connotes death, purification, and rebirth. Fuller further underscores her alchemical theme at the end of "Boding raven," for her image of "soul . . . seeking light / Seeking secure the source of light" recalls the alchemical union of soul-as-Luna and Sol. While Fuller continued to explore this mystical union of female and male in other poems, in the context of her gender theory in *Woman*, this union is observed in woman's withdrawal (alchemical death) from the masculine world and her subsequent discovery of and union with her own masculine nature.

Fuller also returned to her primary source of inspiration, Leila, in 1844. In "Leila in the Arabian zone," Fuller links Leila with the goddess figures of Io, Isis, Diana, Hecate, and Phoebe, "only Leila's children are" (*EF* 233). This connection of Leila with the goddesses anticipates an important observation that Fuller makes in *Woman*: " 'The mothers'— 'The mother of all things,' are expressions of thought which lead the mind towards this side of universal growth" (*EF* 301). In these two passages Fuller intimates a "return to the mothers," an idea that Goethe emphasizes in *Faust II* and that recalls the alchemical concept of *prima materia*, the first matter of all things from which the alchemists often attempted to extract the seed of gold. This return to "the mothers" signals a recognition of the female power(s) that Fuller refers to in *Woman* as Minerva and the Muse (*EF* 311).

Thus far we have observed a number of the alchemical tropes that

Fuller incorporated into her poems of 1844. The most striking use of these tropes, however, occurs in "Double Triangle, Serpent and Rays":

> Patient serpent, circle round,
> Till in death thy life is found;
> Double form of godly prime
> Holding the whole thought of time,
> When the perfect two embrace,
> Male & female, black & white,
> Soul is justified in space,
> Dark made fruitful by the light;
> And centred in the diamond Sun,
> Time & Eternity are one. (*EF* 233)

In this short poem we are first presented with the image of the uroboros, the mercurial serpent, from whose alchemical death new life arises.[23] Next, the alchemical *prima materia* ("godly prime") and the chemical marriage of Sol and Luna are evoked in the "embrace" of "the perfect two," the "Male & female, black & white." Fuller's use of "black & white" recalls the colors associated with the alchemical *nigredo* and *albedo* and a reconciliation of opposites that generates the diamond center (the conjunction of "Male & female" located in the "Double Triangle" of the poem's title), the mystical union of soul "justified in space." While Fuller's double triangles suggest a further reconciliation of opposites, "Time & Eternity" (earth and heaven),[24] this image also recalls the frontispiece of Johannes Kirchweger's *Aurea Catena Homeri* (1723), with its two urobori (linked together tails in mouths) circled around two superimposed triangles (representing the elements of fire and water and constituting a symbol of the human soul).[25] For Fuller, the ideal state of the soul was imaged by a sacred marriage, an alchemical-like conjunction (reconciliation) of opposites.

Fuller takes her theme of the mystical marriage a step further in "Winged Sphynx," where she illustrates the alchemical wedding of heaven and earth. Fuller's subject in this poem, the sphinx, an obscure hieroglyph (even by alchemical standards) for the philosophers' stone,[26] joins heaven and earth in an alchemical marriage of the material (the lion's body) and the spiritual realm (wings) as the sphinx "Assumes at last the destined wings, / Earth & heaven together brings" (*EF* 234). In the first section of this poem, Fuller, through the voice of the sphinx, summarizes the spiritual change that she has experienced: "Through brute nature upward rising, / Seed up-striving to the light, / Revelations still surprising, / My inwardness is grown insight" (*EF* 234). In language that carries an alchemical subtext, Fuller next recounts the process of the sphinx's (and Fuller's own) spiritual transformation,

Still I slight not those first stages,
Dark but God-directed Ages;
  In my nature leonine
Labored & learned a Soul divine;
  Put forth an aspect Chaste, Serene,
Of nature virgin mother queen;
  Assumes at last the destined wings,
Earth & heaven together brings. (*EF* 234)

Fuller's words recall the first stage of the opus—the black ("Dark") stage of the *nigredo*—that leads into the whiteness of the *albedo*, where the sphinx puts "forth an aspect Chaste, Serene, of nature virgin mother queen."

In the final lines of Fuller's poem the sphinx offers a riddle of its own, reminiscent of the cryptic passages from the alchemists:

While its own form the riddle tells
That baffled all the wizard spells
  Drawn from intellectual wells,
Cold waters where truth never dwells:
  —It was fable told you so;—
  Seek her in common daylight's glow. (*EF* 234)

Here Fuller first berates cold-hearted (male) intellectuals who, through the ages, have reported to solve the mysteries of nature. These lines also recall an alchemical epigram from Michael Maier's *Atalanta Fugiens*: "Vile refuse is the [philosophers'] Stone, they say, and lies / There on the roads for rich and poor alike."[27] The connection between the passages from Fuller and Maier becomes clear if we think of the philosophers' stone as an incredulous tale for intellectuals, but for those initiated into the hermetic secret, the stone that weds heaven and earth can be found in the "common daylight," "on the roads for rich and poor alike." Still another alchemical reading that illuminates this passage is found by comparing the answer to the sphinx's riddle concerning the three ages of man with the passage from the *Rosinus ad Sarratantam Episcopum* that intimates that the philosophers' stone is to be found within man.[28] Fuller incorporates this idea into *Woman* where she intimates that woman has the potential to initiate the union of heaven and earth by uniting her own male and female attributes.

Among her other poems of 1844, Fuller's "My Seal Ring," with its image of Mercury mastering the alchemical serpent (*EF* 234), and "Sub Rosa-Crux," with its occult references to the "Knights of the Rosy Cross" and the tomb of Christian Rosenkreutz with its "undying lamp" (*EF* 236–37), illustrate Fuller's continuing use of alchemical tropes.[29] A close examination of these two poems reveals that their alchemical themes are not fully developed. However, these references do suggest that Fuller was reading material on the Rosicrucians in 1844, for she also makes reference in *Woman* to the "Rosicrucian lamp" that "burns unwearied, though condemned to the solitude of the tombs; and to its permanent life, as to every truth, each age has in some form borne witness" (*EF* 268–69).[30] It seems appropriate that Fuller was incorporating references (no matter how brief) to this hermetic organization into her writing, for Fuller's goal in *Woman*, like the goal of the Rosicrucians, was the birth of a golden age (both politically and socially) for the human race.[31]

In contrast to "My Seal Ring" and "Sub Rosa-Crux," the poems "Lead, lunar ray" and "To the Face Seen in the Moon" display Fuller's further use of alchemical tropes to illustrate her vision of the transformation of self. In the first stanza of "Lead, lunar ray," Fuller's imagery anticipates the "Knights of the Rosy Cross" in "Sub Rosa-Crux":

> Lead, lunar ray:
> To the crossing of the way
> Where to secret rite
> Rises the armed knight
> My champion for the fight. (*EF* 235)

As Steele observes, Fuller awaits a champion, the masculine side of Fuller's self, who will take her to the "throne" of the "phoenix king" (*EF* 236).[32] Later, in stanza four, the mystical marriage of Sol and Luna is imaged in Fuller's union of "lunar ray" and sun that yields "the golden grain" (*EF* 236), the seed of gold.[33]

In stanzas five and six Fuller moves to the image of nestlings (Fuller's "thought[s]") that must "Let [their] wings grow strong" for the flight to the "phoenix king" (*EF* 236). Here, Fuller's bird imagery has an interesting connection to the alchemical opus, for it recalls both the poet's previous use of the raven, vulture, and dove in "Boding raven of the breast" and continues the alchemical bird/color sequence from raven-vulture/black, to dove/white, to phoenix/red-gold. According to the author of "The Book of Lambspring," "of the Dove is born a Phœnix, / Which has left behind blackness and foul death" (*HM* 1: 290). Furthermore, the goal of Fuller's poem suggests a union between Fuller (her "thought") and the phoenix king, a reconciliation of opposites that Fuller further develops in "To the Face Seen in the Moon."

In "To the Face," Fuller moves from her evocation of the moon to her intuition that the heavenly maternal orb enfolds a secret the poet has discovered in her own nature:

> Oft, from the shadows of my earthly sphere
> I looked to thee, orb of pale pearly light,
> To loose the weariness of doubt and fear
> In thy soft Mother's smile so pensive bright,
> Thou seemedst far and safe and chastely living . . .
> But, if I stedfast gaze upon thy face
> A human secret, like my own, I trace,
> For through the woman's smile looks the male eye. (*EF* 240)

Fuller's image of the moon anticipates her later observation that woman, like the alchemical union at the end of the opus, is hermaphroditic in nature. Furthermore, the man-of (in)-the-moon correlates with Sol, the alchemical sun, and directs Fuller's attention toward

> His cave,
> Teaching anew the truth so bright, so grave
> Escape not from the middle earth
> Through mortal pangs to win immortal birth,
> Both man and woman, from the natural womb,
> Must slowly win the secrets of the tomb. (*EF* 240–41)

Here the "grave" upon which Fuller puns recalls the alchemical tomb, or alembic, the secrets of which (e.g., the philosophers' stone and the *elixir vitae*) must be won with patience. Once the alchemical union of Sol and Luna is achieved, the two spheres in Fuller's poem rise "fragrant, clear, / [as] the worthy Angel of a better sphere" (*EF* 241). The "worthy Angel," the symbol of Fuller's union, evokes the alchemical hermaphrodite (the philosophers' stone) that emerges from the alchemical vessel with the promise of a transfigured or regenerated earth: "In unpolluted beauty mutual shine / Earth, Moon and Sun the Human thought Divine, / For Earth is purged by tameless central fire" (*EF* 241).

In the second section of the poem, Fuller proclaims:

> I have learned to wait,
> Nor in these early days snatch
> at the fruits of late.
> The Man from the Moon
> Looks not for an instant Noon,
> But from its secret heart
> Slow evolves the Art
> Of that full consummation needed part. (*EF* 241)

In these lines Fuller intimates that she, like the alchemists, has learned patience with her "Art" (spiritual transmutation), which is brought about through the union of male and female.³⁴ Thus, in the last section of the poem, Fuller awaits her own Apollo (the alchemical sun), and from their "union shall spring / The promised King" (*EF* 241), the stone of transmutation.³⁵

The promise of a transfigured earth as it is reflected by the appearance of the hermaphrodite in both the *opus magnum* and the "worthy Angel" of "To the Face Seen in the Moon" is also at the very heart of *Woman in the Nineteenth Century*. In this gender essay Fuller skillfully crafts a work based on the alchemical theme *solve et coagula*, dissolve and make whole.³⁶ Although Gatta has observed that, "The metastructure of *Woman in the Nineteenth Century* can be simply described . . . as a teleological progression from specters of radical dualism at the outset to a vision of unific harmony and mystical marriage at the end,"³⁷ an alchemical reading of Fuller's revisionist essay focusing on the theme of *solve et coagula* enhances Gatta's observation and places *Woman* in the context of Fuller's previous treatment of alchemy.

Indeed, the preceding explication of "Double Triangle, Serpent, and Rays" coupled with Fuller's frontispiece to *Woman*, an emblematic adaptation of "Triangle," affords the reader an alchemical foundation for reading Fuller's essay. Just as the alchemical serpent connotes death and rebirth (*solve et coagula*), the harmony of the two interlocking triangles of Fuller's poem and frontispiece suggests a union of male and female that radiates ("rays") harmony throughout the universe. In *Woman*, Fuller figuratively dissolves the roles of woman in past ages (alchemical dross) and suggests a new role (and image) for woman crystallized in the present and projected onto the future. As Fuller notes in her preface: "The action of prejudices and passions, which attend, in the day, the growth of the individual, is continually obstructing the holy work that is to make the earth a part of heaven. By Man I mean both man and woman: these are two halves of one thought" (*EF* 245). Here, the union of male and female, like that of Sol and Luna in alchemy, produces the "one [great] thought" that will "make the earth a part of heaven"—the alchemical union of heaven and earth. As Fuller notes later in the essay: "Male and female represent the two sides of the great radical dualism. But, in fact, they are perpetually passing into one another. Fluid hardens to solid, solid rushes to fluid. There is no wholly masculine man, no purely feminine woman." Again Fuller's words evoke the alchemical marriage (the reconciliation of opposites) of Sol and Luna and the alchemical hermaphrodite that is their offspring.³⁸ Fuller recognized two different aspects of this male-female union. The first was the literal union between the sexes, but the second (and more important for Fuller) was the union of male and female elements within woman herself. As Fuller states: "The growth of man [woman] is twofold, masculine and feminine" (*EF* 343). Only after woman integrated the male and female aspects of her own personality would she achieve a wholeness of self (the union) tantamount to discovering the philosophers' stone.

Before Fuller's alchemical union could be achieved, two important stages in this great work (Fuller's opus) had to occur: woman must be separated from the dross of patriarchy and she must discover the transmutative force of her own nature (her own seed of gold). Once these stages were accomplished, the "Sacred Marriage" that concludes *Woman* could be affected.

While the idea of recovering the purified and purifying spirit (the seed of gold) of woman recurs throughout her essay, Fuller's first reference to this process is located in a passage she quotes from Louis Claude de Saint Martin:

> The ministry of man implies, that he must be filled from the divine fountains which are being engendered through all eternity, so that, at the mere name of his master, he may be able to cast all his enemies into the abyss; that he may deliver all parts of nature from the barriers that imprison them; that he may purge the terrestrial atmosphere from the poisons that infect it; that he may preserve the bodies of men from the corrupt influences that surround, and the maladies that afflict them. (*EF* 251)[39]

Although the context of this passage is decidedly religious, its subtext resonates with the language of alchemy. It is the alchemist who "deliver[s] all parts of nature," especially the seed of gold and the golden nature of all metals, "from the barriers that imprison them," who "purge[s] the terrestrial atmosphere from the poisons that infect it" (e.g., purges the dross from metals and brings forth their golden nature), and who "preserve[s] the bodies of men from the corrupt influences" (an attribute of the *elixir vitae*).

Fuller, undoubtedly aware of both the religious and alchemical implications of Saint Martin's statement, synthesizes these two seemingly diverse interpretations in *Woman*. According to Fuller, woman needs to free herself from patriarchal dominance; to achieve this, woman must withdraw within herself and reconcile her own male and female attributes. This action would culminate in an inner spiritual union tantamount to the alchemical marriage of Luna and Sol. The microcosm, as Fuller seems to be aware, had to be transformed before the macrocosm. Adapting this idea to her own vision of gender transformation, Fuller proclaims that woman first has to discover the regenerative power within herself before she can transmute and transform the world around her.

In an alchemical context, Fuller first calls for woman to free herself from the dross of patriarchy, or as Saint Martin stated, "from the barriers that imprison [her]." As for this dross, the barriers that hamper woman's progress toward spiritual perfection, Fuller writes, "If there *is* misfortune in woman's lot, it is in obstacles being interposed by men, which do *not* mark her state; and, if they express her past ignorance, do not her present needs" (*EF* 268). The dross of patriarchy, according to Fuller, must be dissolved in order for woman to discover her own golden nature (perfection). As Fuller states earlier in *Woman*:

> We would have every arbitrary barrier thrown down. We would have every path laid open to woman as freely as to man. Were this done and a slight temporary fermentation allowed to subside, we should see crystallizations more pure and of more various beauty. (*EF* 260)

Fuller's words, like those of Saint Martin that she quotes earlier in her text, evoke the language of the alchemists. Were the barriers, or imperfections, imposed on woman by man dissolved ("thrown down"), Fuller claims, figurative chemical reactions, such as "fermentation" and "cyrstallizations," would produce a marriage of heaven and earth, "divine energy would pervade nature . . . [and] a ravishing harmony of the spheres would ensue" (*EF* 260).[40]

Thus it is woman's inherent value as a true, authentic being that Fuller sees as the key to perfection on earth. Before this "harmony of the spheres" occurs, according to Fuller, woman needs to discover her own perfection. After this discovery is affected, Fuller observes: "Perhaps the next generation, looking deeper into this matter, will find that contempt is put upon old maids, or old women at all, merely because they do not use the elixir which would keep them always young" (*EF* 299). Again, we can hear the alchemical resonance of Fuller's text: if woman can free herself from the dross of male domination and thus discover the perfection inherent within herself, she will discover a power akin to the *elixir vitae*.

The key to the discovery of this power recalls the alchemical process of *solve et coagula*. Woman must be separated from the obstacle(s) that prevent her from achieving perfection; in Fuller's words, "We must have units before we can have union" (*EF* 301). Indeed, this idea is so central to Fuller's text that she reiterates it a few pages later:

> Union is only possible to those who are units. To be fit for relations in time, souls, whether of man or woman, must be able to do without them in the spirit.
>
> It is therefore that I would have woman lay aside all thought, such as she habitually cherishes, of being taught and led by men.

I would have her, like the Indian girl, dedicate herself to the Sun, the Sun of Truth, and go no where if his beams did not make clear the path. I would have her free from compromise, from complaisance, from helplessness, because I would have her good enough and strong enough to love one and all beings, from the fulness, not the poverty of being. (*EF* 312)

Once woman achieves spiritual enlightenment, or, in alchemical terms, once she discovers the equivalent of the philosophers' stone within herself, she will possess the power to transmute her surroundings. As Fuller states:

But men do *not* look at both sides, and women must leave off asking them and being influenced by them, but retire within themselves, and explore the groundwork of life till they find their peculiar secret. Then, when they come forth again, renovated and baptized, they will know how to turn all dross to gold, and will be rich and free though they live in a hut, tranquil, if in a crowd. Then their sweet singing shall not be from passionate impulse, but the lyrical overflow of a divine rapture, and a new music shall be evolved from this many-chorded world. (*EF* 313)

After woman's inner work is complete, says Fuller, she will, like the alchemists, "know how to turn all dross to gold, and will be rich and [most important] free." Indeed, once woman discovers the divine power within herself, a further union, a union between man and woman, can take place:

That now the time has come when a clearer vision and better action are possible. When man and woman may regard one another as brother and sister, the pillars of one porch, the priests of one worship.
I have believed and intimated that this hope would receive an ampler fruition, than ever before, in our own land. (*EF* 344)

Fuller's image of man and woman as brother and sister recalls the alchemical brother and sister union of Sol and Luna that produces the philosophers' stone.

This alchemical marriage of Sol and Luna can also be located in "For the power to whom we bow,"[41] the poem with which Fuller concludes her essay. Here Fuller encourages her readers to seek out the royal couple:

Ask for the Castle's King and Queen;
Though rabble rout may rush between,

> Beat thee senseless to the ground,
> In the dark beset thee round;
> Persist to ask and it will come,
> Seek not for rest in humbler home;
> So shalt thou see what few have seen
> The palace home of the King and Queen. (*EF* 348–49)

With these lines Fuller reminds the reader that the way to the spiritual marriage of male and female (the goal of *Woman*) may be arduous and fraught with peril, but if the seeker persists, the goal (the palace of the King and Queen) will be attained. In alchemical terms, the opus is filled with obstacles, not the least of which is the *nigredo*, the darkness at the onset of the opus that signals the initial death of the *prima materia* (and the spiritual torture of the adept). Yet if the alchemist persists, the marriage of the King and Queen (Sol and Luna) will be achieved and the philosophers' stone will be manifest.

A final image of this alchemical union is located in "The Sacred Marriage," a poem that Fuller included in the appendix to *Woman*. Here Fuller substitutes for the King and Queen "Twin stars that mutual circle in the heaven, / Two parts for spiritual concord given, / Twin Sabbaths that interlock the Sacred Seven" (*EF* 378). The twin stars, like Fuller's previous tandems of triangles, Sun and Moon, and King and Queen, evoke the union of opposites in the *opus magnum*. As symbols of the alchemical couple, the twin stars, interlocking the "Sacred Seven" metals of the opus, are an appropriate concluding image to *Woman*, for their union offers the promise of a transfigured world: "A world whose seasons bloom from pole to pole, / A force which knows both starting-point and goal, / A Home in Heaven,—the Union in the Soul" (*EF* 378).[42]

In *Woman in the Nineteenth Century*, Fuller's intent is to urge the spiritual (and at times physical) separation (*solve*) of woman from patriarchy in order for woman to discover the transmutative, regenerative, power (the seed of gold) within her. Once this power is recognized and harnessed, Fuller claims, woman will intuitively know how to use it to change the world around her. As we have observed, Fuller closes the text of *Woman* with "For the power to whom we bow" and the appendix with "The Sacred Marriage." Both of these poems can be read in two distinct alchemical contexts. The first reading emphasizes the union of opposites within woman's soul. The second reading emphasizes the harmonious union between the sexes, a union that can be accomplished only after woman has enacted the sacred marriage within herself. Thus, by the end of *Woman*, we find that Fuller has indeed written "the secret" she had intimated in "Leila"; she has written the formula for the transmutation of the human race. Having journeyed far, Fuller has beheld the "palace home of the King and Queen" and returned with "the secret of moral and mental alchymy."

NOTES

1. Emerson may very well have been influenced by his reading of Johann Wolfgang von Goethe and Jacob Boehme.
2. Ralph Waldo Emerson, *The Journals and Miscellaneous Notebooks of Ralph Waldo Emerson*, Vol. 10 (311).
3. Ralph Waldo Emerson, "Beauty" (282).
4. John Gatta, *American Madonna* (33–34). See also Jeffrey Steele, "Freeing the 'Prisoned Queen' " (137, passim).
5. This passage recalls Goethe's observation in *History of Color-Theories*: "It leads to very pleasant thoughts if one makes a free adaptation of what we may call the poetical part of alchemy" (quoted in Gray, 164).
6. In *Woman in the Nineteenth Century*, Fuller makes reference to Boehme (*EF* 301), Saint Martin (*EF* 251), Godwin (*EF* 284), and Goethe (*EF* 315–18). See also Fuller, "Goethe."
7. *The 'Key' of Jacob Boehme*, a condensed version of the principal points of Boehme's philosophy, is an excellent example of Boehme's adaptation of alchemical thought to theology, as is the passage that Fuller quotes from Saint Martin in *Woman* (*EF* 25).
8. Fuller may also have read W. Godwin's *Lives of the Necromancers*.
9. Although Fuller may have adopted the image of the carbuncle from Novalis, as Gatta (*American Madonna*, 37) suggests, she also may have been influenced by Hawthorne's imagery in "The Great Carbuncle" (1837).
10. In the context of artistic inspiration, Fuller has made a discovery of the power of the self, what Emerson called "self-reliance."
11. The name Leila may have been inspired by Leili (or Lily), from Goethe's *Märchen*, who, like Leila, possesses qualities of the philosophers' stone. Additionally, in *Faust I*, Fuller would have found the phrase: "There was a Scarlet Lion, intrepid wooer, / Wed to the Lily in a tepid ewer" ("Outside the City Gate," lines 1042–43).
12. Interestingly, in a journal entry of October 1842, Fuller referred to her love for her friend Barker as "a carbuncle (emblematic gem) which cast light into many of the darkest caverns of human nature" (*EF* 23). However, this passage refers to Fuller's relationship with Barker before the Barker-Ward nuptials. By abandoning Barker as an outward source of inspiration, Fuller was forced to look inward, where she discovered the persona of Leila.
13. Fuller further develops this theme in *Woman in the Nineteenth Century*.
14. Fuller may be echoing Emerson in this passage, as Gatta (*American Madonna* 37) suggests, but in the context of "Leila," Fuller's imagery is decidedly alchemical.
15. Steele (137).
16. Quoted in Steele (159).
17. A similar image occurs in "Raphael's Deposition From the Cross":

>   Leila, take thy wand again;
>   Upon thy arm no longer rest . . .

>   Slowly drop the pearly tears;
>   At last the Rosary appears
>   A Ruby heart its clasp appears
>   With cross of gold and diamond
>   Like to that upon the wand. (*EF* 240)

Here, the ruby heart recalls the deep red of the carbuncle in Fuller's earlier writing.

18. See Maier, Emblem 43 (191). The epigram for this emblem is as follows:

>   The vulture perches on the mountain peak,
>   Ceaselessly crying "I am white and black;
>   Yellow and red I am, and do not lie,"
>   The raven is the same, who wingless flies
>   In dark of night and in the light of day,
>   For of your art both this and that are chief.

For commentary on this emblem and epigram, see De Jong (272). For further background on the alchemical raven, see Abraham, "Raven" (163–64) and "Vulture" (213), in *Dictionary*; and Fabricius (98, 102, 105, 108–9, 114–15, 146–47, 186).

19. Fuller's explicit equation of love with the carbuncle recalls Hawthorne's theme of the transmutative and regenerative powers of love and/or the philosophers' stone.

20. Philalethes *Ripley Reviv'd* (178) equates the dove with the white swan of the *albedo*. For further background on the alchemical dove, see Abraham, *Dictionary* (58–59); and Fabricius (127, 241–42, passim). Fuller's images of the sphinx and phoenix in "Winged Sphynx" and "Lead, lunar ray" are also important tropes that continue the alchemical sequence. Additionally, the humility of the linnet (*EF* 228) evokes the humble, pure spirit of the alchemist awaiting the rebirth or creation of the philosophers' stone.

21. For more on the violet, see *The Herder Symbol Dictionary* (209–10).

22. See De Jong (51); and Abraham, "Purple Tincture" (1591–60), in *Dictionary*. In *The "Practica*," Basilius Valentinus notes that the tincture of the philosophers' stone "is of a colour intermediate between red and purple" (*HM* 1: 348).

23. Although I do not intend to examine Goethe's influence on Fuller at this time, I would suggest that Goethe's *Märchen*, especially the the serpent that encircles (by seizing the end of its tail with its teeth) the body of a near-dead youth to save his life, was a primary source for Fuller's serpent image in "Double Triangle, Serpent and Rays." Fuller's "Double Triangle" would become the emblem to *Woman*, a gender-role essay in which Fuller reworks alchemical metaphor to underscore the means of women's liberation from patriarchy.

24. As Philalethes (*Ripley Reviv'd* [278]) notes, the stone is "a reconciliation of Contraries, a making of friendship between Enemies."

25. For further background on the double triangle, see Cirlot (351). The Kirchweger figure is reprinted in Gray (Frontispiece). According to Gray, Kirch-

weger's book was studied by Goethe, but there is no evidence to suggest that Fuller had seen this book. Fuller, however, could certainly have come across a similar symbol of the uroboros in any illustrated book on alchemy, such as "The Book of Lambspring" (*HM* 1: 287) and Maier, Emblem 14 (133). See also De Jong (132–35).

26. See the frontispiece to Johann Joachim Becher's *Institutiones chimicae prodromae* (1664) and the frontispiece to Becher's *Oedipus chimicus* (1664), both reprinted in Fabricius (32; *Oedipus chimicus* also reprinted in De Rola, plate 388, 223). See also Maier, Emblem 39 and accompanying epigram (183); for commentary on Emblem 39, see De Jong (255).

27. Maier (177).

28. See Fabricius (208). Also see De Jong (246–47); and Hitchcock, *Remarks on Alchemy* (39).

29. Rosicrucians were alchemists who were believed to possess the secret of the philosophers' stone and hence the power to wed heaven and earth. Christian Rosenkreutz was the mythical father of Rosicrucianism and the purported author of the Rosicrucian text *The Chemical Wedding of Christian Rosenkreutz* (1616).

30. Although Fuller's references to Rosicrucian legend in "Sub Rosa-Crux" and *Woman in the Nineteenth Century* may have come from *The Chemical Wedding* or Goethe's Rosicrucian poem *Die Geheimnisse* (1784–1786), in all probability Fuller's source was William Godwin's *St. Leon*. For more on *Die Geheimnisse*, see Gray (199–200, 292).

31. See McIntosh (45); and Yates (1, 57).

32. Steele (166). In alchemy, it is Mercury who subdues the serpent (uroboros). See illustration in "The Book of Lambspring" (*HM* 1: 279).

33. Whereas Fuller's triad of images (plant, soul-thoughts, and birds) intimates regeneration, her images of "golden grain" and "phoenix-king" recall the coded language that the alchemists used to describe the philosophers' stone.

34. Fuller may also have known that alchemy was called "The Great Art."

35. In alchemy the appearance of the king in regal splendor often signified the stone of transmutation. See Maier, Emblem 28 (161), Emblem 31 (167), Emblem 44 (193), and Emblem 48 (201).

36. Aside from specific references to *solve et coagula* in alchemical texts, in Goethe's *Theory of Colors* Fuller could have found the German poet's admonition to "divide what is united and unite what is divided" (quoted in Gray, 90, 277).

37. Gatta, *American Madonna* (18).

38. In *Secrets Reveal'd*, Philalethes also refers to the stone as "our Hermaphrodite, mighty in both Sexes" (2). Later in the work, Philalethes refers to the stone as the "Hermaphorditical Infant" (16). Fuller would have encountered a figure similar to the alchemical hermaphrodite (the homunculus) in *Faust II*. Aside from references to the hermaphrodite in Goethe and Philalethes, Fuller may have found references to human perfection as a combination of the two sexes in Plato and Ovid.

39. The French mystic Saint-Martin was a student of Jacob Boehme, whose own writings are heavily influenced by alchemical philosophy. See Haeffner, "Boehme" (73–74).

40. For background on crystallization as synonym for the philosophers' stone, see Abraham, "Crystallization" (50–51), in *Dictionary*.

41. An earlier Fuller poem that evokes the alchemical marriage of Sol/sun and Luna/moon is her 1841 "River of beauty flowing through the life" with its image of "the all-embracing Sun and Moon" (quoted in Steele, 151).

42. Fuller's reference to "a force which knows both starting-point and goal" suggests the alchemical serpent, the uroboros.

Epilogue

In the preceding chapters we have observed how Taylor, Poe, Hawthorne, and Fuller adapted the tropes and metaphors of alchemy to give form and order to their visions of regeneration. Whether we speak of the soul's regeneration or transmutation through God's Grace, as in Taylor's *Meditations*, Poe's hermetic visions of regeneration via imagination, Hawthorne's alchemical transmutation of the human heart through love, or Fuller's aspiration to liberate the golden spirit from the dross of patriarchy, these writers captured the essence of early America: a land where the human spirit might rise triumphant and renewed. Like the restorative properties of the *elixir vitae*, early America offered the potential of renewal to its people. Indeed, this *topos* is still prevalent today, although instead of regeneration we may speak of the American Dream or the notion of reinventing the self.

The continuing significance of these authors' texts suggests their power to stimulate our own desire for renewal. Taylor's vision of alchemical regeneration recalls the sense of self as soul, illustrated in Thomas Moore's best-seller, *The Care of the Soul*. Poe's use of alchemical tropes underscores the value of imagination as a means of transformation. Hawthorne's alchemy reminds us of the magical quality of love—capable of transforming the coldest, hardest heart into warm flesh and blood. And Fuller's alchemy offers an affirmation of individual dignity and responsibility. Coincidentally, C. G. Jung's work with psychology and alchemy during the mid-twentieth century ushered in a "new age" of spiritual quests for enlightenment recalling the alchemical themes of Taylor, Poe, Hawthorne, and Fuller.[1]

With the advent of the American Civil War, American literary taste outgrew its penchant for allegory, gothic fantasy, and romance. As a literary crossroads as well as a collective initiatory experience, the Civil War marked an end to American innocence (and romanticism) and began the transition to realism and naturalism. It is indeed ironic that following such a traumatic event as the Civil War, American writers lost interest in the theme of regeneration. It is worthwhile to note, however, that the literary adaptation of alchemical philosophy did not completely disappear after the 1860s. The literature of the twentieth century also yields examples of sustained artistic engagement with alchemical tropes, as recent scholarship concerning D. H. Lawrence, Wallace Stevens, and William Butler Yeats attests.[2]

Curiously, during the *fin de siècle*, Americans briefly renewed their interest in alchemy due to discoveries taking place in chemistry and physics.[3] In 1897, Henry Carrington Bolton noted the following in "The Revival of Alchemy":

> Recent discoveries in physics, chemistry, and psychology have given the disciples of Hermes renewed hopes, and the present position of chemical philosophy has given the fundamental doctrine of alchemy a substantial impetus. The favorite theory of a prima materia, or primary matter, the basis of all the elementary bodies, has received new support by the discoveries of allotropism of the elements, isomerism of organic compounds, the revelations of the spectroscope, the practical demonstrations by Norman Lockyer, the experiments on the specific heat of gaseous bodies at a high temperature by Mallard and Le Châtelier, the discoveries of Sir William Crookes (as set forth in his monograph on Meta-elements), the discovery by Carey Lea of several singular allotropic forms of silver, and, most weighty of all, the mass of related facts and phenomena which find their ultimate expression in the periodic law of the elements, so that many chemists of the present day are inclined to believe in the mutual convertibility of elements having similar chemical properties.[4]

Coinciding with these scientific discoveries was the appearance of the mysterious chemist Stephen Henry Emmens, who, in 1899, persuaded the United States Mint to purchase one million dollars worth of gold that Emmens claimed to have transmuted from Mexican silver dollars.[5] An alchemist charlatan? A gullible director of the United States Mint? The less said about this event, the better.

Scientifically documented evidence of the actual transmutation of base matter into gold would have to wait until 1980, when scientists at the Lawrence Berkeley Laboratory used the BEVALAC particle accelerator to transmute bismuth into gold. The cost of this transmutation was more than $10,000, and the amount of gold produced was less than one-billionth of a cent.[6] Although the experiment was "far from cost-effective," as George B. Kauffman notes,[7] at that particular moment, the chemical fantasy of the alchemists became reality.

The zeitgeist of alchemy remains with us to this day. Aside from its continuing popularity as subject matter for present-day writers and readers of science fiction and fantasy, alchemy remains an engaging metaphor. A recent subject-search at Amazon.com produced more than 475 entries containing the term *alchemy*—the subject matter of which ranged from science to finance, from lust to leadership.[8] Perhaps, as we enter a new millennium, *Spiritus Mercurius* still smiles in his house of fire.

NOTES

1. Cohen (64–66) has noted how the hermetic studies of Ethan Allen Hitchcock filtered through the work of Viennese psychoanalyst Herbert Silberer and influenced Jung's alchemical vision.

2. See Leonora Woodman, "D. H. Lawrence and the Hermetic Tradition" and *Stanza My Stone*; and William T. Gorski, *Yeats and Alchemy*. See also Evans Lansing Smith, "Alchemy in Modernism."

3. This does not take into account the occult revival in Europe dating from the mid-nineteenth century.

4. Bolton (208–9).

5. For further background on Emmens, see George B. Kauffman, "The Mystery of Stephen H. Emmens."

6. See Kauffman (71). For further information on this experiment, see Paul Bendix, "All That Glitters . . ." (29–30) and K. Aleklett, et al., "Energy dependence of ^{209}Bi fragmentation in relativistic nuclear collisions" (1044–46).

7. Kauffman (71).

8. A similar search of the Modern Language Association's electronic database (dating back to 1962) yielded more than 380 entries for *alchemy*.

Works Cited

Abel, Darrel. "A Key to the House of Usher." *Twentieth Century Interpretations of "The Fall of the House of Usher": A Collection of Critical Essays*. Ed. Thomas Woodson. Englewood Cliffs, N.J.: Prentice-Hall, 1969. 43–55. Reprint of *University of Toronto Quarterly* 18 (1949): 176–85.

Abraham, Lyndy. *A Dictionary of Alchemical Imagery*. Cambridge, England: Cambridge University Press, 1998.

———. *Marvell and Alchemy*. Aldershot, England: Scolar, 1990.

"Alchymy." *The Retrospective Review* 14 (1826): 98–135.

Aleklett, K., et al. "Energy dependence of ^{209}Bi fragmentation in relativistic nuclear collisions." *Physical Review C* 23 (1981): 1044–46.

Ammann, Peter J. "The Musical Theory and Philosophy of Robert Fludd." *Journal of the Warburg and Courtauld Institutes* 30 (1967): 198–227.

Ashmole, Elias, ed. *Theatrum Chemicum Britannicum: Containing Severall Poeticall Pieces of Our Famous English Philosophers, who have written the Hermetique Mysteries in their owne Ancient Language*. 1652. Reprint, Kila, Mont.: Kessinger, 1991.

Bendix, Paul. "All that Glitters . . ." *LBL Magazine* 5, no. 3 (1980): 29–30.

Bensick, Carol Marie. *La Nouvelle Beatrice: Renaissance and Romance in "Rappaccini's Daughter."* New Brunswick, N.J.: Rutgers University Press, 1985.

Benton, Richard P. "Is Poe's 'The Assignation' a Hoax?" *Nineteenth-Century Fiction* 18, no. 2 (1963): 193–97.

Bloomfield, William. "Bloomfields Blossoms: or, The Campe of Philosophy." *Theatrum Chemicum Britannicum*. Ed. Elias Ashmole. Kila, Mont.: Kessinger, 1991. 305–23.

Boehme, Jacob. *The "Key" of Jacob Boehme: With an Illustration of the Deep Principles of Jacob Behmen*. Trans. William Law. Grand Rapids, Mich.: Phanes, 1991.

Bolton, Henry Carrington. "The Literature of Alchemy." *Pharmaceutical Review* 19 (1901): 150–55, 195–99.
Bonus, Petrus. *The New Pearl of Great Price: A Treatise Concerning the Treasure and Most Precious Stone of the Philosophers.* Ed. Janus Lacinius, 1546. Trans. Arthur Edward Waite. 1894. Reprint, London: Stuart, 1963.
Burns, Shannon. "Alchemy and 'The Birth-mark.'" *American Transcendental Quarterly* 42 (1979): 147–58.
Butler, Jon. "Magic, Astrology, and the Early American Religious Heritage, 1600–1760." *The American Historical Review* 2 (1979): 317–46.
Chandler, Alice. "'The Visionary Race': Poe's Attitude Toward His Dreamers." *ESQ: A Journal of the American Renaissance* 60 (1970): 73–81.
Chaudhuri, Supriya. "Jason's Fleece: The Source of Sir Epicure Mammon's Allegory." *Review of English Studies*, n.s., 35 (1984): 71–73.
Cirlot, J. E. *A Dictionary of Symbols.* Trans. Jack Sage. 2nd ed. New York: Dorset, 1971.
Clack, Randall A. "The Alchemy of Love: Hawthorne's Hermetic Allegory of the Heart." *ESQ: A Journal of the American Renaissance* 41 (1995): 307–38.
———. "'Strange Alchemy of Brain': Poe and Alchemy." *A Companion to Poe Studies.* Ed. Eric W. Carlson. Westport, Conn.: Greenwood Press, 1996. 367–87.
———. "The Transmutation of Soul: The *Opus Alchymicum Celestial* and Edward Taylor's 'Meditation 1:8.'" *Seventeenth-Century News* 50 (1992): 6–10.
Cohen, I. Bernard. "Ethan Allen Hitchcock: Soldier-Humanitarian-Scholar: Discoverer of the 'True Subject' of the Hermetic Art." *Proceedings of the American Antiquarian Society* 61 (1951): 29–136.
Cooper, James Fenimore. *The Pioneers or the Sources of the Susquehanna.* Ed. James Franklin Beard. Albany, N.Y.: State University of New York Press, 1980.
Cramer, Daniel. *The Rosicrucian Emblems of Daniel Cramer: The True Society of Jesus and the Rosy Cross: Here are forty sacred emblems from Holy Scripture concerning the most precious name and cross of Jesus Christ.* Trans. Fiona Tait, 1617. Reprint, Grand Rapids, Mich.: Phanes, 1991.
Craven, J. B. *Doctor Robert Fludd: The English Rosicrucian—Life and Writings.* N.p.: Occult Research, n.d.
Cunnar, Eugene R. "Donne's 'Valediction: Forbidding Mourning' and the Golden Compasses of Alchemical Creation." *Literature and the Occult: Essays in Comparative Literature.* Ed. Luanne Frank. Arlington, Tex.: University of Texas at Arlington Press, 1977. 72–110.
Damon, S. Foster. "De Brahm: Alchemist." Ed. Barton Levi St. Armand. *Ambix: The Journal of the Society for the History of Alchemy and Chemistry* 24 (1977): 77–88.
Debus, Allen G. *The Chemical Philosophy: Paracelsian Science and Medicine in the Sixteenth and Seventeenth Centuries.* 2 vols. New York: Science History Publications, 1977.
———. *The English Paracelsians.* New York: Watts, 1966.
———. "John Woodall, Paracelsian Surgeon." *Ambix: The Journal of the Society for the History of Alchemy and Chemistry* 10 (1962): 108–18.

———. "The Paracelsian Compromise in Elizabethan England." *Ambix: The Journal of the Society for the History of Alchemy and Chemistry* 8 (1960): 71–97.

De Crèvecoeur, Hector Michel-Guillaume St. Jean. *Letters from an American Farmer*. 1782. Reprint, London: J. M. Dent, 1926.

De Jong, H.M.E. *Michael Maier's* Atalanta Fugiens: *Sources of an Alchemical Book of Emblems*. Leiden, Netherlands: Brill, 1969.

Del Fattore, Joan. "John Webster's *Metallographia*: The Source for Alchemical Imagery in the *Preparatory Meditations*." *American Literature* 18 (1983–1984): 231–41.

De Rola, Stanislas Klossowski. *The Golden Game: Alchemical Engravings of the Seventeenth Century*. New York: Braziller, 1988.

Disraeli, Isaac. *Curiosities of Literature*. 2 vols. New York: Crowell, 1881.

Dobbs, Betty Jo Teeter. *Alchemical Death and Resurrection: The Significance of Alchemy in the Age of Newton*. Washington, D.C.: Smithsonian Institution, 1990.

———. *The Foundations of Newton's Alchemy or "The Hunting of the Greene Lyon."* Cambridge, England: Cambridge University Press, 1975.

———. "Studies in the Natural Philosophy of Sir Kenelm Digby, Part 1." *Ambix: The Journal of the Society for the History of Alchemy and Chemistry* 18 (1971): 1–25.

———. "Studies in the Natural Philosophy of Sir Kenelm Digby, Part 2." *Ambix: The Journal of the Society for the History of Alchemy and Chemistry* 20 (1973): 143–63.

———. "Studies in the Natural Philosophy of Sir Kenelm Digby, Part 3." *Ambix: The Journal of the Society for the History of Alchemy and Chemistry* 21 (1974): 3–28.

Dove-Rume, Janine. "Hawthorne, l'alchimiste, et son Grande' Oeuvre, *The Scarlet Letter*." *Information sur les sciences sociales* 30 (1991): 157–78.

Eliade, Mircea. *The Forge and the Crucible*. Trans. Stephen Corrin. 2nd ed. Chicago: University of Chicago Press, 1978.

Emerson, Ralph Waldo. "Beauty." *The Conduct of Life: The Complete Works of Ralph Waldo Emerson*. Vol. 6. Boston: Houghton Mifflin, 1903. 267–90.

———. *The Journals and Miscellaneous Notebooks of Ralph Waldo Emerson: 1847–1848*. Vol 10. Ed. William H. G. Gilman et al. Cambridge, Mass.: Harvard University Press, 1973.

Fabricius, Johannes. *Alchemy: The Medieval Alchemists and Their Royal Art*. Rev. ed. Wellingborough, England: Aquarian, 1989.

Fideler, David. "The Rose Garden of the Philosophers." *Gnosis: A Journal of the Western Inner Traditions* 8 (1988): 40–44.

Findlay, Ian. "Edward Bulwer-Lytton and the Rosicrucians." *Literature and the Occult: Essays in Comparative Literature*. Ed. Luanne Frank. Arlington, Tex.: University of Texas at Arlington Press, 1977. 137–46.

Franklin, Benjamin. *The Papers of Benjamin Franklin*. 33 vols. Ed. Leonard W. Labaree et al. New Haven: Yale University Press, 1959–1997.

———. *The Writings of Benjamin Franklin*. 10 vols. Ed. Albert Henry Smyth. New York: Macmillan, 1905–1907.

Fuller, Margaret. *The Essential Margaret Fuller*. Ed. Jeffrey Steele. New Brunswick, N.J.: Rutgers University Press, 1992.

———. "Goethe." *The Dial* 2 (July 1841): 1–41.

Gatta, John, Jr. *American Madonna: Images of the Divine Woman in Literary Culture*. New York: Oxford University Press, 1997.

———. "Aylmers' Alchemy in 'The Birthmark.'" *Philological Quarterly* 57 (1978): 399–413.

———. *Gracious Laughter: The Meditative Wit of Edward Taylor*. Columbia Mo.: University of Missouri Press, 1989.

"The Glory of the World; or, Table of Paradise; That Is to Say, A True Account of the Ancient Science Which Adam Learned From God Himself; Which Noah, Abraham, and Solomon Held as One of the Greatest Gifts of God; Which Also All Sages, At All Times, Preferred to the Wealth of the Whole World, Regarded as the Chief Treasure of the Whole World, and Bequeathed Only to Good Men; Namely, The Science of the Philosopher's Stone." *Hermetic Museum, Restored and Enlarged*. Ed. Arthur Edward Waite. Vol. 1. York Beach, Me.: Samuel Weiser, 1991. 165–243.

Godwin, Joscelyn. *Athanasius Kircher: A Renaissance Man and the Quest for Lost Knowledge*. London: Thames, 1979.

———. Introduction. *Atalanta Fugiens: An Edition of the Emblems, Fugues and Epigrams*, by Michael Maier. Trans. and Ed. Joscelyn Godwin. Grand Rapids, Mich.: Phanes, 1989.

———. *Robert Fludd: Hermetic Philosopher and Surveyor of Two Worlds*. Grand Rapids, Mich.: Phanes, 1991.

Godwin, William. *Lives of the Necromancers; or, An Account of the most Eminent Persons in Successive Ages Who Have Claimed for Themselves, or to Whom Has Been Imputed by Others, The Exercise of Magical Power*. 1876. Reprint, New York: Gordon, 1976.

Goethe, Johann Wolfgang von. *Faust: A Tragedy*. Trans. Walter Arndt. Ed. Cyrus Hamlin. New York: Norton, 1976.

———. *Goethe's Fairy Tale of The Green Snake and the Beautiful Lily* [*Märchen*]. Trans. Donald Maclean. Grand Rapids, Mich.: Phanes, 1993.

Gorski, William. *Yeats and Alchemy*. Albany, N.Y.: State University of New York Press, 1996.

Grabo, Norman S. *Edward Taylor's Christographia*. New Haven: Yale University Press, 1962.

Gray, Ronald D. *Goethe the Alchemist: A Study of Alchemical Symbolism in Goethe's Literary and Scientific Works*. Cambridge, England: Cambridge University Press, 1952.

Haeffner, Mark. *The Dictionary of Alchemy: From Maria Prophetissa to Isaac Newton*. London: Aquarian, 1991.

Hawthorne, Julian. *Nathaniel Hawthorne and His Wife: A Biography*. 2 vols. 3rd ed. Boston: Osgood, 1885.

Hawthorne, Nathaniel. *The Centenary Edition of the Works of Nathaniel Hawthorne*. Ed. William Charvat et al. 23 vols. Columbus: Ohio State University Press, 1962–1994.

———. *The Love Letters of Nathaniel Hawthorne: 1839–1863*. Washington, D.C.: NCR Microcard Editions, 1972.

Hennelly, Mark. "Hawthorne's *Opus Alchmicum*: 'Ethan Brand.'" *ESQ: A Journal of the American Renaissance* 22 (1976): 96–106.

The Herder Symbol Dictionary: Symbols from Art, Archaeology, Mythology, Literature, and Religion. Trans. Boris Matthews. Wilmette, Ill: Chiron, 1978.

Hess, Jeffrey A. "Sources and Aesthetics of Poe's Landscape Fiction." *American Quarterly* 22 (1970): 177–89.

Hitchcock, Ethan Allen. *Fifty Years in Camp and Field: Diary of Major-General Ethan Allen Hitchcock, USA.* Ed. W. A. Croffut. New York: Putnam, 1909.

———. *Remarks upon Alchemy and the Alchemists, Indicating a Method of Discovering the True Nature of Hermetic Philosophy; And Showing that the Search after the Philosopher's Stone Had Not for Its Object the Discovery of an Agent for the Transmutation of Metals.* Boston: Crosby, 1857.

Hoeller, Stephan A. *Freedom: Alchemy of a Volunteer Society.* Wheaton, Ill: Quest Books, 1992.

Hoffman, Daniel. *Poe Poe Poe Poe Poe Poe Poe.* Garden City, N.Y.: Doubleday, 1972.

Hudson, Ruth Leigh. "Poe and Disraeli." *American Literature* 8 (1936–1937): 402–16.

Hull, Raymona E. "Hawthorne and the Magic Elixir of Life: The Failure of a Gothic Theme." *ESQ: A Journal of the American Renaissance* 18 (1972): 97–107.

Jacobs, Robert. *Poe: Journalist and Critic.* Baton Rouge, La.: Louisiana State University Press, 1969.

———. "Poe's Earthly Paradise." *American Quarterly* 12 (1960): 404–13.

Jantz, Harold. "America's First Cosmopolitan." *Proceedings of the Massachusetts Historical Society* 84 (1972): 3–25.

Jonson, Ben. *The Alchemist. Ben Jonson's Plays and Masques.* Robert M. Adams. New York: Norton, 1979. 176–274.

Jung, C. G. *Alchemical Studies.* Vol. 13 of *The Collected Works of C. G. Jung.* Trans. R.F.C. Hull. Ed. Herbert Read et al. 2nd ed. Princeton, N.J.: Princeton University Press, 1967.

———. *Mysterium Coniunctionus: An Inquiry into the Separation and Synthesis of Psychic Opposites in Alchemy.* Vol 14 of *The Collected Works of C. G. Jung.* Trans. R.F.C. Hull. Ed. Herbert Read et al. 2nd ed. Princeton, N.J.: Princeton University Press, 1970.

———. *Psychology and Alchemy.* Vol. 12 of *The Collected Works of C. G. Jung.* Trans. R. F. C. Hull. Ed. Herbert Read et al. 2nd ed. Princeton, N.J.: Princeton University Press, 1968.

Kauffman, George B. "The Mystery of Stephen H. Emmens: Successful Alchemist or Ingenious Swindler?" *Ambix: The Journal of the Society for the History of Alchemy and Chemistry* 30 (1983): 65–88.

Kesselring, Marion L. "Hawthorne's Reading, 1828–1850." *Bulletin of the New York Public Library* 53 (1949): 55–71, 121–38, 173–94.

Ketterer, David. "'Circle of Acquaintance': Mistress Hibbins and the Hermetic Design of *The Scarlet Letter*." *English Studies in Canada* 9 (1983): 294–311.

———. "The Sexual Abyss: Consumation in 'The Assignation.' " *Poe Studies* 19, no. 1 (1986): 7–10.
Kittredge, George Lyman. "Dr. Robert Child the Remonstrant." *Publications of the Colonial Society of Massachusetts* 21 (1919): 1–146.
Kleiman, Edward. "The Wizardry of Nathaniel Hawthorne: *Seven Gables* as Fairy Tale and Parable." *English Studies in Canada* 4 (1978): 289–304.
Lambspring. "The Book of Lambspring." *Hermetic Museum Restored and Enlarged*. Ed. Arthur Edward Waite. Vol. 1. York Beach, Me.: Samuel Weiser, 1991. 271–306.
Lawrence, D. H. *Studies in Classic American Literature*. 1923. Reprint, New York: Viking, 1961.
Leventhal, Herbert. *In the Shadow of the Enlightenment: Occultism and Renaissance Science in Eighteenth-Century America*. New York: New York University Press, 1976.
Linden, Stanton J. *Darke Hierogliphicks: Alchemy in English Literature from Chaucer to the Restoration*. Lexington, Ky.: University Press of Kentucky, 1996.
Lindsay, Vachel. "The Wizard in the Street (Concerning Edgar Allan Poe)." *The Recognition of Edgar Allan Poe: Selected Criticism Since 1829*. Ed. Eric W. Carlson. Ann Arbor: University of Michigan Press, 1966. 101–2.
Luther, Martin. *The Table Talk of Martin Luther*. Trans. and Ed. William Hazlitt. London: Bell, 1883.
Madathanas, Heinrich. "The Golden Age Restored: Having Now Appeared a Second Time, Flourished Beautifully, and Brought Forth Fragrant and Golden Seed. This Rare and Precious Seed Is Shewn and Imparted to All the Sons of True Wisdom and the Doctrine." *Hermetic Museum, Restored and Enlarged*. Ed. Arthur Edward Waite. Vol. 1. York Beach, Me.: Samuel Weiser, 1991. 51–67.
Maier, Michael. *Atalanta Fugiens: An Edition of the Emblems, Fugues and Epigrams*. Trans. and Ed. Joscelyn Godwin. Grand Rapids, Mich.: Phanes, 1989.
Marlowe, Christopher. *The Tragical History of Doctor Faustus*. Vol. 5 of *The Works and Life of Christopher Marlowe*. Ed. Frederick S. Boas, 1932. Reprint, New York: Goddian, 1966.
Martin, Luther. "Hawthorne's *The Scarlet Letter*: A is for Alchemy?" *American Transcendental Quarterly* 58 (1985): 31–42.
Marvell, Andrew. "To His Coy Mistress." *The Complete Poems of Andrew Marvell*. Ed. Alexander B. Grosart. Vol. 1. London: Fuller Worthies' Library, 1872. 106–8.
Mather, Cotton. *Magnalia Christi Americana*. 2 vols. Ed. Kenneth B. Murdock. Cambridge, Mass: Harvard University Press, 1977.
McIntosh, Christopher. *The Rosicrucians: The History and Mythology of an Occult Order*. 2nd ed. Northamptonshire, England: Crucible, 1987.
McLean, Adam. *The Alchemical Mandala: A Survey of the Mandala in the Western Esoteric Traditions*. Grand Rapids, Mich.: Phanes, 1989.
McPherson, Hugo. *Hawthorne as Myth-Maker: A Study in Imagination*. Toronto Ontario, Canada: University of Toronto Press, 1969.
Meikle, Jeffrey L. "Hawthorne's Alembic: Alchemical Images in *The House of*

the Seven Gables." ESQ: A Journal of the American Renaissance 26 (1980): 173–83.
Merkur, Daniel. "The Study of Spiritual Alchemy: Mysticism, Gold-Making, and Esoteric Hermeneutics." *Ambix: The Journal of the Society for the History of Alchemy and Chemistry* 37 (1990): 35–45.
Miller, Edwin Haviland. *Salem Is My Dwelling Place: A Life of Nathaniel Hawthorne.* Iowa City: University of Iowa Press, 1991.
Mitchell, John. "Michael Maier's Alchemical Quadrature of the Circle." *Alexandria* 1 (1991): 72–75.
Moore, John Robert. "Poe's Reading of *Anne of Geierstein.*" *American Literature* 22 (1951): 493–96.
Moore, Thomas. *The Care of the Soul: How to Add Depth and Meaning to Your Everyday Life.* New York: HarperCollins, 1998.
Morton, Charles. *Compendium Physicae.* Vol. 33 of the *Collections of the Colonial Society of Massachusetts.* 1687. Reprint, Boston: Colonial Society of Massachusetts, 1940.
Newman, William. *Gehennical Fire: The Lives of George Starkey, an American Alchemist in the Scientific Revolution.* Cambridge, Mass.: Harvard University Press, 1994.
———. "Newton's *Clavis* as Starkey's *Key.*" *Isis* 78 (1987): 564–74.
———. "Prophecy and Alchemy: The Origin of Eirenaeus Philalethes." *Ambix: The Journal of the Society for the History of Alchemy and Chemistry* 37 (1990): 97–115.
Nicholl, Charles. *The Chemical Theatre.* London: Routledge, 1980.
Norton, Thomas. "The Ordinall of Alchimy." *Theatrum Chenicum Britannicum.* Ed. Elias Ashmole. Kila, Mont.: Kessinger, 1991. 2–106.
Oreovicz, Cheryl Z. "Edward Taylor and the Alchemy of Grace." *Seventeenth-Century News* 34 (1976): 33–36.
———. "Investigating 'The America of Nature': Alchemy in Early American Poetry." *Puritan Poets and Poetics: Seventeenth-Century American Poetry in Theory and Practice.* Ed. Peter White. University Park, Pa.: Pennsylvania State University Press, 1985. 99–110.
Paracelsus [Theophrastus Bombastus von Hohenheim]. *The Hermetic and Alchemical Writings of Aureolus Phillippus Theophrastus Bombast of Hohenheim, Called Paracelsus, The Great.* 2 vols. Ed. L. W. de Laurence and Arthur Edward Waite, 1894. Reprint, Kila, Mont.: Kessinger, 1991.
Partlitz, Simeon [Partlicius]. *A New Method of Physick: or, A Short View of Paracelsus and Galens Practice: In 3 Treatises.* Trans. Nicholas Culpeper. London: n.p., 1654.
Pharmacopeia Londinensis: or, The London Dispensatory. Trans. Nicholas Culpeper, 1649. Reprint, London: Churchill, 1702.
Philalethes, Eirenaeus [George Starkey]. "The Fount of Chemical Truth." *Hermetic Museum, Restored and Enlarged.* Ed. Arthur Edward Waite. Vol. 2. York Beach, Me.: Samuel Weiser, 1991. 261–69.
———. "The Metamorphosis of Metals." *Hermetic Museum, Restored and Enlarged.* Ed. Arthur Edward Waite. Vol. 2. York Beach, Me.: Samuel Weiser, 1991. 227–45.

———. *Ripley Reviv'd: or, an Exposition upon Sir George Ripley's Hermetico-Poetical Works*. London: William Cooper, 1678.

———. *Secrets Reveal'd, or an Open Entrance to the Shut Palace of the King [Introlitus Appertus ad occlusum regis palatium]*. London: William Cooper, 1669.

Pitcher, Edward W. "Poe's 'The Assignation': A Reconsideration." *Poe Studies* 13, no. 1 (1980): 1–4.

Poe, Edgar Allan. *Collected Works of Edgar Allan Poe*. 3 vols. Ed. Thomas Ollive Mabbott. Cambridge, Mass.: Harvard University Press, 1969–1978.

———. *Edgar Allan Poe: Essays and Reviews*. Ed. G. R. Thompson. New York: Library of America, 1984.

———. *The Letters of Edgar Allan Poe*. 2 vols. Ed. John Ward Ostrom. New York: Gordian, 1966.

Pollin, Burton R. *Discoveries In Poe*. Notre Dame, Ind.: University of Notre Dame Press, 1970.

———. "Poe's 'Von Kempelen and His Discovery': Sources and Significance." *Etudes Anglaises* 20 (1967): 12–23.

Poynter, F.N.L. "Nicholas Culpeper and the Paracelsians." *Science, Medicine, and Society in the Renaissance*. Ed. Allen G. Debus. Vol. 1. London: Heinemann, 1972. 201–20.

Rainwater, Catherine. " 'This Brazen Serpent Is a Doctors Shop': Edward Taylor's Medical Vision." In *American Literature and Science*, ed. Robert J. Scholnick, 18–38. Lexington, Ky.: University Press of Kentucky, 1992.

Rattansi, P. M. "Paracelsus and the Puritan Revolution." *Ambix: The Journal of the Society for the History of Alchemy and Chemistry* 11 (1963): 24–32.

Read, John. *The Alchemist in Life, Literature, and Art*. London: Nelson, 1947.

———. *Prelude to Chemistry: An Outline of Alchemy, Its Literature, and Relationships*. New York: Macmillan, 1937.

Reid, Alfred S. "Hawthorne's Humanism: 'The Birthmark' and Sir Kenelm Digby." *American Literature* 38 (1966): 337–51.

Richard, Claude. "Ou L'Indicibilité de Dieu: Une lectuere de 'Ligeia.' " *Delta* 12 (1981): 11–34.

Roberts, Marie. *Gothic Immortals: The Fiction of the Brotherhood of the Rosy Cross*. London: Routledge, 1990.

Robinson, Danny. "Hawthorne in the Boston Athenaeum." *The Nathaniel Hawthorne Society Newsletter* 10, no. 1 (1984): 1–2.

Rosenberg, Liz. " 'The Best That Earth Could Offer': 'The Birth-mark,' A Newlywed's Story." *Studies in Short Fiction* 30 (1993): 145–51.

Ruland, Martin. *A Lexicon of Alchemy or Alchemical Dictionary Containing a Full and Plain Explanation of All Obscure Words, Hermetic Subjects, and Arcane Phrases of Paracelsus*. 1612. Reprint, Kila, Mont.: Kessinger, 1991.

Sachs, Viola. "The occult language and scripture of the New World." *Social Science Information* 23, no. 1 (1984): 129–41.

———. "The occult, magic, and witchcraft in American culture." *Social Science Information* 22, no. 6 (1983): 941–45.

Sachse, Julius F. *The German Pietists of Provencial Pennsylvania, 1694–1708.* 1895. Reprint, New York: AMS, 1970.
St. Armand, Barton Levi. "Poe's Emblematic Raven: A Pictorial Approach." *ESQ: A Journal of the American Renaissance* 22, no. 4 (1976): 191–210.
———. "Poe's 'Sober Mystification': The Uses of Alchemy in 'The Gold-Bug.'" *Poe Studies* 4, no. 1 (1971): 1–7.
———. "Usher Unveiled: Poe and the Metaphysics of Gnosticism." *Poe Studies* 5, no. 1 (1972): 1–8.
Sheppard, H. J. "Gnosticism and Alchemy." *Ambix: The Journal of the Society for the History of Alchemy and Chemistry* 6 (1957): 86–101.
———. "The Mythological Tradition and Seventeenth Century Alchemy." *Science, Medicine, and Society in the Renaissance: Essays to Honor Walter Pagel.* Ed. Allen G. Debus. Vol. 1. London: Heinemann, 1972. 47–59.
Siebel, Kathy, and Thomas M. Davis. "Edward Taylor and the Cleansing of AQUA VITAE." *Early American Literature* 4 (1969–1470): 102–9.
Slotkin, Richard. *Regeneration Through Violence: The Mythology of the American Frontier, 1600–1860.* Middletown, Conn.: Wesleyan University Press, 1973.
Smith, Evans Lansing. "Alchemy in Modernism." *Cauda Pavonis: Studies in Hermeticism*, n.s., 13 (1994): 11–18.
Sollors, Werner. "A Defense of the 'Melting Pot.'" *The American Identity: Fusion and Fragmentation.* Ed. Rob Kroes. Amsterdam: University van Amsterdam Press, 1980. 181–214.
Stanford, Donald. "Edward Taylor." *Major Writers of Early American Literature.* Ed. Everett Emerson. Madison: University of Wisconsin Press, 1972. 59–91.
———. "The Giant Bones of Claverack, New York, 1705." *Proceedings of the New York State Historical Association* 40 (1959): 47–61.
Steele, Jeffrey. "Freeing the 'Prisoned Queen': The Development of Margaret Fuller's Poetry." In *Studies in the American Renaissance*, ed. Joel Myerson, 137–175. Charlottesville, Va.: University Press of Virginia, 1992.
Stich, Klaus P. "Hawthorne's Intimations of Alchemy." *ATQ: The American Transcendental Quarterly*, n.s., 5 (1991): 15–30.
Stiles, Ezra. *Literary Diary.* 3 vols. Ed. Franklin Bowditch Dexter. New York: Scribner, 1901.
Swann, Charles. "Alchemy and Hawthorne's *Elixir of Life Manuscripts.*" *Journal of American Studies* 22 (1988): 371–87.
Taylor, Edward. *The Poems.* Ed. Donald Stanford. New Haven: Yale University Press, 1960.
———. *The Poetical Works of Edward Taylor.* Ed. Thomas H. Johnson. Princeton, N.J.: Princeton University Press, 1966.
Thompson, C.J.S. *The Lure and Romance of Alchemy.* 1932. Reprint, New York: Bell, 1990.
Thompson, G. R. *Poe's Fiction: Romantic Irony in the Gothic Tales.* Madison: University of Wisconsin Press, 1973.
———. "Poe's Flawed Gothic." *New Approaches to Poe: A Symposium.* Ed. Richard P. Benton. Hartford, Conn.: Transcendental Books, 1970. 38–58.
Tompson, Benjamin. *Benjamin Tompson 1642–1714: First Native-Born Poet of*

America, His Poems. Ed. Howard J. Hall. Boston: Houghton Mifflin, 1924.

Turnbull, G. H. "George Stirk, Philosopher by Fire (1628?–1665)." *Publications of the Colonial Society of Massachusetts* 38 (1947–1951): 21–53.

Valentinus, Basilius. *The "Practica," with Twelve Keys, and an Appendix Thereto, Concerning The Great Stone of the Ancient Sages.* Ed. Michael Maier, 1618. *Hermetic Museum, Restored and Enlarged.* Ed. Arthur Edward Waite. Vol. 1. York Beach, Me.: Samuel Weiser, 1991. 311–57.

Van Leer, David M. "Aylmer's Library: Transcendental Alchemy in Hawthorne's 'The Birth-mark.'" *ESQ: A Journal of the American Renaissance* 22 (1976): 211–20.

Vivan, Itala. "An Eye into the Occult in Hawthorne's Text: The Scar in the Letter." *Quaderni di lingue e letterature* 8 (1983): 71–107.

Waite, Arthur Edward, ed. *Hermetic Museum, Restored and Enlarged: Most Faithfully Instructing All Disciples of the Sopho-Spagyric Art How That Greatest and Truest Medicine of The Philosopher's Stone May Be Found and Held.* 2 vols. 1893. Reprint, York Beach, Me.: Samuel Weiser, 1991.

———. *Raymund Lully: Illuminated Doctor, Alchemist and Christian Mystic.* London: Rider, 1922.

———. *The Real History of the Rosicrucians Founded on Their Won Manifestoes, and on Facts and Documents Collected From the Writings of Initiated Brethren.* 1887. Reprint, Blauvelt, N.Y.: Steinerbooks, 1997.

Walsh, James J. *Education of the Founding Fathers of the Republic: Scholasticism in the Colonial Colleges.* New York: Fordham University Press, 1935.

Weathers, Willie T. "Edward Taylor and the Cambridge Platonists." *American Literature* 26 (1954): 1–31.

Webster, C. "English Medical Reformers of the Puritan Revolution: A Background to the 'Society of Chymical Physitians.'" *Ambix: The Journal of the Society for the History of Alchemy and Chemistry* 14 (1967): 16–41.

Webster, John. *Metallographia or, An History of Metals.* 1671. Reprint, New York: Arno, 1978.

West, Muriel. "Poe's 'Ligeia.'" *The Explicator* 22, no. 2 (1963): 15–16.

———. "Poe's 'Ligeia' and Isaac D'Israeli." *Comparative Literature* 16, no. 1 (1964): 19–28.

Westfall, Richard S. "Alchemy in Newton's Library." *Ambix: The Journal of the Society for the History of Alchemy and Chemistry* 31 (1984): 97–101.

Wilkinson, Ronald Sterne. "The Alchemical Library of John Winthrop, Jr. (1606–1676) and His Descendants in Colonial America, Part 1." *Ambix: The Journal of the Society for the History of Alchemy and Chemistry* 11 (1963): 33–51.

———. "The Alchemical Library of John Winthrop, Jr. (1606–1676) and His Descendants in Colonial America, Part 2." *Ambix: The Journal of the Society for the History of Alchemy and Chemistry* 13 (1966): 139–86.

———. "George Starkey, Physician and Alchemist." *Ambix: The Journal of the Society for the History of Alchemy and Chemistry* 11 (1963): 121–52.

———. "The Hartlib Papers and Seventeeth-Century Chemistry." *Ambix: The*

Journal of the Society for the History of Alchemy and Chemistry 17 (1970): 85–111.

———. "Hermes Christianus: John Winthrop, Jr. and Chemical Medicine in Seventeenth Century New England." *Science, Medicine and Society in the Renaissance: Essays to Honor Walter Pagel.* Ed. Allen G. Debus. Vol. 1. London: Heinemann, 1972. 221–41.

———. "New England's Last Alchemists." *Ambix: The Journal of the Society for the History of Alchemy and Chemistry* 10 (1962): 128–38.

———. "The Problem of Identity of Eirenaeus Philalethes." *Ambix: The Journal of the Society for the History of Alchemy and Chemistry* 12 (1964): 24–43.

Woodall, John. *The Surgions Mate, or a Treatise Discovering faithfully and plainely the due contents of the Surgions Chest, the uses of the instruments, the vertues and operations of the Medicines, the cures of the most frequent diseases at Sea.* London: n.p., 1617.

Woodman, Leonora. "D. H. Lawrence and the Hermetic Tradition." *Cauda Pavonis: Studies in Hermeticism*, n.s., 8 (1989): 1–6.

———. *Stanza My Stone: Wallace Stevens and the Hermetic Tradition.* West Lafayette, Ind.: Purdue University Press, 1983.

Yates, Frances A. *The Rosicrucian Enlightenment.* London: Routledge, 1972.

Young, Edward J. "Subjects for Master's Degree in Harvard College from 1655–1791." *Proceedings of the Massachusetts Historical Society* 18 (1880): 119–151.

Zolla, Elémire. "Septimius Felton e la letteratura alchemica inglese e americana." *Rivista di estetica* (1966): 17–55.

Index

Alchemy: chemical process, 2–3; as Christian allegory, 4–5; history of, 1–2; and mysticism, 3–5, 65; and the seven planets, 49
Alchemical colors, 3
Alchemical conjunctio, 54, 60, 70, 111 n.45, 132 n.41
Alchemical garden, 65
Alchemical grave, 28, 59
Alchemical hermaphrodite, 61, 80 n.33, 124, 131 n.38
Alchemical mercury, 55, 131 n.32
Alchemical phoenix, 63, 82 n.63
Alchemical prison, 63
Alchemical raven, 118, 130 n.8
Alchemical rose, 26, 58, 110 n.31
Alchemical stages, 2–3
Alchemical swan, 76
Alkahest, 19
Ammann, Peter J., 52
Antimony, 50
Aqua Vitae, 20
Arbor Philosophica (philosophers' tree), 65, 72
Arnold of Villanova, 2
Ashmole, Elias (*Theatrum Chemicum Britannicum*), 45
Aurora Consurgens, 54, 99, 117

Aurum Potabile, 19
Aurum Vitae Red (the Red Elixir), 14

Becher, Johann Joachim: *Institutiones chimicae prodromae*, 131 n.26; *Oedipus chimicus*, 131 n.26
Bloomfield, William: "Bloomfields Blossoms," 27, 50
Bolton, Henry Carrington, 134
Bonus, Petrus, 10 n.6, 29–30, 111 n.47
Burns, Shannon, 97, 111 n.33

Cauda Pavonis (peacock's tail), 26, 107
Chandler, Alice, 69, 79 n.21
Cohen, I. Bernard, 135 n.1
Cooper, James Fenimore: *The Pioneers*, 44
Cramer, Daniel: *The Rosicrucian Emblems of Daniel Cramer*, 110
Culpeper, Nicholas, 17; *Culpeper's School of Physick*, 37 n.17

Danforth, Samuel, 42, 45, 110 n.32
De Brahm, John William Gerar, 43
De Crèvecoeur, Hector Michel-

Index

Guillaume St. Jean: *Letters from an American Farmer*, 6, 43–44
De Jong, H.M.E., 21, 119
Disraeli, Isaac: *Curiosities of Literature*, 45, 47 n.18
Dorn, Gerhard, 5

Eliade, Mircea, 9 n.2
Emerson, Ralph Waldo: "Beauty," 113–14
Emmens, Stephen Henry, 134

Fideler, David, 76
Fludd, Robert, 52; "Truth's Golden Harrow," 38–39 n.39; "Clavis," 63
Franklin, Benjamin, 42–43
Fuller, Margaret: "Boding raven of the breast," 118–19, 122; "Double Triangle, Serpent and Rays," 120, 124, 130 n.23; "For the power to whom we bow," 127–28; "Lead, lunar ray," 122, 130 n.20; "Leila," 115–17; "Leila in the Arabian zone," 119; "My Seal Ring," 121; "Now wandering on a tangled way," 118; "Raphael's Deposition From the Cross," 129–30 n.17; "River of beauty flowing through the life," 132 n.41; "The Sacred Marriage," 128; "Sub Rosa-Crux," 121; "Summer on the Lakes," 114; "To the Face Seen in the Moon," 122–24; "Winged Sphynx," 120–21, 130 n.20; "With equal sweetness the commissioned hours," 118; *Woman in the Nineteenth Century*, 117, 118, 119, 124–28

Gatta, John, Jr., 21, 97, 111 n.33, 115, 124, 129 n.14
"The Glory of the World," 78 n.4, 81 n.49
Godwin, Joscelyn, 87
Godwin, William, 44, 45, 79 n.23, 131 n.30
Goethe, Johann Wolfgang von, 119. Works: *Die Geheimnisse*, 131 n.30; *Faust*, 129 n.11; *Histories of Color-Theories*, 129 n.5; *Märchen*, 129 n.11, 130 n.23; *Theory of Colors*, 131 n.36
Gray, Ronald D., 4, 130–31 n.25

Hawthorne, Nathaniel: "The Artist of the Beautiful," 98–99; "The Birthmark," 84, 88, 97–98; "Dr. Heidigger's Experiment," 109 n.6; "Earth's Holocaust," 89–90; "Egotism; or, The Bosom-Serpent," 96–97; "Ethan Brand," 93–94; "The Golden Touch," 99–102; "The Gorgon's Head," 87–88; "The Great Carbuncle," 84, 94; *The House of the Seven Gables*, 103–7; "Man of Adamant," 92–93; *The Marble Faun*, 88; "The May-Pole of Merry Mount," 90–92, 110 n.19; *Notebooks*, 84; "Peter Goldthwaite's Treasure," 94–96, 110 n.29; "Rappaccini's Daughter," 98; "Sir William Pepperell," 83–84, 109 n.3; *The Scarlet Letter*, 84, 103; "A Select Party," 109 n.5; "Septimius Felton," 108; "Septimius Norton," 84–85; "The Threefold Destiny," 110 n.22; "A Virtuoso's Collection," 85, 86
Hawthorne, Sophia, 90, 110 n.14
Hennelly, Mark, 93, 94
Hermes Trismegistus, 1
Hess, Jeffrey A., 72
Hitchcock, Ethan Allen, 45, 89, 90, 109–10 n.14
Hoeller, Stephan A., 110 n.21
Hoffman, Daniel, 79 n.21
Hull, Raymona E., 83

Jacobs, Robert, 68, 72
Jonson, Ben: *The Alchemist*, 85–86, 109 n.11, 111 n.47
Jung, C. G., 10 n.5, 39 n.48, 55, 117, 133

Kauffman, George B., 135
Kelpius, Johannes, 9, 11 n.31
Ketterer, David, 53–54

Khunrath, Heinrich, 39 n.55; *Ampitheatrum sapientiae aeternae*, 52–3, 77, 79 n.12, 82 n.73
Kircher, Anthanasius, 46–47 n.18
Kirchweger, Johannes: *Aurea Catena Homeri*, 120, 130–31 n.25
Kleiman, Edward, 104, 111–12 n.51

Lambspring: "The Book of Lambspring," 110 n.32, 122, 131 nn.25, 26, 32
Lawrence, D. H., 50
Libavius, Andreas: *Commentariorum Alchymiae*, 76, 82 n.74
Linden, Stanton, 14–15
Lindsay, Vachel, 78
Lull, Raymond, 69, 81 n.54
Luther, Martin , 4–5

Mabbott, Thomas Ollive, 81 n.54
Madathanas, Heinrich: "The Golden Age Restored," 38
Maier, Michael: *Arcana arcanissima*, 86–87; *Atalanta Fugiens*, 38 n.37, 39 nn. 44, 47; 56, 59, 79 n.22, 80 nn. 29, 30; 81 n.56, 109 n.5, 110 n.32, 111 n.47, 121, 130 n.18, 131 nn.25, 26, 35; *Summum bonus*, 38 n.37; *Symbola aureae mensae*, 80 nn.34, 48; 81 n.49
Martin, Luther, 103, 111 n.45
Martyr, Peter, 5–6
Marvell, Andrew, 64
Mather, Cotton, 7
Meikle, Jeffrey L., 111 n.48, 112 n.51
Michelspacher, Steffan: *Cabala*, 38 n.37
Moore, John Robert, 82 n.64
Moore, Thomas, 133
Morton, Charles: *Compendium Physical*, 41
Mylius, Johann Daniel: *Anatomia auri sive turocinium medico-chymicum*, 81 nn.49, 55; *Opus Medico-chymicum*, 110 n.20; *Philosophia reformata*, 65, 80 n.34, 80 n.39, 81 nn.49, 57; 111 n.36

Norton, Thomas, 4, 2

Oreovicz, Cheryl Z., 35

Paracelsus (Theophrastus Bombastus von Hohenheim), 15, 17, 27, 30, 60–61, 111 n.47
Partlitz, Simeon: *A New Method of Physick*, 17, 18
Pharmacopoeia Londinensis (*The London Dispensatory*), 17, 18
Philalethes, Eirenaeus (George Starkey), 45; "The Fount of Chemical Truth," 20, 63; "The Metamorphosis of Metals," 116; *Ripley Reviv'd*, 4, 10 n.12, 33, 60, 76, 130 nn.20, 24; *Secrets Reveal'd*, 61, 131 n.38
Pitcher, Edward W., 53
Poe, Edgar Allan: artist as alchemical mediator, 68–69, 78; concept of the Supernal, 66–68. Works: "Annabel Lee," 64; "The Assignation" ("The Visionary"), 51–55; "Chapter of Suggestions," 66–67; "The Colloquy of Monos and Una," 61–63, 80 n.41; "A Descent into the Maelström," 46 n.18; "The Domain of Arnheim," 68–69, 72–78; "Dream-land," 67–68; "Eleonora," 69–71, 81 n.57; "The Fall of the House of Usher," 59–61; "The Gold Bug," 71–72; "Ligeia," 55–59; "Marginalia," 65–66, 69; "The Philosophy of Furniture," 79 n.17; "The Pit and the Pendulum," 80 n.37; "The Poetic Principle," 67; "Review of Longfellow's *Ballads and Other Poems*," 66; "Sonnet—To Science," 44; "Von Kempelen and His Experiment," 49–50
Pollin, Burton R., 78 n.1, 81 n.54
Pordage, John, 30

Quintessence (Fifth Element), 36 n.8, 61

Richard, Claude, 79 n.20
Rosicrucians, 5, 77, 109 n.3, 121–22, 131 n.29
Rosinus ad Sarratatam Episcopum, 31, 121
Ruland, Martin: *The Lexicon of Alchemy*, 4, 20, 51, 63, 109 n.11

Sachs, Viola, 44
Saint Martin, Claude de, 125, 131 n.39
Schweighardt, Theophilus: *Speculum Sophicum Rhodo-Stauroticum*, 109 n.3
Seed of Gold, 116
Solve et Coagula, 50, 124
St. Armand, Barton Levi, 59, 64–65, 71, 79 n.24, 80 n.43, 81 nn.53, 59; 82 n.63
Steele, Jeffrey, 115, 117, 122
Stich, Klaus P., 93, 94
Stiles, Ezra, 8, 41–42, 43

Tabula Smaragdina (Emerald Tablet), 1, 80 n.47
Taylor, Edward: Alchemical paradigm, 21. Works: "The Description of the Great Bones Dug Up at Claverack," 4; *Preparatory Meditations*: 1.2, 31; 1.4, 25–26; 1.7, 15–17; 1.9, 14; 1.10, 19–21; 1.14, 33; 1.23, 32–33; 1.24, 24; 1.28, 22; 1.30, 25; 1.34, 28; 1.35, 35; 1.48, 22–24; 2.2, 33–34; 2.4, 28; 2.5, 25; 2.12, 25; 2.21, 27–28; 2.25, 24; 2.32, 29; 2.33, 32–33; 2.45, 33; 2.54, 38 n.35; 2.60, 26–27; 2.68[B], 21, 37 n.23; 2.82, 24; 2.93, 24; 2.126, 34–35; 2.144, 38 n.35; 2.153, 16–17, 24; "The Return," 31–32
Theatrum Chemicum, 72
Tompson, Benjamin: "Funeral Tribute," 7; *New England's Tears for her Present Miseries*, 8
Thompson, G. R., 79 n.25
Tractatus Aureus Hermetis Trismegisti, 75

Uroboros, 96, 117, 120, 132 n.42

Valentinus, Basilius: "The Practica," 39 n.49, 130 n.22; *The Triumphal Chariot of Antimony*, 50
Van Leer, David M., 111 n.33

Webster, John: *Metallographia*, 15–16, 18–19, 25, 27, 36 n.4, 37–38 n.27, 38 n.31
Winthrop, John, Jr., 7–8
Winthrop, Wait Still, 109 n.4
Woodall, John: *The Surgions Mate*, 17, 37 n.18

Young, Edward J., 41

About the Author

RANDALL A. CLACK is Visiting Assistant Professor of English at Shippensburg University of Pennsylvania and has previously taught at the University of Connecticut, Elizabeth City State University, and Southern Polytechnic State University. His articles have appeared in such journals as *ESQ: A Journal of the American Renaissance* and *Seventeenth-Century News*.

**Recent Titles in
Contributions to the Study of American Literature**

The Short Fiction of Kurt Vonnegut
Peter J. Reed

Enchanted Places: The Use of Setting in F. Scott Fitzgerald's Fiction
Aiping Zhang

Solitude and Society in the Works of Herman Melville and Edith Wharton
Linda Costanzo Cahir

The Immigrant Experience in North American Literature: Carving out a Niche
Katherine B. Payant and Toby Rose, editors

American Literary Humor During the Great Depression
Robert A. Gates

PS
2177
.A43
C57
2000